From Burke and Wordsworth to the Modern Sublime in Chinese Literature

Comparative Cultural Studies,
Steven Tötösy de Zepetnek, Series Editor

The Purdue University Press monograph series of Books in Comparative Cultural Studies publishes single-authored and thematic collected volumes of new scholarship. Manuscripts are invited for publication in the series in fields of the study of culture, literature, the arts, media studies, communication studies, the history of ideas, etc., and related disciplines of the humanities and social sciences to the series editor via email at <clcweb@purdue.edu>. Comparative cultural studies is a contextual approach in the study of culture in a global and intercultural context and work with a plurality of methods and approaches; the theoretical and methodological framework of comparative cultural studies is built on tenets borrowed from the disciplines of cultural studies and comparative literature and from a range of thought including literary and culture theory, (radical) constructivism, communication theories, and systems theories; in comparative cultural studies focus is on theory and method as well as application. For a detailed description of the aims and scope of the series including the style guide of the series link to <http://docs.lib.purdue.edu/clcweblibrary/seriespurdueccs>. Manuscripts submitted to the series are peer reviewed followed by the usual standards of editing, copy editing, marketing, and distribution. The series is affiliated with *CLCWeb: Comparative Literature and Culture* (ISSN 1481-4374), the peer-reviewed, full-text, and open-access quarterly published by Purdue University Press at <http://docs.lib.purdue.edu/clcweb>.

**Volumes in the Purdue series of Books in Comparative Cultural Studies
<http://www.thepress.purdue.edu/comparativeculturalstudies.html>**

Yi Zheng, *From Burke and Wordsworth to the Modern Sublime in Chinese Literature*
Agata Anna Lisiak, *Urban Cultures in (Post)Colonial Central Europe*
Representing Humanity in an Age of Terror, Ed. Sophia A. McClennen and Henry James Morello
Michael Goddard, *Gombrowicz, Polish Modernism, and the Subversion of Form*
Shakespeare in Hollywood, Asia, and Cyberspace, Ed. Alexander C.Y. Huang and Charles S. Ross
Gustav Shpet's Contribution to Philosophy and Cultural Theory, Ed. Galin Tihanov
Comparative Central European Holocaust Studies, Ed. Louise O. Vasvári and Steven Tötösy de Zepetnek
Marko Juvan, *History and Poetics of Intertextuality*
Thomas O. Beebee, *Nation and Region in Modern American and European Fiction*
Paolo Bartoloni, *On the Cultures of Exile, Translation, and Writing*
Justyna Sempruch, *Fantasies of Gender and the Witch in Feminist Theory and Literature*
Kimberly Chabot Davis, *Postmodern Texts and Emotional Audiences*
Philippe Codde, *The Jewish American Novel*
Deborah Streifford Reisinger, *Crime and Media in Contemporary France*
Imre Kertész and Holocaust Literature, Ed. Louise O. Vasvári and Steven Tötösy de Zepetnek
Camilla Fojas, *Cosmopolitanism in the Americas*
Comparative Cultural Studies and Michael Ondaatje's Writing, Ed. Steven Tötösy de Zepetnek
Jin Feng, *The New Woman in Early Twentieth-Century Chinese Fiction*
Comparative Cultural Studies and Latin America, Ed. Sophia A. McClennen and Earl E. Fitz
Sophia A. McClennen, *The Dialectics of Exile*
Comparative Literature and Comparative Cultural Studies, Ed. Steven Tötösy de Zepetnek
Comparative Central European Culture, Ed. Steven Tötösy de Zepetnek

Yi Zheng

From Burke and Wordsworth to the Modern Sublime in Chinese Literature

Purdue University Press
West Lafayette, Indiana

Copyright 2010 by Purdue University. All rights reserved.

Printed in the United States of America.

Library of Congress Cataloging-in-Publication Data

Zheng, Yi, 1961-
 From Burke and Wordsworth to the Modern Sublime in Chinese Literature / Yi Zheng.
   p. cm. -- (Comparative Cultural Studies)
 Includes bibliographical references and index.
 ISBN 978-1-55753-576-4
 1. Sublime, The, in literature. 2. English poetry--18th century--History and criticism. 3. English poetry--19th century--History and criticism. 4. Chinese poetry--20th century--History and criticism. 5. Comparative literature--English and Chinese. 6. Comparative literature--Chinese and English. 7. Romanticism--England. 8. Chinese poetry--English influences. I. Title.
 PR575.S77Z47 2011
 820.9'384--dc22
                          2010044536

This book is dedicated to Hagar Gal and Ofer Gal.

Contents

Acknowledgments	ix
Introduction to *From Burke and Wordsworth to the Modern Sublime in Chinese Literature*	1
Chapter One Envisioning a Culture of the Sublime Aesthetic	12
Chapter Two The Imperative of the Romantic Aesthetic and Burke's Inquiry into the Sublime	24
Chapter Three Wordsworth's Poetic *Prelude* to Modern History	40
Chapter Four The Construction of the Sublime as an Aesthetic Movement across Time and Place	68
Chapter Five Guo Moruo and the Reformation of Modern Chinese Poetry in a Sublime Poetics	83
Chapter Six Rewriting *Qu Yuan* and towards a Sublime Denouement	104
Conclusion	124
Works Cited	129
Index	139

Acknowledgments

I owe many individuals and institutions special thanks: I thank Jonathan Arac who read numerous versions of the manuscript and who is not only my mentor, but also my intellectual role model; I thank Paul A. Bové, Stephen Carr, Henry Kripps, and Ronald Judy for their insightful comments; Sheldon Hsiaopeng Lu and Jean Carr for intellectual conversations and encouragement; and I am indebted to the intellectual and personal support of the late Carol Kay. I thank the Porter Institute for Comparative Poetics at Tel Aviv University, the Wissenschaftskolleg in Berlin, and the Collegium Hungaricum in Budapest for postdoctoral and senior fellowships, exciting projects, intellectual nurturing, and discussion; I thank Andrew Plaks and Sally Humphreys for reading and commenting on different versions of the manuscript. I am grateful to my friends and colleagues, Hui Zhang and Meir Shahar, from the Department of East Asian Studies, Tel Aviv University, for good times in sometimes streneous circumstances. In Australia, I thank Mabel Lee for comments on parts of the manuscript and her generosity. I thank Stephanie H. Donald, David Goodman, Louise Edwards, and the China Centre of the University of Technology (Sydney), Adrian Vickers, Jeffrey Riegle, the School of Languages and Cultures, and Margaret Harris at the University of Sydney for institutional, intellectual, and financial support. And I am grateful to Wang Yiyan, Jon Kowallis, and Gao Yuanbao for conversations on modern Chinese literature and poetry. I am especially grateful to the editor of the Purdue University Press monograph series of Books in Comparative Cultural Studies series, Steven Tötösy de Zepetnek, for his interest in my work for his series. I also thank the anonymous readers from Purdue University Press for their comments and suggestions and Agnieszka Stefanowska (Sydney) for editorial assistance.

Most importantly, I thank my family for their love and for making my intellectual life possible: I thank my mother Zheng Shufang and my late father Liu Deren for having taught me the love of books when it was thought unwise to do so in China during the Cultural Revolution and I thank my fellow bookworms Hagar Gal and Ofer Gal to whom I dedicate my book.

An earlier version of chapter 4 was published in *Modern Chinese Literature and Culture* 16.1 (2004): 153-91. I thank Kirk Denton and the two anonymous reviewers for their comments and suggestions and the permission to reuse the material and a part of chapter 3 was published in *Travelling Facts*. Ed. Baillie, Dunn and Yi Zheng. Frankfurt: Campus, 2004. 92-123. I thank Campus Verlag for permission of republication.

Introduction

Guo Moruo (1892-1978) is arguably one of the most important modern Chinese poets (see, e.g., Roy), whose career spanned the major part of the twentieth century. In an account of what had awoken his interest in poetry, he credited the nineteenth-century US-American poet Henry Wadsworth Longfellow (1807-1882), whose poem "The Arrow and the Song" he had read in his high school English textbook, as his first poetic inspiration: "The poem struck me as exceedingly refreshing. It was as if I were seeing poetry for the first time. Now I can no longer remember the original lines . . . but the general impression lingers. . . . It was simply a repetition of parallels, but it had illuminated me with the true spirit of poetry. It also rekindled my interest in what was for me the overly familiar, and aesthetically indifferent because having been read-to-a-pulp *Shijing* (Book of Songs), especially *Guofeng* (Ballads). For the first time I felt the same freshness, the same beauty" (*Guo,* "Wode zuoshi jingguo" 138-39). Over the years, Guo acquired knowledge and appreciation of such authors as Longfellow, Whitman, Tagore, Goethe, and Qu Yuan (see Gálik, *Milestones* 43-72; Zheng 153-98). However, his particular personal poetic tribute to writers elucidates more than the origins of Guo's poetic career. The torturous route of Guo's poetic awakening demonstrates the nonlineal movement between new poetic beginnings and their cultural aesthetic sources, as well as the historical complexity of the beginnings of modern Chinese literature, including the seminal presence of literary cultures of other places and times. It also shows that poetic impact is not a presence of dominance, of simple impact and response. Instead, Guo's story highlights the complicated travail between tradition and modernity and between Chinese and Western poetics. For what Guo recalls in his early poetic awakening is not just Longfellow's parallel structure, but that certain translatable spirit which has led to a rediscovery of his own poetic origin. Guo's poetic development provides surprising illuminations of what is usually considered an exceedingly iconoclastic Chinese literary modernity. At least as it is represented by the New Culture Movement (1914-1920s, at times referred to as the May Fourth Movement because of its culmination on 4 May 1919 in a massive movement of protest against Western imperialism and the warlord governments of China), an intellectual and cultural revolution in early Republican China known for its iconoclastic and reformist zeal. More fundamentally, however, the passage offers translocal glimpses into the very foundation of the institution of modern literature and aesthetic culture as it was formulated in different temporal and geographic locations. As an example of a personal literary vision in times of dramatic historical change, it illustrates the intricate relations between origins and developments in the formation of cultural modernities across time and space. Since Guo's modern poetic awakening vis-à-vis both Euro-American Romanticism and a recuperated classical Chinese sublime tradition, Guo has embarked on a massive project of cultural transformation with like-minded poets and cultural critics. They aimed to reform poetry in particular and culture in general. At the center of this project lay the revision of a modern aesthetics of the sublime, invoking the historical and poetic figure of grandeur and greatness, but stressing the excessive capacity—the sublime's aesthetic ability to overwhelm, scatter and carry over affectively—of such ideal figuration, which is then charged with the potential to offer imaginative possibilities for new historical directions.

In my book I address the modern formation of an aesthetic culture of the sublime as part of Guo's project in early twentieth-century China. I also examine the philosophical and aesthetic formations of the sublime in Europe from the late eighteenth to the mid-nineteenth centuries as the Chinese moment's modern historical precursor. I analyze the aspirations and dilemmas of modern Chinese literary culture as demonstrated in the transformation of the aesthetics of the sublime in Guo's attempt to revolutionize Chinese poetic sensibility. This approach sets up the European and the Chinese as distinct but historically intertwined and discursively analogous moments, a juxtaposition that highlights these moments' historical-aesthetic commensurability. This comparative commensurability (see L. Zhang , *Mighty Opposites* 7-8, 149) is historically aesthetic in the sense that both the earlier European reformulation of the sublime and its later Chinese transformation are movements dependent on the historical situation at the moments of their figuration, as well as on the excessive and capacious nature of the sublime as an aesthetic property.

In the first half of the book I trace the Romantic construction of the sublime—how it is figured as a cultural and historical redirection—in the late eighteenth- to mid-nineteenth-century English aesthetic and poetic texts in conjunction with its continental counterparts. In the second half, I treat the sublime aesthetics' early twentieth-century Chinese transformation by the poet "of the times," Guo Moruo. Guo's rewriting and infusion of the Romantic aesthetics of the sublime into a nascent modern Chinese poetics is envisioned as a poetic reconstruction, as well as a cultural redress, of the historical trauma of modernity. Hence it is a project comparable to Burke's aesthetic inquiry into the sublime in historical crisis and to Wordworth's revision of a modern poetics as a prelude to a new historical direction. I do not examine the process of formation and transformation of aesthetic ideals and figures as a monolineal progress. Instead, my approach is to show that the perceived European influence on modern Chinese literature "involves a far more complicated process than the simple transmission of a literary model from one culture to another; that reception of influence is frequently predicated on intrinsic conditions and needs; that an influence cannot take place unless there is pre-existing predisposition" (Yeh, "Chayi de youlu" 94). In his study, *Milestones in Sino-Western Literary Confrontation*, Marián Gálik defines "influence" as "confrontations," a process to be understood "in the broadest possible connections and parallels, in all their essential motions and contexts" (4). Gálik elaborates through the Soviet comparatist A.S. Bushmin that "literary continuity [*snyatie, Aufheben*]" in the encounter of two or more literatures as "the highest contact-taking," which, as "a creatively mastered-tradition, is in its essence in a dissolved, or philosophically speaking, in a 'cancelled' state" (4). This understanding of influence, for Gálik, is to shift the emphasis to the "receiving end . . . if we divide the word *Aufheben* in its Hegelian connotation into its three meaningful components, i.e., to cancel, to preserve and to lift up, then it becomes clear that the process (which may be understood as influence) may imply a new phenomenon which becomes relevantly modified in the prism of the receiving literary and social context, primarily in connection with the creative abilities of the receiving subject and the needs of the receiving literary structure" (4).

To be influenced in this sense is to make a historically implicated choice, which presupposes rather than undermines creative activities (cancels out then lifts up what might be in the original). To emphasize predisposition is to foreground the needs and agencies of the new writers, adaptors, and translators who in this sense are not merely on the receiving end of knowledge, model, or form. I argue that what is foregrounded when one privileges preexisting predispositions is the historical condition and possibility of any chosen cultural project, be it an original formulation, translation, or re-creation. When Guo explains that it was not the original lines, but, rather, a lingering general impression of Western poetry that redirected him to a modern Chinese poetic rejuvenation, he spells out the quintessence of what he calls his literary "supranationalism" in line with the early twentieth-century Chinese New Culture Movement (see Shih 14). The original in these cases of cultural rather than literal linguistic translation, adaptation, or re-creation is most often seen as references to and possibilities of a zeitgeist. I demonstrate that this is the case with Guo's transformation of sublime aesthetics in his attempt to rejuvenate a modern Chinese poetics, in particular, to create a modern Chinese poetic sensibility, and similarly so when the late eighteenth- and mid-nineteenth-century European aesthetic philosophers and poets tried to figure an aesthetics or begin a new poetic tradition responsive to and able to redeem, redirect a terrifying modern history. The latter, I show, is exemplified in the texts of Burke and Wordsworth. My study, then, is comparative in the sense that it juxtaposes two distinctly different cultural moments and thus I analyze their discursive and aesthetic formations by framing them together in their historical linkage to the arrival of modernity. The "commensurability" of the two parts, as I mention earlier, is in our shared modern history. Hence it is a historical, as well as aesthetic commensurability, demonstrated in the like-minded critical and creative responses to events of their times by key cultural figures at the different but historically entwined ends. I demonstrate that it is in relation to analogous historical pressures that the European and Chinese aesthetes or poets resort to the cultural capacity of the sublime as an aesthetic property. Whether through original aesthetic reformulation or anxious transformative poetic recreation, these aesthetic attempts at historical redress represent two comparable cultural moments geographically separated but historically linked, albeit along different temporal registers, by the experience of what might be called the encounter with modernity.

Thus, I do not treat European Romanticism as a block term of vague and all-encompassing Western cultural precedence, understood as overwhelming dominance, to modern Chinese counterparts. Rather, the European aesthetic treaties and poems are studied as historical texts in specific historical contexts, put in relation historically and aesthetically with the similarly historically situated Chinese texts. This orientation also dictates that the study delves into detailed textual analysis of pivotal (pre-)Romantic European aesthetic and poetic texts of the sublime, as well as Guo's poetic theory and compositions as Romantic sublime's timely historical recreation. By such historically informed textual and aesthetic analysis, I aim to make clear that it is in textual aesthetic figurations that the sublime is figured in European Romanticism as a culturally capacious aesthetic category whose hyperbolic agency is then reinvoked and experimented with poetically by Guo when he attempts to transform the sublime into modern Chinese poetics. In other words, Guo is not influenced by inspired European or US-American Romantic souls (see R. Liu, "Whitman's Soul" 172-86; Ou, "Pantheistic Ideas" 187-96) but, rather, likewise attracted to and consequently refigured the sublime aesthetics' capacious agency. Thus the historical significance of the modem figuration of the sublime—why and how it is reevoked and reformulated at these different but related historical junctures—cannot be made clear without a careful study of its actual figuration and refiguration, and without a localized examination of the structuration of its modus operandi. At the same time, such textual aesthetic analysis shows that inter- and intraliterary studies do not have to be at the opposite ends of the spectrum. History, as it were, can be glimpsed, comprehended, and rethought, through, in, and in between poetic lines. And conversely, aesthetic cultural projects, including their modus operandi, are seldom envisioned for their own sake. Critical readings of aesthetic and poetic texts will show that the protocols of the Romantic aesthetics of the sublime exemplify the necessary interrelations and multidirectional passage between aesthetic ideals, cultural interests, historical origins and ends. Cultural and historical circumstances, in this sense, are not just outside but in the texts.

In this way, I investigate two main issues: the relationship between the figuration of aesthetic ideal and historical change and the transformation of ideas and cultural-aesthetic forms in different temporal and geographic locations. These, in turn, are examined in particular along the recurrent motif of aesthetic and poetic beginnings and their sources of origins in both European and Chinese texts. Thus, the notion of beginnings as a historical-aesthetic and social-cultural concern is central to the book's conceptual frame. Edward W. Said argues that while the idea of "origin" is divine, mythical, and privileged, "beginning" is secular and humanly produced. In his treatise on the role of the intellectual goal of criticism, he traces the ramifications and diverse understandings of the concept of beginning through history. For

Said, a beginning is a first step in the intentional production of meaning and the production of difference from preexisting traditions. It authorizes subsequent texts as it both enables them and limits what is acceptable. In his book, *Beginnings*, Said postulates that eighteenth- to nineteenth-century European novels represent a major attempt in Western literary culture to give beginnings an authorizing function in experience, art, and knowledge. This authorizing function of beginnings, which is the legitimation, as well as the first step of difference vis-à-vis tradition, can also be employed to understand the cultural preoccupation and historical aspiration of Romantic aesthetic culture. It explains the recurrent need for new primordial ground, the repeated struggle for a historically as well as poetically viable commencement poetics and the persistent search for sources of aesthetic and cultural transformation in both European and Chinese Romantic texts. It also sheds light on the obsession with the figure of death and monuments and with the longing for new epic heroes in the figuration of the sublime in these aesthetic and poetic texts.

I suggest in my critical and historical analysis of figures and texts as diverse as Burke's *Inquiry into the Origins of Our Ideas of the Sublime and Beautiful*, Wordsworth's *Prelude*, and Guo's experimental poem "Fenghuang Niepan (Nirvana of the Phoenix)" and his verse drama, *Qu Yuan* that the modern aesthetic turn is a deliberate historical hyperbolization of the sense of literary agency. Such agency is, in turn, imaginatively and affectively constructed as a means to redress different cultures' traumatic encounter with the modern moment, what Friedrich Schiller calls the cultural wounds of history (39). I demonstrate that, imagined as a project of affective and moral transformation, the Romantic reinvention of a modern aesthetics promulgates not only a different aesthetic ideal but also a different social function for literary culture at moments of historical crisis. This is seen in such cultures' manifest preoccupation with sublime aesthetics, which is conceived as a cultural project to counter the terrors brought about by modern history. In this aesthetic figuration of history as a mutilated wardrobe of inheritance, the process of history is understood to be brutally disruptive but nonetheless a precedent that has to be reckoned with, often only with the help of a new cultural imagination. This understanding of history is also seen in the sublime's cultural translation in early twentieth-century China when the latter was suddenly and violently brought face to face with the trauma of modernity.

In my study I show that by turning to the sublime, both the modern European aesthetes and Chinese poets are making a privileged and hyperbolic case for literary aesthetic culture as an imaginative resolution to historical crisis. My analysis draws on contemporary theories and critical works from both the fields of Anglo-American scholarship and studies of modern Chinese literature and culture, including critical sources published in Chinese. In this sense, the secondary materials are as essential as the primary sources since they foreground the nature of the cultural and historical transformations discussed here and serve as examples of the entanglement between tradition and contemporaneity, the West and the East. The concept of modernity—central to the construction and understanding of Romantic and sublime discourse, as well as its temporal and geographic crossings—is understood as "contested." This understanding has become consensual in recent scholarship as well as general cultural discourse. As Charles Laughlin summarizes in his introduction to *Contested Modernities in Chinese Literature*, the problem of understanding modernity and its correlations in twentieth-century China goes beyond the contentions in European and Anglo-American debates. There, it is not only a case of contentions in dates, places of germination, forms of manifestation, and historical ideological orientations in evaluating its implications, but also one involving understanding and evaluating the impact of semicolonialism, the "Orientalist" nature of Western Sinology as well as our contemporary global situation (Laughlin 1). Recent scholarship on modern Chinese history has traced modernity's economical and cultural emergence in China to a much earlier period, namely, the late Ming and Qing dynasties, just as there are disputes in the dating and implication of the beginning of European modernity. However, while taking into account these new understandings, I keep to the characterization of modernity as traumatic processes and moments of discontinuity in Chinese as well as European history. This is because I intend to explore aesthetic and poetic texts in their cultural historical contexts, that is, in the context of how modernity as a concept and historical moment was understood and treated by the studied historical cultural figures and their times. And, hence, I engage such treatment as historical aestheticism—an ambitious and imaginative aesthetic construction motivated and underwritten by historical anxieties and events. I show that cultural modernity is also contested in what are usually read as established canonic texts of modern reaction (all authors treated are key figures in and of their variously located modern moments). I will therefore maintain the sense of modernity first as Burke and Wordsworth had it, namely, as the social and cultural aftermath of the whole set of events culminating in, or becoming the aftermath of, the French Revolution; and then as the Chinese May Fourth intellectual tradition (the New Culture Movement) defines it in relation to its own and the world's social cultural history. These are what were meaningful to Burke's sublime as an exemplary aesthetics; to Wordsworth's attempt to lay a modern poetic ground upon which history can "rise once more"; and to Guo's transformation of the aesthetics of the great into one of dark destruction rather than poetic uplift as originally intended.

For the Chinese May Fourth tradition, for example, of which Guo is an avant-garde figure, to begin its account of a modern cultural history with 1842, the year when China signed the Nanjing Treaty with Great Britain, the first of a whole series of unequal treaties that conceded territorial rights to the modernized Western powers, is to emphasize that Chinese modernity is reactive. It is an account centered on national and individual survival in a new historical context. And the ensuing modernization project is therefore about whether to embrace Western Enlightenment understood as democracy and science, or to struggle against Western imperialism. In short, it has defined itself with and against the impingement of a modern West. What is also important is that this account delineates a local-national modern cultural revolution as an aftermath and redress of traumatic worldwide political and historical events. This is what underwrites the "timely spirit" which drove Guo and his fellow cultural practioners' efforts to reinvent a modern Chinese poetics. Reaction to and redress of the processes and consequences of industrialization, of the French Revolution, and colonial expansion are also central in both Burke's (pre) Romantic aesthetic figurations and Wordsworth's major poetic texts. And the obsession with the sublime aesthetics along different temporal lines, for all parties, as a cultural reaction to modernity highlights the sense of historical crisis at the heart of such aesthetic-poetic (re)formulations.

The term *modernity* is thus alluded to in the book, that is, reiterated from primary aesthetic and poetic texts and contemporary theoretical works, as reference to both past events and their discursive configurations. It is employed simultaneously as a cultural figure that figures its own discourse and the historical difference it signals. This means that it is also evoked as a historical moment commonly perceived to be discontinuous from its previous moments in both its European and Chinese accounts. And as seen in both European Romantic and early twentieth-century Chinese cultural texts, modernity is figured as an ongoing extreme situation. To adhere to this Romantic and New Culturalist construction, therefore, is to adhere to a historically informed position. It is not a position that demands one share the overall perception of the trajectory of modernity and history by the studied historical cultural figures, but a critical understanding of their sense of trauma and disjunction as the germinating factor in modern action and reaction. This understanding is enhanced by the comparative nature of the project. Because of the constant transposition of events and meanings, sources and recreations, origins and ends, it is difficult to entertain any ideas of their anteriority or detachment. The notion of translation, consequently, is central in structuring understandings of their movements and interrelation. The departure of the concept of translation here is Lydia Liu's elaboration of "translingual practice" as "coauthorship" and reinvention (46), a dynamic process of meaning making and culture building on the historical contact between China and the West. However, its use throughout the chapters is not restricted to translingual or even transcultural practices. Translation in its employment here is first derived from the discussed historical texts, for its connotation of the establishment of correspondence between historical events and poetic beginnings and ends, as in Wordsworth's structural poetic modus operandi and Guo's cultural transformation from sources of the remote in both time and space. This sense of translation as a structure of correspondence, rather than mere linguistic or textual traversal, is stressed and reiterated throughout the study because of its promise of structural and discursive transposition. Transposition is defined as a movement of dynamic meaning making and system of transference. Translation, then, is a "schema of configuration," but more generally cultural and historical than narrowly national linguistic as Naoki Sakai defines it (3). It emphasizes that new beginnings, as the starting point of difference in the movement of aesthetic ideals and figures, are always predicated on the centrality of other places and times. It is in this sense of cultural and historical transfiguration that Burke establishes a historical and aesthetic distance and figures his aesthetic philosopher as historical director and negotiator; Wordsworth defines his poet as translator; and Guo reforms a modern Chinese poetry as multisourced, of sublime historical ends but contrary cultural-aesthetic impulses.

The juxtaposition of texts from different temporal and geographical locations also demands elaboration of what might appear to be methodological or structural idiosyncrasies. In chapters 1, 2, and 3, which deal with the European primary and secondary materials, I delve more directly into the discussion on the protocols of the Romantic aesthetics of the sublime as major countercurrents of a modern cultural poetics-politics in Anglo-American Romantic studies. In chapters 4, 5, and 6—where I treat the new figuration of such a sublime aesthetic ideal in the modern Chinese poetic revolution, I delineate the contours of their arguments and contentions in order to provide contextual narratives of their situation and implication, since much of the material has not been previously dealt with in English. The task to inform in the later chapters is undertaken with some discomfort. In the course of writing, I felt the necessity of providing background knowledge to an audience who might otherwise be unfamiliar with the location and hence the meaning of the discussion, notwithstanding the historical linkage that underlines the aesthetic and cultural traversals foregrounded. This is, of course, less a personal complaint than part of the complexity inherent in a cross-cultural, comparative discussion: it illustrates the need to communicate as well as the dilemma of the "other" interlocutor in face of the asymmetry in the transfer of knowledge. After all, the project is undertaken as an attempt to contribute to the building of comparative literary study and to extend the inquiry into Chinese cultural modernity beyond the circle of Chinese studies. As the present endeavor, which has traced the historical and imaginative entanglement between the East and West, past and present, demonstrates, traveling in more than one direction is the only way to make sense of our modern condition. Therefore, I hope the differences will at least highlight the complications of such an undertaking and invite further interest and attention to the problem as well as the possibilities.

The recurrent concerns in literary and cultural studies about the relationship between aesthetic figuration and historical difference, about the implications of the temporal and cultural crossing of ideas and concepts and aesthetic ideals, is what underwrites the passage between the diverse texts, figures, and their discussions. This is a project that seeks to add new insights and dimensions to ongoing debates. The juxtaposition of materials and deliberations that otherwise do not directly influence one another foregrounds the historical linkage between two distinct cultural moments encompassing vast temporal and spatial differences. What links the revision of literary-aesthetic culture at the turn of the eighteenth century in England and the formulation of a modern poetics in the New Culture Movement in China more than a hundred years later is their implication in shared modern history, which conditions but does not determine the kind of "general impression" of the former upon the latter. Shumei Shih, in her account of twentieth-century Chinese literary modernism, has treated this implication as manifested in modern China's semicolonial condition, which, for her, predetermines its modern cultural predilections (Shih 1-48). The May Fourth Chinese intellectuals, however, defined and defended their choices otherwise.

Introduction

In their accounts, their allowance of their varied but collective "general impression" of and from the modernizing West to be the resources for a modern Chinese cultural rejuvenation are inevitable, although not always loved, personal as well as collective choices in the face of a historical crisis. Thus, although they vary in their moment of social and cultural concerns, as well as in their particular aesthetic permutations, the English and the Chinese Romantic sublime are nevertheless perceived similarly as the redress of the threat and trauma of modernity. The shared preoccupation with the sublime also allows the writers each in their turn to wrestle with and make sense of issues—including historical or poetic origins and ends, tradition and the present moment, the perception and feelings of terror, might, melancholy and destruction, and rapture and passion, or the limit and possibility of poetic creation—which are all central in the construction of such an aesthetics. The example of its later (Chinese) transfiguration also highlights the possibilities and limitations of the earlier (European) project and reshapes the debate on aesthetics and historical change which is most often undertaken exclusively within the confines of the cultural modernity of Europe and Anglo-America. In my study I seek a revision.

As a comparative study of primary texts across languages and cultures, this volume serves the aims and scope of the Purdue University Press monograph series of Books in Comparative Cultural Studies, a series that emphasizes a contextual approach in the study of culture in all of its products and processes and is theoretically and textually as well as historically based. It also serves the series' area of interests by bringing into focus lesser-known literature (at least in English) in a comparative context. Yingjin Zhang, in his groundbreaking revision of a Chinese comparative literature, has called for a critical engagement with literary and cultural theory on the part of its practitioners while studying Chinese texts with a self-reflexive position (Y. Zhang 5-7). I examine both Chinese and European texts to understand anew our shared modern history, as well as to reconceptualize aesthetic theories and their historical modus operandi. I also aim to break new grounds by reengaging the "older" comparative taxonomy, that is, by structuring historically different cultural texts as parallel cases of a related theme, but not tracing direct crossings of influences temporally and spatially. By this I demonstrate that influences are often misnomers for choices, for new formulations conditioned by historical predisposition.

In chapters 1 and 2, I treat the subject schematically while grounding it in historical debates. It begins with the reinvention of the aesthetic field from the late eighteenth to the mid-nineteenth centuries in Europe. By concentrating on Burke's figuration of the origins of the sublime and the beautiful as a problem of historical choice and situating it in relation to Schiller's letters *On the Aesthetic Education of Man* and Kant's philosophy of the aesthetic judgment, I postulate that the construction of the modern sublime as an aesthetic redemption of history begins in medias res of a general sense of crisis. The ambition of such an aesthetic construction, therefore, is nothing less than the relocation and redirection of a modernity that has hardly begun but has gone amiss. In the Burkean aesthetical-political reconstruction, the urgency to relocate the historical question of direction as an ontological question of the status of being and the natural, scientific question of bodily function is to reestablish the origin of particular, chosen histories as the primeval ground upon which a straying modernity can be legitimately, "naturally" rectified and refounded. This construction is an arduous attempt to restore nature upon the ruins of history and render history second nature. The sublime aesthetics refigured as such becomes an offering of redress for the "wound upon modern humanity" inflicted by "culture itself" (Schiller 39) and an aesthetic imperative that attempts to exceed the limits of history.

In chapter 3, I explore Wordsworth's poetic composition of his personal and at the same time historical anxieties of modernity into a structure of what he calls the "spots of time" (*The Prelude: 1799, 1805, 1850* 429) where he can culturally and imaginatively restore history. The discussion begins with the question of direction in Wordsworth's structuration of *The Prelude,* conceived as the poetic "prelude" of new historical directions. It suggests that the poet's commencement poetics, his seminal restlessness, and the widely discussed problem of beginning in his text are not only a center point of Wordsworth's poetic means but also vital to his poetic ends. For the construction of the end, the limit, and the direction of poetic passage in *The Prelude* is central to the understanding of the purpose and interest of Wordsworth's longest poem as a Romantic text. The problem of "preluding" history as the "rush of poetic numbers" remains for the poet ostensibly a question of finding new directions in the face of the cultural and historical impasse that is an aftermath of the French Revolution. I conclude from the discussion that the poetic direction of *The Prelude,* with its worldly concerns of history and revolution, becomes a matter of figuring a sublime poetics, a task predicated on the function of the poet as translator. The sublime telos of Wordsworth's poetics is a poetics of translation, which appears much less a picture of harmonizing totality as is understood in Anglo-American Romantic studies, than a willful imposition of the translatability between kinds. And it is only in such a relation of translation that Wordsworth rebuilds the sense of the sublimity of poetic power and figures the poetic imperative of historical redirection.

In chapter 4, I aim to demonstrate that both because of its own perceived capacious (excessive) property and the particular cultural affective demands of modern times, the aesthetics of the sublime is readily and emphatically refigured and transformed across geographies and ideologies. These claims are built on the philosophical and aesthetic theory of Jean-Luc Nancy, which directs attention to the emergence and structure of the modern sublime as an aesthetic movement of unlimitation (in philosophical terms) that takes place on the border of the limit, and as a cultural assertion whose ambition is to reground historical direction. This thesis is further developed by examining the modern passage of the sublime aesthetics as a timely spirit, which idealizes capacious movement in the birth of a "new" Chinese literary culture in the early twentieth century. It explores the implications of the new culture's preoccupation with its own timeliness, and with itself as a reactive cultural story of ambitious but at the same time melancholic historical beginning.

In chapter 5, I discuss the transformation of the Romantic aesthetics of the sublime as a modern aesthetic ideal constructed in the New Poetry movement, which, in turn, is imagined as a cultural response to the burdens of modernity, by tracing as its example the poetic works and literary vision of Guo and in particular his reconstruction of a sublime aesthetics in figuring a poetics of the times and a new Chinese epic culture-hero. Here, I focus on the implications of cultural translation and on the movement between historical direction and aesthetic ideal, the temporal and the spatial. I demonstrate that in forging a timely poetics in his first poetry collection *Nüshen* (The Goddess), and in particular the much celebrated poem "Fenghuang Niepan (Nirvana of the Phoenix)," which ends in defiance and celebration of destruction rather than sublime poetic resolution, Guo's transformative poetic act unleashes all that is dark and obscure in the modern figuration of the sublime and brings into sharp relief the implications of the historical aesthetic formation.

In chapter 6, I continue to discuss Guo's reprieve of tradition embodied in his lifelong refiguration of the historical poet Qu Yuan. These verse dramas are often acclaimed as the most passionately iconoclastic and sublime in modern Chinese literary history. I trace and analyze Guo's contrary tendencies for the aesthetics of the sublime and the beautiful when he evokes and recasts Qu Yuan (340-278 BC) as the great original Chinese poet. While beginning with Guo's earlier dramatic verse, *Xianglei,* I concentrate on the "Ju song (Ode to the Orange)" and the "Leidian song (Thunderstorm Monologue)" in his later historical poetic drama, *Qu Yuan.* This provides the framework to explore the cultural significance of the supplementary structure of the aesthetic principles in these two poetic compositions as Guo's attempt to create a modern Chinese poetics. Guo's verse drama, however, ends up looking like a poetic journey of terror and rage that precariously reaches towards its moment of sublime affect, a moment brought about by a poetic substitution and dramatic resolution of compromise. Guo, like Burke, at the moment when the sublime cannot be resolved poetically or dramatically, turns to the sentiment of the beautiful as solution, as closure. From this central structure of poetic substitution that is excessive but compromising, the chapter concludes that the end of Guo and his fellow New Culturalists' espousal and transformation of an aesthetic movement of unlimitation (a sublime poetics) against the terrors of modernity is a hyperbolic construction of a different literary agency. It is an imaginatively capacious but destructive agency, which reiterates but exceeds the possibilities as well as the "dark" "obscurity" of the original. Envisioned as a counteraction against both the imposition of the West and their own bankrupt cultural "tradition," Guo's aspirations and dilemmas in translating and refiguring a sublime poetics for a different society, as well as for himself as the "New" poet, epitomize those of the modern Chinese intellectuals in their attempt to transform and reinvent, out of pain and anxiety, a cultural modernity.

Chapter One

Envisioning a Culture of the Sublime Aesthetic

In contemporary philosophy, aesthetics as an established philosophical enquiry has two applications: a restricted sense of the study of beauty in art and nature and a general reference to the whole process of human perception and sensation—those feelings of pleasure and pain that are not simply reducible to clearly defined intellectual concepts (Malpas 34). In his study of Lyotard's idea of art, the sublime, and the postmodern, Malpas also points out that as a particular discipline of inquiry, aesthetics emerged during the eighteenth century in Europe and since then formed a key part of the work of many Anglo-European thinkers (34). One can further observe that in recent cultural, literary, and philosophical discussions, whether about the debates on modernity and postmodernity with which Malpas is concerned or about particular aesthetic tenet's historical formulation across time and space, aesthetics is almost always used both as a philosophy of art and as a general account of perception and feeling.

The point of interest in this chapter is the coming-to-be of the modern aesthetics of the sublime as a particular historical formation. It is discussed as a historical-aesthetic process that becomes important culturally in eighteenth-century Europe and is later thought of and sought after similarly in a cultural and poetic revolution in early twentieth-century China. By general consent, the discussion of the sublime, sometimes called the aesthetics of greatness, is perhaps the single most important concern of eighteenth-century English aesthetics. While at the same time, at least according to Samuel Holt Monk, "no single definition of the term would serve in any single decade for all writers . . . but the word naturally expressed high admiration, and usually implied a strong emotional effect, which, in the latter years of the century, frequently turned on terror" (233). For Burke, who clearly specifies in his *Philosophical Enquiry into the Origin of Our Ideas of the Sublime and Beautiful* (1757), "terror is in all cases whatsoever the ruling principle of the sublime" (58). This terror-grounded formulation of the aesthetics of the sublime highlights the sense of crisis in the (pre-)Romantic longing for historical and literary greatness. It reveals the historical concern in the concerted aesthetic movement, which can be described as a historical aestheticism. In what follows, I explore such historical-aesthetical tendencies in the English and continental European (pre-)Romantic construction of a modern aesthetic culture, that is, aesthetic, literary, and cultural figurations originally and imaginatively set up as timely redemption of a crisis-ridden modern history.

Historical aestheticism

Burke's (in)famous description of the spectacle of the French Revolution is as historical, in the sense that it is about a neighboring event, as it is aesthetic: "As to us here our thoughts of everything at home are suspended, by our astonishment at the wonderful Spectacle which is exhibited in a Neighboring and rival Country—what Spectators, and what actors! England gazing with astonishment at a French struggle for Liberty, and not knowing whether to blame or to applaud! The thing indeed . . . has still something in it paradoxical and Mysterious. The spirit it is impossible not to admire; but the old Parisian ferocity has broken out in a shocking manner" (Burke, "To the Earl of Charlemont" 10). Burke's concern is more with the affect of the splendors of the French struggle for liberty on the English audience. For him it is as if the historical event is staged for its implications, which depend on its power of affection and evocation for reflection. Burke is both moved and wary, he admires the spirit but fears its ferocity, just as he had aspired to and was fearful of its excess in his theory of the sublime. His task, therefore, is to comprehend and redirect the spectacular historical show, for and on behalf of his audience.

The relationship between aesthetic figuration and historical change awaiting redirection, as staged dramatically here by Burke and echoed elsewhere in contemporary aesthetic debates, is the central question of aesthetic-literary modernity in Europe at the turn-of-the-eighteenth to the nineteenth centuries. It continues to be one of the most important questions in the writing of literary and aesthetic histories. Its intersection is the recurring theme in recent cultural discussions and is deemed vital in understanding the institution of modern aesthetic culture. Indeed, in their study of the emergence of modern literature in early German Romanticism, Philippe Lacoue-Labarthe and Nancy locate the beginnings of the modern literary institution in the aftermath of a "triple crisis": the social and moral crisis of the bourgeoisie, with newfound access to culture; the political crisis of the French Revolution; and the Kantian critique urgently in need of its own critical recasting (4-5). In their delineation, the Kantian crisis of the subject is located not in philosophy but in a radical modernity, and the project of early German (Jena) Romanticism opens up "not a crisis in literature, but a general crisis and critique" for which literature or literary theory is the "privileged locus of expression" (5). It is privileged because it presents itself as the most properly critical formulation of the crisis of modern history. The Romantic ambition, literary or philosophical (they become one in the Jena project), therefore, is concerned little with the invention of genres and erection of aesthetic doctrines, it is "always" the result of the ambition "for an entirely new social function for the writer . . . and consequently for a different society" (6).

The interest of Lacoue-Labarthe and Nancy's historical aesthetic study of the Jena project is in their establishment of a theory of literature in Romanticism. For them it is a "literature" reformulated as the "privileged locus of expression" of the crisis of modern history (5). They define the Romantic project by placing it against the background of specific social, political, and philosophical crises, but develop the social function of the writer as, and in, the continuous philosophical recasting of the Kantian (loss of the) subject. The building up of the literary absolute as the ultimate social function of Romanticism, for them, lies in its radical displacement, resurrection, and redefinition of philosophy. Lacoue-Labarthe and Nancy account for the establishment of the literary absolute as a philosophical aftermath relocated in the crisis of history. It points to an understanding of Romanticism radically different from the kind that reads its advent as literature's move to autonomy or therapeutic restitution. They highlight the correlation between aesthetic figuration and historical change. More importantly, their account exemplifies the story of the "reordering of the field of aesthetic experience" (Price 262) in Europe from the late eighteenth into the mid-nineteenth centuries. This reordering is marked by "an intensification of interest in the mental image and in the difficulties of assimilating it to the problems of ontology and epistemology, on the one hand, and to those of ethics, on the other" (Ferguson 1). It is a reordering of perception and experience which betrays an historical anxiety in its presentation as a philosophic-categorical aftermath, a process that is defined by Malpas as the coming-into-being of aesthetics. In fact, "the intensification of interest" marks the advent of a modern aesthetics that attempts to inaugurate "an era which disowns the historical inheritance that defines it" (Bourke 199). Richard Bourke's insight places the Romantic aesthetic movement accurately at its historical junction and points out that at its center is a desire for and at the same time an anxiety about historical discontinuity. And while for Bourke the difficulties of historical as well as poetic continuity as experienced by the Romantics are brought about by the disruption of the French Revolution, for Lacoue-Labarthe and Nancy, the Romantic is introduced as an aesthetic reprieve in which the literary becomes the privileged locus of expression of the crisis of modernity. Such aesthetic movement is a culturally capacious reconstruction whose point of departure consists in a deliberate hyperbolization of literary agency as a means to counteract the social, political, and cultural problems of the modern moment. This, I argue, is also what defines and underwrites the historical aestheticism—a reinvoked and redefined aesthetic imperative as historical direction—embedded in the texts and conceptual implications of a host of late eighteenth-century European aesthetic philosophers from Schiller to Burke.

Lacoue-Labarthe's and Nancy's reading foregrounds the sense of crisis in the urgently emphatic formulation of an aesthetic modernity. Their account also displays that the modern reordering, or rather, reinvention of the aesthetic field is preoccupied with the motif of beginnings and the centrality of historical and cultural translation. The latter often manifests itself as an operating structure of transference in the conceptual underpinning and textual modus operandi of key aesthetic texts. For example, in Lacoue-Labarthe's and Nancy's understanding, the end of the Jena project is dependent upon the location of its beginnings, and the hyperbolization of literary agency as the very critical formulation of modernity is the translation of an historical anxiety into an epistemological problem. However, this translation is not what Jerome McGann diagnoses as the displacement of history when he exposes the "grand illusion" of Romanticism. The Romantic for McGann is the turn of the "imagination and nightmares of a poetic freedom" from "the ruins of culture and history" (91). Proceeding from the idea of the Romantic hyperbolization of literary agency, however, I would argue in what follows that this turn is, rather, an aesthetic practice of "rich distance": William Gilpin's "beautiful distance" extols the "obscurity" that makes it possible to observe objects without seeing their "awkwardness," whereas I am invoking the richness of a distance that blurs fine distinctions and allows alteration—the replacing and displacing of the distances (Gilpin 34; see also Harrison 62-67) that try to reengage the disruptions, legacies, and challenges of culture and history.

Understood as such, the Romantic preoccupation with beginnings as the first concern in the process of the literary reformulation is the locus of the interchange between the aesthetic and the historical. As beginnings are structures of intentions, attitudes, and feelings, and according to Said, they are the first instance of difference, "they make a way along the road" (13). The question of beginnings is thus a question of the will to difference, as well as a question of boundaries—of the end, the limit, and the directions of a given trajectory. It is precisely in its preoccupation with beginnings that the modern aesthetic, emerging in the late eighteenth-century Europe where the excitement as well as terrors of dramatic changes reigned, is set up as the most properly critical formulation of the crisis of modern history. And because of its beginnings in such concerns of the crisis of history, European Romanticism, the inaugurating composition of the modern aesthetic imperative, is understood as a reaction formation. It is seen as "a complex of responses to certain conditions which Western society has experienced and continued to experience since the middle of the eighteenth century" (Butler 184). For instance, in response to the modern condition, Friedrich Schiller conceives the aesthetic as the historical detour of a cultural redress. His *Letters on the Aesthetic Education of Man* stress the immediacy of a timely conception of an historical aestheticism to heal the wound inflicted by "culture itself" upon modern humanity (35). In this proposal of an "aesthetic education of man," the aesthetic is instrumental to the realization of a history that has inevitably lost its innocence and harmony on its way to maturity, a history that cannot be redirected otherwise. In the *Letters*, Schiller defines the aesthetic as the only "impulse" that would move rationality and sensuousness, unhappily divorced in modern times, toward a somewhat dialectic emergent, the "sublime humanity." Thus Schiller establishes the task of the aesthetic philosopher as the director of history: "Given then, I shall reply to the young friend of Truth and Beauty who wants to learn from me how he can satisfy the noble impulse in his breast in the face of all the opposition in his century—give the world on which you are acting the direction towards the good, and the quiet rhythm of time will bring about its development" (53).

In Schiller's project, the act of rectification stresses both the sense of agency and a progressive history, but it is foremost an art of education, of radical redirection, as well as conservation of the "time-honored." Its radicality is cast in the "quiet rhythm of time." As a blueprint for the feat of the aesthete, philosopher, or poet, it rests on a deliberate distancing: the prerequisite for the emergent director of the history of modernity is his refuge in the sanctuary of the ruins of antiquity, the ever lost glory of Greece, a classic—ruined—civilization as wilderness, as invigorating outside to the effeminate, mundane, and deprecated "modern culture." Schiller cries out with unconcealed sentiments against the tendencies of his "time": "No doubt the artist is the child of his time; but woe to him if he is also its disciple, or even its favorite. Let some beneficent deity snatch the infant betimes from his mother's breast, let it nourish him with the milk of a better age and suffer him to grow up to full maturity beneath the distant skies of Greece. Then when he becomes a man, let him return to his century as an alien figure; but not in order to gladden it by his appearance, rather, terrible like Agamemnon's son, to cleanse it" (51).

Schiller's proposal is the call for a new barbarian, whose rearing is tortuous. It echoes the Romantic longing for the originary elsewhere. The golden age of the classical past is invoked to engender him as the avant-guardian—the vanguard and custodian—of a future modernity. Schiller's indulgence in aesthetic barbarism is not nostalgic, but progressive. It is the will to redirect the progress of history, to counteract the terror of modernity, which highlights the cleansing project of his cultural avant-guardianism. Though in the end the Schillerian ideal of human nobility, which can be achieved through the aesthetic solution of politics, is beauty and freedom, his proposal of cultural redemption is by way of the sublime: the project of cleansing is an affective traversal and translation of terror.

The beginning of a modern aesthetics of the sublime from Burke to Kant

The theme and variations of the sublime are the privileged loci of expression of the modern aesthetic as it has developed in Europe since the eighteenth century. In fact, Martin Price's charting of the reordering of the field of aesthetic experience coincides with the moment when the picturesque moves toward the sublime (262). It is no accident that the key figure of English reaction to modernity, Burke, is also the key figure in the English theorization of the sublime. If Schiller's cultural notion of avant-guard demonstrates the modern ambition of historical aestheticism by relocating the past to guard and guide the present course, Burke's aesthetic figuration is born directly out of his sense of historical crisis. Luke Gibbons suggests, in his pioneering study of Burke's engagement with Irish politics and culture, that "as an aesthetics of extreme situations, Burke's theory of the sublime may be seen not only as a philosophical enquiry but also as a fraught, highly mediated response to the turbulent colonial landscape of eighteenth-century Ireland" (23). For him, this explains Burke's obsession with theatricality and terror as something essential in the experience of the sublime, something "orchestrating exemplary actions" (26), and his figuration of public executions as the most exemplary of events that function as the ultimate "dramaturgy of the real" (5-7). In Gibbons's remapping, Burke's theory of the sublime is a philosophical response to a keenly felt historical problem, culminating in an aesthetics of exemplary events as an intersection between the epistemological and the historical. Still, like many others before him, Gibbons concludes from this that "Burke's aesthetics often picks up where his politics leaves off" (6). I suggest, however, that Burke's figuration of an aesthetics of exemplary events demonstrates that, for him, the aesthetic is not only supplementary to political discourse, but it also represents in the first instance an historical imagination. In Burke's construction of the sublime as an aesthetics that orchestrates exemplary actions, the aesthetic is the very stage upon which history can be redirected culturally and affectively, just as the effect of his exemplary events is through the theatricality of the real.

Burke begins his cultural address of the crisis of modernity as a *Philosophical Enquiry into the Origin of Our Ideas of the Sublime and Beautiful*. However, his fears and exaltations, his exaggerated obsession with tastes, smells, touches, and gratifications, come to be understood, later, in an aesthetic epistemology, as a "homespun psycho-physiology" (Eagleton, "Aesthetics and Politics" 53); his eager and timely inquiry into the ideas of the sublime and beautiful becomes records of a Kantian "bathos of experience" (qtd. in Ferguson 2). Frances Ferguson's treatment of Burke illustrates his modern fate. While Eagleton shows contempt for Burke's concerns with the "mere debased modes of access to the world" ("Aesthetics and Politics" 33), Ferguson juxtaposes Burke with Kant and locates the Burkean "bathos" in his insistence on the model of sensory testimony but finds he makes no "thorough-going distinctions" (2). Thus, his aesthetic philosophy is cast as empiricism turned against itself. Whereas the Kantian aesthetics, the other philosophically and culturally monumental project, for her, "not only addresses such a central problem of empiricist aesthetics—the relative standing of objects and representations—but goes a long way toward resolving it by the simple argument of structure" (2)

The construction of a Burkean empiricism-turned-against-itself leading to the triumph of the Kantian transcendental structure, is, of course, one of the usual stories in modern European philosophy. It casts the Burkean and Kantian differences simply in epistemological terms, and shows a certain lack of interest in situating the historical grounding of both the Burkean and Kantian turn to aestheticism. I will demonstrate that, in fact, for neither Burke nor Kant is "the relative standing of objects and representations" the interest of their argument, or the central problem of their aesthetics. For the Burkean inquiry, the difficulties of classification leading to dark obscurity of concept are the foremost topic of discussion. Whereas although the project of the Kantian aesthetic is the movement that erects the argument of structure, the triumph and interest of Kant's form is much less the distinction between the aesthetic objects and the real than the establishment of the a priori of an artificial system. His form is a restructuring of the subject and reconstruction of a regulative structure in the face of the "bathos of experience," the challenge and threat of modernity. In brief, although the Burkean and Kantian differences in constituting a modern aesthetic beginning may appear epistemological ones, the contested nature of these lies in their different cultural philosophical choices in reaction to historical anxiety: what is usually construed as an intra-aesthetic debate in the post-Romantic account of the sublime should be better understood as an historically situated cultural story.

Kant begins to define the sublime as the relations between "our" limitedness and the chaotic, terrifying limitlessness of the beyond: "We may describe the sublime thus: it is an object (of nature) the representation of which determines the mind to think the unattainability of nature regarded as a presentation of ideas" (*Critique of Judgment* 108). The gesture of concession, of deference to a determinate insufficiency, however, is only the first step in the structure of mastery: this effort—and the feeling of the unattainability of the idea by means of the imagination—is itself a presentation of the subjective purposiveness of our mind in the employment of the imagination for its supersensible destination (*Critique of Judgment* 108). In Slavoj Žižek's reading, this is a unique point in Kant's system, a point at which "the gap between phenomenon and Thing-in-itself, is abolished in a negative way, because in it the phenomenon's very inability to represent the Thing adequately *is inscribed in the phenomenon itself*" (203) and the paradox of the sublime is the mediation of this inability, a "successful presentation by means of failure, of the inadequacy itself" (204). However, Kant's structure of the sublime paradox does not end with the mediation of the a priori inadequacy. It is a process of final conquest. In his sublime, this effort to first demonstrate then overcome a human inadequacy by revealing it is a step in an a priori design that "forces us" to realize something supersensible whose purposiveness the feeling of the sublime displays, and meanwhile accedes to the dominion of reason. And this accession to law and reason is our "aesthetic judgments upon the sublime." This act of mastery depends very much on its structuring process. This is probably why the mathematical sublime is usually privileged in Kant's case on empiricist aesthetics. Kant's "series," progression, is often put forward against Burke's "dark dread" and "obscurity": "The account of the mathematical sublime differs from this in using the example of the series (much as Burke had used the counting of columns or pillars) to insist upon the inevitability of exceeding the experiences that one actually had. The mathematical sublime, therefore, differs crucially from Burke's account of sublime obscurity, which involves the dread of some unperceived power potentially concealed in darkness" (Ferguson 24). Kant's turning away from the empirical infinite—the unknown beyond—to the erection of a "completely different" artificial system, in this sense, is a systematic harnessing, a conquering mount. Burke has counted the pillars, but it is up to Kant to structure a system of "series" that establishes progression and "insists upon inevitability." Hence, in Kant's mathematical sublime the boundless or the indefinitely bounded may be "potentially concealed in darkness," but they can be measured by and in mathematical representations. One can further suggest that in such measurement, consequently, the human and historical fear of the empirically unknown and unaccountable is redressed, mounted in an artificial structure that reestablishes it in a different system. The nature of the movement, as I suggest earlier, is a process of transposition, not the masking of the dark void, or "postponement of the encounter with the Thing" (Žižek 204). Since what is established is "the discovery of the relationship between finitude and infinitude. . . . And more important, the relationship between finitude and infinitude rests upon an assertion of the possibility of reassembling these discrete units into a unity, of insisting that a one can be made out of this many . . . Similarly, Kant's account of the dynamical sublime, 'on nature regarded as might,' relies on a connection between distinct explanatory systems to restate the extensional terms of the mathematical sublime in intensional or causal terms" (Ferguson 25-26).

If one follows such a reading, the Kantian transcendental procedure is by no means escapist. It goes beyond putting things in abeyance, and is later recast in the neo-Kantian tradition as the mounting of explanatory systems that structure the real or potential infinitude in thoroughgoing "extensional," "intensional," and "causal" terms, a structuring that insists on inevitability, progressiveness, and conquering "thought" as human freedom. But this reading does not take into consideration that the transition from the purely mathematical to the dynamic, upon which the ambition and interest of Kant's aesthetic judgment erects itself, is by no means easy or conclusive in his analytic of the sublime. As Paul de Man demonstrates in his "Phenomenality and Materiality in Kant," the move to extension shows the necessity to move from the purely formal back to the phenomenal, as the sublime, being "the largest" conceptually, "can never be accessible to the senses. But it is not pure number either, for there is no such thing as a 'greatest' in the realm of number. It belongs to a different order of experience" (de Man, "Phenomenality" 86) Thus the necessity of extending the model of the mathematical sublime to the model of the dynamic sublime marks a shift, a discontinuity in Kant's systematic formal account of the sublime and of the aesthetic judgment. This shows us that the extension of Kant's purely formal structure, upon which the experience of sublime is predicated, not only has at its center a disruption, but also is a move, not unlike its Burkean or many other contemporary counterparts, towards the affective. The move towards the affective rejoins Kant with his contemporary aesthetes. It points to the historicity—the dilemma and urgency of its modernity—in this philosophical aesthetic turn. In Kant's necessary extension to the dynamic sublime, the kinetics of the sublime is treated at once, almost abruptly, as a question of power (*Critique of Judgment* 99-104). The section actually begins with the word "might" and is followed by a dramatic building up of the interplay between might, mighty resistance, and fear. The natural and the aesthetic sublime are related in scenes of violent confrontation and can only be resolved in imaginations of conquest:

> Bold, overhanging, and as it were threatening rocks; clouds piled up in the sky, moving with lightening flashes and thunder peals; volcanoes in all their violence of destruction; hurricanes with their track of devastation; the boundless ocean in a state of tumult; the lofty waterfall of a mighty river, and such like—these exhibit our faculty of resistance as insignificantly small in comparison with their might. . . . and we willingly call these objects sublime, because they raise the energies of the soul above their accustomed height and discover in us a faculty of resistance of a quite different kind, which gives us courage to measure ourselves against the apparent almightiness of nature. (*Critique of Judgment* 100-01).

In the extension, the dialectic of reason and imagination, upon which the moral dimension is introduced and predicated, is maintained (Kant, *Critique of Judgment* 108-09), but only through the mediation of affects, moods, and feelings:

> The satisfaction in the sublime of nature is then only *negative* (while that in the beautiful is *positive*), viz. a feeling that the imagination is depriving itself of its freedom . . . *Astonishment* that borders upon terror, the dread and holy awe which seizes the observer at the sight of mountain peaks rearing themselves to heaven, deep chasms and streams raging therein, deep-shadowed solitudes that dispose one to melancholy meditations—this, in the safety in which we know ourselves to be, is no actual fear but only an attempt to feel fear by the aid of the imagination, that we may feel the might of this faculty in combining with the mind's repose the mental movement thereby excited, and being thus superior to internal nature—and therefore to external—so far as this can have any influence on our feeling of well-being. (*Critique of Judgment* 109)

In Kant's treatment of the "satisfaction" of the sublime, both its initial effect and subsequent transformation are accounted for in affective terms: it begins as one of "astonishment that borders upon terror;" a "dread and holy awe"; but in the safety of our knowledge of our actual place elsewhere, this "is no actual fear but only an attempt to feel fear by the aid of imagination," which in turn is transformed into a feeling of re-posed superiority, an enhanced sense of "our feeling of well-being" (109). This transformation of terror into the satisfaction of the sublime is "a play, a trick of the imagination," but Kant goes on to connect it to reason and morality as a transitional progression:

> In fact, a feeling for the sublime in nature cannot well be thought without combining therewith a mental disposition which is akin to the moral. . . . But in aesthetic judgments upon the sublime this dominion is represented as exercised by the imagination, regarded as an instrument of reason . . . But this idea of the supersensible, which we cannot *know* but only *think* nature as its presentation—is awakened in us by means of an object whose aesthetical appreciation strains the imagination to its utmost

bounds, whether of extension (mathematical) or of its might over the mind (dynamical). (*Critique of Judgment* 108-09).

This elevation of the imagination from a metaphysical to a transcendental principle is not only accomplished in affective terms. But in these affective terms, it takes on the form of a reconquered mastery. Kant's aim in it is that "it achieves a gain in power that is larger than what it sacrifices." The loss of empirical freedom becomes in the process the gain in critical freedom. Such an accomplishment of the aim of the sublime is a complicated and somewhat devious procedure, in which the empirical and the transcendental are translatable rather than separate categories.

The Kantian transcendental procedure seems therefore a reconciliation of "the movement of the affect" and "the codified, formalized, and stable order of reason" (de Man 86). On what grounds, then, does Kant take the Burkean affective "empiricism" for granted and to task? First, one must notice that it is only after he has erected his transcendental principle by reconciling the affective with the formal, albeit somewhat abruptly, that Kant compares it to the Burkean system: "We can now compare the above transcendental exposition of aesthetical judgments with the physiological worked out by Burke and by many clearheaded men among us," he propounds in the "Analytic of the Sublime" in the *Critique*, "in order to see whither a merely empirical exposition of the sublime and beautiful leads" (118). The misdirection of such an exposition, for him, however, is not its methodology of empiricism predicated upon the movement of the affective, as he has no problem with the Burkean inferences based on feelings, affects, and sensations: "Burke, who deserves to be regarded as the most important author who adopts this mode of treatment . . . confirms this explanation, not only by cases in which the imagination, in combination with the understanding, can excite in us the feeling of the beautiful or of the sublime, but by cases in which it is combined with sensation" (*Critique of Judgment* 118-19). Kant not only seems to find no fault with Burke's affective language, which speaks about feelings and refers to bodily movements and sensations as well. He also finds in the latter's procedure the necessary combination of imagination and understanding, although he designates its proper space as that of psychological observation pertaining to the study of empirical anthropology: "As psychological observations, these analyses of the phenomena of our mind are exceedingly beautiful and afford rich material for the favorite investigations of empirical anthropology" (*Critique of Judgment* 119). Such semireluctant acknowledgment of his empiricist legacy, however, does not prevent him from consenting to the necessary link between the corporeal and the intellectual, and their unity in the affective: "And so, as Epicurus maintained, all *gratification* or *grief* may ultimately be corporal, whether it arises from the representation of the imagination or the understanding, because life without a feeling of bodily organs would be merely a consciousness of existence, without any feeling of wellbeing or the reverse" (*Critique of Judgment* 119).

Since Kant reaffirms rather than objects to Burke's procedure of the sublime, which emphasizes the feeling of life, what, then, is his location of its misdirection and his own departure from it? "If, however, we place the satisfaction in the object altogether in the fact that it gratifies us by charm of emotion, we must not assume that any *other* man agrees with the aesthetical judgment which *we* pass, for as to these each one rightly consults his own individual sensibility. But in that case all censorship of taste would disappear" (*Critique of Judgment* 119). What Kant fears is the threat of irreconcilability between individuation and social agreement, which erodes all censorship of taste. It is on this account that he will not allow the proliferation of mere egoistical validation and insists instead on the necessity of a judgment "according to its inner nature—i.e., on account of itself" which "may exact the adhesion of everyone" (*Critique of Judgment* 119). Hence, the central problem of the Kantian aesthetic judgment is the question of such judgment's grounding. It is the necessity to establish the very basis for an "unconditioned command" for the judgment of tastes on which a critical freedom, as the very link between the project of reason and the project of morality, depends: "if we regard it as a judgment which may exact the adhesion of everyone," Kant pronounces in unambiguous terms, "then there must lie at its basis some *a priori* principle (whether objective or subjective) to which we can never attain by seeking out the empirical laws of mental changes" (*Critique of Judgment* 120). The dread of the proliferation of individuation, which threatens the very possibility of the correspondence between things, and the anxiety for a regulative structure determine the need for grounding, for an unconditioned command of some a priori principle in the establishment of Kant's aesthetic judgment. And it is also what leads to his departure from the Burkean methodological empiricism: "For these only enable us to know how we judge, but do not prescribe to us how we ought to judge" (*Critique of Judgment* 120).

The genealogy of the deliberation on who better charts the path for the modern sublime in European aesthetic (philosophical as well as literary) history shows that the choice is not only about the comfort of the a priori over indulgence in dark obscurity, a choice borne out at least in the triumph of the former in modern Anglo-American philosophical and aesthetic studies. It is also about definitions of the concept of the aesthetic as a reactive formulation of modernity. The difference between the veneration of the Kantian transcendental procedure and the implications of the Burkean reactive establishment of sympathetic correspondence is a difference in historical vision. It is also a difference in understanding the place of the aesthetic in that vision. While the former envisions the use of the aesthetic as a structuration of historical progression by mounting an artificial system upon the perceived onslaught of a crisis, the latter attempts to establish the translatability between history and the aesthetic vision, and to redirect the aesthetic affect of history as theatricality of human drama. The misconception of both Kant and Burke, in this sense, leads to misunderstandings not only of the Romantic sublime but also of the institution of modern aesthetic culture. Since both have professed the affective turn, the difference between the Kantian and Burkean sublime is a difference in their structure of reaction towards the trauma of modernity. Hence, the Kantian construction of the sublime is also an historical aestheticism. While Kant resorts to the might in nature as supplement to his regulative structure, Burke settles on the difficulties of classification as the departure of his inquiry. Burke prefers to begin and end with dark obscurity, which, for him, is the quintessence of the sublime, especially in its modern construction. An excursion into the Burkean aesthetic inquiry, in this sense, is an excursion into the anxiety of modernity at the moment when it was most crucially, historically affective in Europe, in some of its most immediate and original manifestations.

Chapter Two

The Imperative of the Romantic Aesthetic and Burke's Inquiry into the Sublime

Burke's aesthetic system of sympathetic correspondence

How, then, does Burke establish his aesthetic judgment? Upon what ground does he set up his explanatory system on taste, and does it accede to the Kantian dread of the proliferation, infinity, and rampant individuation that incapacitate "all censorship on tastes" and social agreement? Burke's introduction sets out to ground the argument for the universality or commonalty of taste: "All men are agreed to call vinegar sour, honey sweet, and aloes bitter; and as they are all agreed in finding these qualities in those objects, they do not in the least differ concerning their effects with regard to pleasure and pain. They all concur in calling sweetness pleasant, and sourness and bitterness unpleasant" (*Enquiry* 14).

Here, Burke begins with the relationship between one's experience and the objects that prompt them, and with concerns about the changes that communication between persons effect in the relationship between persons and objects, but does not seem to pursue them to the end. However, the Burkean move to redefine what it might mean to give an explanation of taste, I suggest, is not a slippage of categories, nor is it a movement that is established by default. The Burkean "sublime obscurity" of inquiry is a roundabout movement that coyly, self-vexingly, establishes sequences that may secure "generalization on the basis of social enumeration" (Ferguson 62). What Burke ends up pursuing is not the ontological or empirical standings of objects and feelings but a comparative judgment. This Burkean comparative judgment stresses not only the relativity of classification but also the necessity to establish both distinction and correspondence between things and events, human sensations and the representations of them. Burke's introduction on taste is a typical Romantic move of supplementation, described by Coleridge as serpentine "or like the path of the sound through the air; at every step he pauses and half recedes, and from the retrogressive movement collects the force which again carries him onward" (*Biographia Literaria*

2: 11). By such receding movement forward, Burke tries to reground taste and his *Enquiry* every step along the way. The introduction does begin with the exigency of the principles of judgment and the commonality of human experience: "On a superficial view, we may seem to differ very widely from each other in our reasonings, and no less in our pleasure: but notwithstanding this difference, which I think to be rather apparent than real, it is probable that the standard both of reason and taste is the same in all human creatures. For if there were not some principles of judgment as well as of sentiment common to all mankind, no hold could possibly be taken either on their reason or their passions, sufficient to maintain the ordinary correspondence of life" (*Enquiry* 1).

Like Kant, Burke also stresses the desirability of "some principles of judgment as well as sentiment common to all mankind" so that a relative hold can be taken on human reason and passions. But in his attempt to ascertain these principles, Burke does not begin "from a position that argues the naturalness of taste, or the ways in which aesthetic experience provides evidence of the reality of things in the world" (Ferguson 63). For him, the ground for the commonality of things, judgments, and feelings begins with a probability, a calculation, of social agreement. It expresses the wish not of "thorough-going distinction" or "explanatory systems" but of sustenance of "the ordinary correspondence of life." It exhibits a will to establish—to induce possibilities of the relationship between things, judgments, and feelings. The passage that establishes the universality of human taste establishes it as social agreement and cultural negotiation: "All men are agreed to call vinegar sour, honey sweet, and aloes bitter; and as they are all agreed in finding . . . They all concur in calling sweetness pleasant, and sourness and bitterness unpleasant" (*Enquiry* 14). By positing tastes as negotiation, as restatement, the Burkean position does not allow for the opposition between individuation and social formation, aesthetic experience and "the reality of things in the world." What might seem irksome ironies, inherent in a wrongly chosen philosophical tradition that unwittingly undoes both Burke's position and his accomplishment, are the carefully constructed grounds and willed conclusions of his argument. It switches from difference of kinds, to difference of degrees, so that a sequential relationship—that one thing can be led to or translated into another—can be induced to maintain correspondence between things, judgments, and feelings. By grounding tastes on the pale of "individual physiology" and social negotiation, and playing excessively with the surplus and vicissitudes of naming and induction, Burke is able to "enquire" into and reground a timely historical and political question as an ontological and empirical one. In his detailed reading into the rhetorical labyrinths of Burke's foundational aesthetic text, Tom Furniss suggests that Burke's contradictions and inconsistencies are symptomatic of a strenuous engagement with the ideological problems endemic to the period. For example, by insisting on both the acquirability of taste and "the commonality of human faculties as the basis of aesthetic experience and taste . . . [Burke] develops simultaneously a rhetorical mechanism which will allow cultural and social differences to be generated in what looks like a natural fashion" (74). What Burke aspires to is both the possibility of comparison and the distinction of judgment, and the correspondences which they maintain, and which in turn maintain them.

Refiguring the legislative function of the sublime as social negotiation

The Burkean game of translation and refiguration is capacious but precarious. He repeatedly elaborates on the necessity of human agency and imagination in setting up laws, and then reminds us how they in turn function as "invariable principles" governing our action and feelings. That is, if we do not proceed to "suppose" that taste has fixed principles, and imagination laws, "our" labor may be judged useless. In other words, "our" otherwise "absurd undertaking" only becomes legitimate if we are aware and insist on our presupposition as negotiation (*Enquiry* 12). An "enquiry" as such, hence, begins on the principle of "supplementarity" in the Derridian sense, although not as an enigma of language or Western metaphysics in general, but a choice of departure with specific, timely historical burdens. Or one can suggest that the Derridian principle is but a reiteration of the Colerigean construction of re-grounding each step along the way. And the Burkean structure of inquiry more typically Romantic than "homespun": "The term Taste, like all other figurative terms, is not extremely accurate: the thing which we understand by it, is far from a simple and determinate idea in the minds of most men, and it is therefore liable to uncertainty and confusion. I have no great opinion of a definition, the celebrated remedy for the cure of this disorder. For when we define, we seem in danger of circumscribing nature within the bounds of our own notions . . . instead of extending our ideas to take in all that nature comprehend" (12). To begin with "figurative terms" is to commit simultaneously to the dangers of confusion and the excess of extension. As Furniss elaborates: "This oscillation can be seen as a micro-drama of the aesthetic and political problems the *Enquiry* is grappling with: how is it possible to write a clear, rational enquiry about an aesthetic experience which, by definition, escapes from or exceeds definition only to come to the central questions, which are: To what extent, and with what consequences, can a rational enquiry about an aesthetic which is supposed to extend our ideas 'to take in all that nature comprehends' become itself an example of such an aesthetic?" (75). Burke's *Enquiry* as a timely cultural treatise acts out rather than resolves the promises and dilemmas of such an aesthetic: "The passion caused by the great and sublime in *Nature*, when those causes operate most powerfully, is astonishment; and astonishment is that state of the soul, in which all its motions are suspended, with some degree of horror . . . Hence arises the great power of the sublime . . . Indeed terror is in all cases whatsoever, either more openly or latently, the ruling principle of the sublime" (95-101).

The task of the *Enquiry* is to trace the "origins" of "our ideas" of the sublime and beautiful and develop theoretical principles that demonstrate and govern their function and affect. Burke begins accordingly by attempting to establish a series of distinctions: "The passions which belong to self-preservation, turn on pain and danger

... they are delightful when we have an idea of pain and danger, without being actually in such circumstances ... whatever excites this delight, I call sublime ... Beauty ... is a name I shall apply to all such qualities in things as induce in us a sense of affection and tenderness, or some other passion the most nearly resembling these" (*Enquiry* 51). These definitions define the sublime and the beautiful as definitely opposite to each other: "They are indeed ideas of a very different nature, one being founded on pain, the other on pleasure; and however they may vary afterwards from the direct nature of their causes, yet these causes keep up an eternal distinction between them" (124). So the passions of pleasure and pain, which are the foundations of the ideas of the beautiful and sublime, are conceived by Burke as simple and not relational passions: pleasure does not result from the removal of pain nor pain from the removal of pleasure. This notion of the simplicity of pleasure and pain is a challenge and movement away from Locke's radical empiricism. In the Burkean figuration, neither pleasure nor pain as simple passion is grounded in immediate empirical perception. There is a greater nuance to their operations and that nuance can be perceived in Burke's move to the further distinction of these two passions in terms of their instrumentality and purpose: "*self preservation* and *society*; to the ends of one or the other of which all our passions are calculated to answer. The passions which concern self-preservation turn mostly on *pain* or *danger*" (57). Pain is the passion of self-preservation, insofar as it indicates death, the threat of death or imminent harm. Therefore those objects or events that excite the "ideas" of pain and danger are terrible and "whatever is in any sort terrible, or is conversant about terrible objects, or operates in a manner analogous to terror, is a source of the sublime" (58). It is important to note that while for Burke pleasure and pain are ideas, the source of the sublime is the terrible object, or whatever is conversant about terrible objects, or events and operations that excite terror, thence these ideas. In this regard the grounding of Burke's perception of pleasure and pain remains empirical, in the sense that the idea issues out of a relation of correspondence between the operations of cognition and the world. His examples of terrible events, such as torture and death, are empirical examples. However, as Burke further elaborates, these physical states of pain and death, as instances of terror, are sources of the sublime only with the mediation of distance. In his recapitulation of the origin and function of the sublime, he insists on the necessity of removal, of distantiation from the immediacy of the causes: "they are simply painful when their causes immediately affect us; they are delightful when we have an idea of pain and danger, without actually being in such circumstances" (xviii). In such refiguration, distance and translation become the originating and functioning mechanisms of the affect of the sublime, in which the affectivity of things, events, and sensations depend on the translatability of kinds. Burke seems to have no problem moving from the physical state of pain and danger to having "an idea of pain and danger, without being actually in such circumstances" (xviii), from terrible events to whatever that is conversant with terrible events and sensations. The Burkean aesthetics, in this instance, is an aesthetics of relocation. And this movement, this translatability, points to the mediated nature of Burkean empiricism.

The sublime has such power over us due to its magnitude; it is so great that it fills the mind to the exclusion of all other objects. Horror, then, is the astonishment at the mind's passivity, its loss of activity in the face of greatness, for the power of the sublime is in its "anticipat[ing] our reasonings, and hurry[ing] us on by an irresistible force," rather than being produced by those reasonings (*Enquiry* 57). And because terror robs the mind of its power of acting and reason more than any other passion, what is terrible is sublime. Since the nature of the Burkean sublime is the translation of terror and pain into distanced pleasure, it comes to be only through the traversing of borders, and its overwhelming affect exists in the impossibility of its containment within given categories of human sensation or cognition. And "to make any thing very terrible, obscurity seems in general to be necessary" (57). Hence the truly terrible, and so truly sublime, is that which is great and dark, that which suspends and blurs. In the conception of the sublime, not only is obscurity necessary, because it produces the terrible which openly or latently governs the sublime, but also the very categories of the terrible and the sublime exist in constant motion and impede each other as distinct categories. This is what constitutes for Burke Milton's unsurpassed sublimity: "No person seems better to have understood the secret of heightening, or of setting terrible things, if I may use the expression, in their strongest light by the force of a judicious obscurity, than Milton. His description of Death in the second book is admirably studied; . . . In this description all is dark, uncertain, confused, terrible, and sublime to the last degree" (100-01). Burke proceeds from here to privilege obscurity over clarity in the "*affections* of the mind" (60). This includes the effect of beauty, which, though positively defined as the identification of love, and differentiated from that of the sublime as black and white (237-39), becomes cause of fear once it is developed in an eroticized femininity. The affective power of the Burkean sublime and beautiful thus resides with "the force of judicious obscurity." The distinction of categories functions as a distinction of categories only through their constant traversal between cause and effect, objects and our impressions of them. They impede the very a priori standing of thorough-going distinctions and the dichotomy of cause and effect, things and human sensations. For "it is one thing to make an idea clear, and another to make it *affecting* to the imagination" (101). The principle of the *Enquiry* is that of "we do and must suppose: I am in little pain whether any body chuses to follow the names I give them (sublime or beautiful objects) or not, provided he allows that what I dispose under different heads are in reality different things in nature. The use I make of the words may be blamed as too confined or too extended; my meaning cannot be misunderstood" (5).

One should not overlook Burke's choice of words such as "chuses," "allows," "dispose," and "make use of." After all, whatever "I" dispose under different headings are in reality different things only if somebody allows it. And this is dependent upon the "use I make of the words," upon the correct understanding of "my meaning." The establishment of distinctions, in this sense, establishes itself as a matter of contingent necessity and willful choice. The presence and function of natural and eternal distinctions become dependent upon the establishment of series—the movements of conflation, induction, and extension that enforce sequential relationships between categories and names. It is a movement of "judicious obscurity" that facilitates the possibilities of comparison while regrounding the reign of judgment.

Burke's replacement of the "origins" of the sublime and beautiful in the sensations of the body points to the historicity of the *Enquiry*. It is a situated discourse. As a cultural response to the tendencies of his time, it makes comparable the human body and the body politic, and ventures into articulating the necessity and implications of establishing cultural distinction and moral judgment upon social negotiation. The modern, historical question of direction and choice is thus relocated and bolstered as the natural, "time-honoured" question of being, knowing, and the right action (feeling). Such an attempt begins with "the possibilities and difficulties raised by its ground in a physiological, sensationalist account of aesthetic experience supposedly verifiable by everyone" (Furniss 19). This historical ambition explains why "sublime obscurity" is central in Burke's inquiry. In fact, the very categorization of both the sublime and the beautiful depends on the blurring of the borders between corporal, imaginative, and cognitive experience. Burke's account of the sublime seems to be the culmination and catalyst of the eighteenth- and early nineteenth-century formulations of the sublime in Europe that "typically celebrate the energetic, the obscure, the disruptive, the unlimited, the powerful, and the terrible as a new set of positive aesthetic terms" (Furniss 20). These formulations, according to standard histories of eighteenth-century aesthetics, involve a series of reinterpretations of Longinus but mark a dramatic departure from him, in which an aesthetic psychology replaces a literary rhetoric (Arac 139). And thus a discourse on the power of figures is transformed into the process of transcendental individuation. Burke's *Enquiry* is elevated to the pinnacle of that transformation because his physiological, sensationalist account of the sublime as bodily, imaginative, and cognitive activities seems to anticipate modern psychology (Ryan 265-79). However, Burke's insistence on the verifiable "authenticity" of every man's experience does not quite fit into the story of the displacement of the authority of tradition by emerging individualism.

When Burke complains that "even Longinus, in his incomparable discourse upon a part of this subject, has comprehended things extremely repugnant to each other, under one common name of the *Sublime*" (*Enquiry* 1), he is refiguring a previous "incomparable discourse" as preface to his own inquiry. Even though the solicitation of lineage is figured as protestation, it highlights that "things extremely repugnant to each other" have been comprehended "under one common name." The reference is one of critique and reinvocation. It renders the previous text of Longinus's already "incomparable discourse" as the ruins of a faulty but memorable past, out of which Burke can figure his original inquiry and his place in that cultural history that he seeks to relocate and direct. After all, in Burkean terms, ambition exceeds imitation precisely in our capacity to be "conversant with terrible objects, the mind always claiming to itself some part of the dignity and importance of the things which it contemplates" (49). Ambition exceeds the limits of imitation as a consequence of the sublime. Burke's critical allusion to Longinus, therefore, is not all that different from Pope's exultation that the great rhetorician's "own example strengthens all his laws," for he "is himself the great sublime he draws." For Pope's commentary is not merely on how Longinus has maximized his great laws with his grand style, but on his "achievement of a legislative and representative function, about the fact that he has, in Wordsworth's phrase, 'created the taste by which he is to be enjoyed'" (Ferguson 38). From Pope to Burke and later to Wordsworth, they have all shown an aspiration to the condition of a great sublime, who, in their figuring, is much less an individual genius than an epic culture hero, so that they may share the (mis)fortune of Longinus and "be taken as a metonymy of their culture" (Ferguson 38), or to redress that culture altogether, though both Burke and Wordsworth also aspire to its verifiability by every man. In exemplifying the aesthetics he propounds, Burke's *Enquiry* redefines and relocates what had been defined by the sublime Longinus long ago, that is, that which "typically celebrate[s] the energetic, the obscure, the disruptive, the unlimited, the powerful, and the terrible." As a redefinition, it differs considerably from the original not so much in that the psychological has replaced the rhetorical, but in its practice of cultural avant-guardism: its erection of the legislative function. It attempts to reign in and redirect "the moment of disruptive intensity that for Longinus had been the hallmark of sublimity. For Longinus, the sublime stood out against the "'whole tissue of the composition;' it came with a 'flash' which 'scatter[ed] everything before it'" (Arac 139).

Constructing an exemplary aesthetics from primeval ground

The Burkean sublime is one of simultaneous terror and delight: "delightful horror" is "the most genuine effect, and truest test of the sublime" (*Enquiry* 73). While stressing their simultaneity, Burke does not deny their "contrary" causes—"if the sublime is built on terror, or some passion like it, which has pain for its object; it is previously proper to enquire how any species of delight can be derived from a cause so apparently contrary to it" (134). The prerequisite for the sublime effect is distance: "at certain distances, and with certain modifications, they may be, and they are delightful, as we every day experience" (40). Furniss understands the act of distancing as the "removal of pain and danger," and proposes three possible interpretations: removal can be understood as "removed" (at a certain distance or at one remove); "'removal' can also imply that the delight succeeds the terror *after* the removal of the threat"; and "finally, 'removal' can mean that the act of removal is itself the source of the delight which 'accompanies' it—the sublime therefore being the experience of the threatened self seeming to overcome or master danger through *effort*" (Furniss 25).

While Furniss's reading points to the Burkean sublime as a "moment" or "synchronic structure" that by the act of removal produces both itself and its experiential possibility, it misconstrues in its last instance the overriding spatial and temporal movement that structures the moment, in post-Kantian terms, that is, as mastery and overcoming, whereas Burke not only stresses the simultaneity, but at best describes the movement as derivation or modification. The end of Furniss's construction is to establish the Burkean sublime as that strenuous effort that saves the bourgeois subject from fatal stasis, an effort that might be called self-making labor. Therefore, he likens the Burkean sequence to Thomas Weiskel's three-phase model of the Kantian sublime, where the "phases" are successive and lead to the final overcoming of the mind. Thus, in his terms both the Burkean and the Kantian sublime end with the same conquering closure: for Burke, "the sublime therefore being the experience of the threatened self seeming to overcome or master danger through *effort*"; for Kant, "the third phase [being] a defensive recuperation in which the mind identifies itself with or attributes to itself, through a 'metaphorical transposition,' the qualities of that which had threatened to overwhelm it" (Furniss 25). But here Furniss misconceives the movement in the Burkean structure. The fiction of temporality in the Kantian model establishes the succession that leads "inevitably" to the triumph of the mind. And what is realized in the fiction is the series of progression that verify (as long as one can account for it) the inevitability of the final "reality," the mounting of the mind. The Burkean structure, on the other hand, emphasizes the translatability between kinds: from terror to delight. It is a reciprocal movement between different affects, rather than an inevitable progression towards the triumphant finality of the subject. The "removal" should be understood as an act of distancing, which overrides the boundaries of the spatial and the temporal and figures them as shifting relations. The sequence established like this is not one of different states but one of mutual translatability—one can always move from one to the other, even though the effort may be strenuous (a movement that excludes the "weaker subjects"). While in Kant the crowning phase of the sublime is the vaunting joy of the mind, the Burkean sublime moment is the reciprocal interplay of body and mind: "In all these cases, if the pain and terror are so modified as not to be actually noxious; if the pain is not carried to violence, and the terror is not conversant about the present destruction of the person . . . they are capable of producing delight; not pleasure, but a sort of delightful horror, a sort of tranquility tinged with terror . . . Its object is the sublime" (*Enquiry* 136).

As Burke elucidates, the affect of the sublime is not the mastery of danger or the overcoming of terror. It is "a sort of delightful horror, a sort of tranquility tinged with terror." In other words, even at the most sublime moment, terror has never completely lost its presence. One needs only to recall the Miltonic moment as the foremost instance of the Burkean sublime: "In this description all is dark, uncertain, confused, terrible, and sublime to the last degree." The moment becomes the most sublime because of its obscure simultaneity of darkness, uncertainty, confusion, and terror. Also, for Burke, the insistence on grounding passions and affects on body parts is not just that he is hopelessly caught up with a "silly" and "antiquated" physiology (Weiskel 88). Burke's identification of "the strongest of all passions" as that of "self-preservation," which he figures in the translatability between terror and delight, and locates in the reciprocity of body and mind, is not merely a matter of philosophical and epistemological choice. "The only difference between pain and terror is that things which cause pain operate on the mind, by the intervention of the body;

whereas things that cause terror generally affect the bodily organs by the operation of the mind suggesting danger; but both agree likewise in every thing else" (*Enquiry* 134). What is established in the Burkean classification is a structure of movement and reciprocity, where the difference is one of degree. And neither the physical nor the psychological state of being underlies the ground of his concerns. His claim of neo-Newtonism bespeaks a different anxiety. To read Burke's insistence only in terms of intellectual tradition and philosophical choice is to overlook the significance and urgency of grounding in that willful choice. His configuration of the sublime is dependent upon the ambiguous act of distancing, which establishes the consequences and subtleties of the difference of degrees. It also depends upon the new figuration of terror, and is devised out of terror occasioned by the sense of historical crisis: "The nature of rest is to suffer all the parts of our bodies to fall into a relaxation, that not only disables the members from performing their functions, but takes away the vigorous tone of fibre which is requisite for carrying on the natural and necessary secretions . . . melancholy, dejection, despair, and often self-murder, is the consequence of the gloomy view we take of things in this relaxed state of body" (135).

The nexus of fears Burke is addressing seems to be the endemic social diseases of the disrupted and mutilated body of modernity. Melancholy, dejection, despair, and self-murder, the much feared and discoursed symptoms of late eighteenth-century England, are both the "consequences" and potential causes for the dysfunctioning of "the natural and necessary secretions" of the body politic. Gibbons, on the other hand, locates the sources of Burke's fears in his experience of the British colonization of Ireland, in his appropriation of figures such as "Philoctetes" as the wounded national Irish body (Gibbons 39-82). This certainly explains Burke's preoccupation with terms such as "convulsions" or "paroxysms." And it underscores the Burkean sublime as an aesthetics of crisis, terror, and anxiety, which foretells ruination and catastrophe. However, from whereever one traces their sources, Burke's fears, as he picturesquely depicts, is not the fear of change, as is often ascribed to him, but of the opposite: the lack thereof caused by too much relaxation, by inertia. Thus, it is not difficult to understand his simultaneous attraction to and wariness of the dark energies in the sublime aesthetics and later in the staging of the French Revolution. What constitutes the moment of aesthetic pleasure, and what is good for historical redirection, is "a sort of delightful horror." However, to diagnose the diseases of modernity as the dysfunctioning of "the natural and necessary secretions" of the body is a strenuous effort, an attempt to devise remedies from primeval ground. The urgency to relocate the historical question of direction as an ontological question of the status of being and the natural, scientific question of bodily function is to reestablish the origin of particular, chosen histories as the primeval ground, upon which a straying modernity can be legitimately, "naturally" rectified and refounded. It is an arduous attempt to restore "nature" upon the ruins of history and render history "second nature," an attempt that naturalizes the "choice of inheritance" (Bromwich 46).

Since the Burkean sublime and its attendant comparative judgment are built on the basis of analogy, the moment of sublimity is "more an efficacious fiction than a genuine transcendence" or a middle-class commitment to reaffirm the almost "physical" "common labour" (Furniss 29). However, the sublime occasion as ruse presents serious problems if one reads the Burkean *Enquiry* as a class manifesto that defends the middle-class subject as a kind of heroic laborer, or if one takes Burke's psycho-empiricism too seriously. For either way, the sublime experience and the inquiry into it would look like "something of a shell game" (Ferguson 70). The sublime ruse begins with the condition of "removal." The movement in its production is built on similitudes and resemblances: "Whatever is fitted to produce such a tension [of the nerves], must be productive of a passion similar to terror, and consequently must be a source of the sublime, though it should have no idea of danger connected with it" (*Enquiry* 134). This suggests that the figurative process is crucial to the structure and affect of the sublime moment. This seems substantiated by Burke's notorious use of literary, textual references as empirical examples.

"For murder from his native clime, / Just gains some frontier, breathless, pale, amaz'd; / All gaze, all wonder!" (*Enquiry* 34). The literary example of the Homeric fugitive actually suggests that the central problem here is the problem of the communication of emotional experience. The spectators' apprehension of the fugitive's countenance may testify to the continuation of the latter's terror rather than to his pleasure at escaping the occasion for feeling that terror, but their gaze is in wonderment while he merely stands amazed. Their delight is the distanced witnessing of his terror, a metaphorical participation (in the sense metaphors transfer affectively—carry forward and translate), whether it is immediate or residual. The sublime moment of "All gaze, all wonder!" is occasioned for the spectators and excludes the actual, in this case literary, fugitive. While the wretch does manage a narrow escape, a temporary act of distancing, the spectators are twice removed: from his native clime and his present condition. This is how they participate in his escape and residual terror, and translate them into their delight. While he is staged, "breathless, pale, amaz'd," the very image of the affect of residual terror, they are "All gaze, all wonder!" The communication of emotions does occur at the moment when these emotions have lost a clear connection with their causes, but it occurs at the expense of the distinction between cause and effect, image and thing, representation and empirical experience. The equivocation that engenders the communication is the affect and potential of theatricality, which, as I point out earlier, is essential for the Burkean sublime. This sublime ruse, through its very theatricality, engenders the chain of very "genuine," distinguishable but translatable emotions. What is established in the example that places uncertainly causes and effects, testimonies and experiences, is the equivocation—their distinction and translatability, and the affect and potential of the figurative process. Equivocation and obscurity in this sense are absolutely necessary in the Burkean perception of the "affections of the mind" (*Enquiry* 60), and the most obscure mode of expression for him is by words—language. Thus, if poetry has the upper hand in Burke's system it is because of the vagaries of expression and the slippages of referentiality. This greatness of poetry results from its pointing to the limitations of its own process. Of course, here Burke reverts to nature to make his point: "I think there are reasons in nature why the obscure idea, when properly conveyed, should be more affecting than the clear" (60).

Another example that is often used to illustrate the fallibility of the Burkean "empiricist" aesthetics is his juxtaposition of the spectacle of a staged tragedy and a "real" public execution: "But be its [the tragedy's] power of what kind it will, it never approaches to what it represents. Chuse a day on which to represent the most sublime and affecting tragedy we have . . . unite the greatest efforts of poetry, painting, and music; and when you have collected your audience, just at the moment when their minds are erect with expectations, let it be reported that a state criminal of high rank is on the point of being executed in the adjoining square; in a moment the emptiness of the theatre would demonstrate the comparative weakness of the imitative arts, and proclaim the triumph of the real sympathy" (*Enquiry* 47). It is suggested that Burke evokes the extremity of public execution, the ultimate of death, as the limit to the proliferation of images. Along the peculiar lines of his *Enquiry*, by equivocating matters of kinds into matters of degrees, Burke seems to have placed himself in an impossible position: there will be no end of sensory events and no distinction between such events and the representations of them. He is hovering on the edge of the inevitable pitfall of empiricism. The example, by virtue of its appeal to death over the power of "the most sublime and affecting tragedy," seems to be the last straw against the threat. The emptiness of the theater not only distinguishes the real and the represented, and demonstrates that public execution has a greater attraction and greater hold on its audience than the theater, but also firmly establishes the finality, the absolute power of limit. There is always the ultimate of death. However, one should not forget two things here: first, Burke's sublime aesthetics is an aesthetics of exemplary events, which, by definition, is concerned with but extends the affectiveness of the actual; second, his example of the event of public execution versus theater is contrived to demonstrate the complications of "sympathy" and "delight" for the audience. Public execution, therefore, as occasion for the Burkean sublime, is again a spectator sport. The emptiness of the theater testifies to the greater attraction of public execution, not as imminent death, but as spectacle, as better occasion for the spectators to exercise their "real sympathy"—the sharing of a common humanity defined and minimized by the insurmountable specificity of you and me. The death staged here is real, but only for the executed. If the narrow escape of the Homeric fugitive images the narrow escape of the audience from participating directly in his drama (Jacobus, *Romanticism* 46), the real death of the state criminal only enhances their sense of proximity and the wonders of their subsequent escape. While the prospect of immediate death does provide experience that cannot, by definition, become habitual for the executed, for the spectators, both the immediacy and the actual death nonetheless remain a prospect, out of which they may feel real sympathy, but also salvage a sense of pleasure, "all gaze, all wonders!" After all, they can go to public executions habitually, just like they can choose or not choose to go to the theater. The extremity of death functions as the ultimate ruse, a sublime ruse more affecting than the power of any staged tragedy. Its affect is in its theatricality, the theatricality of the real, which attests to "the comparative weakness of the imitative arts," and establishes death, the ultimate of the real, as art. It is a better form of art, because it is real. This not only exemplifies the Burkean ruse of sublimity, but also the travail of the aesthetic or literary agency. It foregrounds the very capacity of the figurative. The affect of the staged tragedy and the public execution in this sense is comparable, in that the onlookers, so effected, might become actors too. The potentiality of their action is effected in the present moment of their metaphorical participation in the sublime play, if they are neither the executed nor executioner. But the stage of their act is offstage, elsewhere. After all, the sublime requires proximate rather than actual danger, though it demands "no small uneasiness." The immediate act of the audience is not to risk their own necks or cut that of another but engage in the equivocation: "we do not sufficiently distinguish what we would by no means chuse to do, from what we should be eager enough to see if it was once done" (*Enquiry* 47).

Mary Jacobus interprets this as showing not only Burke's insistence on the ambiguities of sublime aesthetics but also his own political ambiguities in front of the historical stage of which he poses himself as both spectator and critic. She believes "Burke comes close to saying that while he would not choose to send Louis XVI to the guillotine, he would leave the theatre to watch the sight" (*Romanticism* 54). Ronald Paulson sees the connection between Burke's *Enquiry* and his later *Reflections on the Revolution in France*. He suggests that Burke's imagery of revolution in the *Reflections* comes from the terrible of his sublime, with precisely the same kind of aesthetic distancing outlined in his *Enquiry*. Paulson shows that Burke projects in his *Reflections* not only a series of sublime scenes but also a sublime plot, with the sense of "removal" at the very center of its structure, only this time to create "immediacy" instead of "security." Thus he concludes that "for Burke revolution is a theatrical performance, just as his hell derives from Milton's poem and painted representations of it, and the whole is a strange aesthetic experience, one important element of which is the inevitable distance of the Englishman from the immediate danger but with the undeniable potential for a reprise on his own soil" (38-57). Paulson's delineation of the correlation between Burke's aesthetic categories and his reflections on the French Revolution demonstrates the symbiosis between aesthetics and politics. It also points back to the very historicity of late eighteenth-century inquiries into the sublime and the beautiful as an aesthetics of modernity. The sublime ruse, as intention and effect, is equivocal indeed. The staged and the real, in such representation, become matters of degrees. And upon such assumptions Burke seeks to refute the "common observation, that objects which in the reality would shock, are in tragical, and such like representations, the source of a very high species of pleasure" (*Enquiry* 14). Instead, we salvage a similar delight from both the reality and dramatization of "the feelings of our fellow creatures in circumstances of real distress . . . we . . . read the authentic histories of scenes of this nature with as much pleasure as romances or poems," and thus the ruin of empires "touches us in history" as much as "in fable" (45). Burke's theory of art, therewith, is also his theory of history. After all, to ensure the transference of affect, Burke needs history as much as he needs tragedy: "The prosperity of no empire, nor the grandeur of no king, can so agreeably affect in the reading, as the ruin of the state of Macedon, and the distress of its unhappy prince. Such a catastrophe touches us in history as much as the destruction of Troy does in fable . . . there is no spectacle we so eagerly pursue, as that of some uncommon and grievous calamity; so that whether the misfortune is before our eyes, or whether they are turned back to it in history, it always touches with delight. This is not an unmixed delight, but blended with no small uneasiness" (45-47).

Turning back to history is like going to a tragedy. Burke explains further that all tragedy needs to do is to remove us from the idea of fiction. The passage may be arguing for the comparative weakness of tragedy in its representation of reality. Burke needs to maintain the respective fiction of history and nature, and in this way reverses the aforesaid by concluding, "But be its power of what kind it will, it never approaches to what it represents." But by the same argument, he renders reality another form of art. Since art imitates reality, the highest form of art is reality, and the highest form of tragedy, history. It is with such a view of Burke's theory of history as theater that Jacobus situates his later, more directly "political" and "historical" *Reflections on the Revolution in France*: "He also installs the *Reflections* on the same equivocal border as the fleeing criminal of Homer's simile, suspended between the real perils of history and the uneasy delights of tragedy" (*Romanticism* 54). Jacobus concludes that Burke hesitates between excesses of revolution and that of his own rhetoric, and that uncertainty is the common point of instability on which his discussion of the theater and his representation of revolution both rest. I would argue, however, that in view of his larger picture of history as theater, Burke's uncertainty shows as much hesitation as willful choice. As many have pointed out, at least as shown in the *Enquiry* and the *Reflections*, the excesses of revolution are not all that separable from the excesses of his own rhetoric. The choice of achieving the sublime ambition of "that glorying and sense of inward greatness" (Jacobus, *Romanticism* 54) by condemning the sending of Louis XVI to the guillotine but condoning the leaving of any staged, therefore secondary theater show to watch the sight, is not merely a choice of voyeurism. The touches of catastrophe in history, like the touches of the destruction of Troy in fables, are genuine. In front of the stage of the theater of history, as in the theater of staged tragedy, onlookers are or can become actors. It is an act that begins as reaction, but opens to new directions. In the face of the events of 1789 in France, Burke positions himself and all England as onlookers, as shown in the opening quotation. Here the revolution in France is staged for the English audience as a "wonderful Spectacle." While England is "All gaze, all wonder," the events in the "Neighbouring and rival Country" are shown as a sublime tragedy that astonishes its spectators with uncertainty—they do not know "whether to blame or to applaud" since "the thing indeed . . . has still something in it paradoxical and Mysterious. The spirit it is impossible not to admire" (Burke, "To the Earl of Charlemont" 10). And Burke knows too well that in the face of the sublime onlookers can become actors too. This is why the placing of the English as audience and the registering of their reaction become central in the onset of his reflections on the revolution in neighboring France. The revolution and its affect are put on stage, set for reinterpretation and possible redirection vis-à-vis the English response.

In this historical drama, Burke sets himself as the off-stage director. Hence the note of equivocal satisfaction on the execution of Louis XVI in January 1793: "the Catastrophe of the Tragedy of France has been completed. It was the necessary result of all the preceding parts of that monstrous Drama" ("To Lord Loughborough" 344). As expert audience and critic (potential director), Burke is satisfied that the tragedy is completed and despite its monstrosity all parts have fallen into place. In his denunciation of the Revolution Society and Price's sermon, the chief target is "their failure to register appropriate emotions in the face of Louis's humiliation in October 1789" (Jacobus, *Romanticism* 47). They are bad audience and potentially dangerous players in any future drama. Their reaction amounts to a "revolution in sentiments, manners, and moral opinions" (47) which inaugurates a modernity that Burke deeply fears and distrusts. It is with an understanding of Burke's aesthetics in politics and politics in aesthetics as such that the young Wordsworth dismisses the *Reflections* as "a philosophical lamentation over the extinction of Chivalry" (Wordsworth, "Letter to the Bishop of Llandaff" 14). In his *Reflections* upon the modern drama in the theater of history, Burke is shamelessly sentimental. Sentiments become the cornerstone of his moral, political, and historical judgments. To demonstrate the erroneous reaction of the Republican audience, Burke only needs to ask "Why do I feel so differently from Dr. Price?" and proceeds to answer his own question—"because it is natural" and because "we are so made as to be affected at such spectacles with melancholy sentiments upon the unstable condition of mortal prosperity, and the tremendous uncertainty of human greatness; because in those natural feelings we learn great lessons; because in events like these our passions instruct our reason; because when kings are hurl'd from their thrones by the Supreme Director of this great drama, and become the objects of insult to the base, and of pity to the good, we behold such disasters in the moral, as we should behold a miracle in the physical order of things. We are alarmed into reflection" (*Reflections* 175).

The plight of kings, and in particular of King Louis XVI, is turned into an instance of the unstable conditions of mortal prosperity. And his fall by revolutionary violence reflects the tremendous uncertainty of human greatness. It is a miraculous show, but analogous to any other human condition, so that when "we" behold such tremendous human disasters, "we are alarmed into reflexion; our minds (as it has long since been observed) are purified by terror and pity" (*Reflections* 175). Once the threatening monstrosity of a violent revolution in a neighboring, existing social order is translated into the natural cycle and contained in the familiar discourse of a God-given human condition, "the way lies clear to represent the French Revolution as a tragic spectacle designed to purge its audience by terror and pity" (Jacobus, *Romanticism* 48). Burke's dramatization of revolution and history evoked much contempt from his contemporaries. Thomas Paine, for example, in replying to the *Reflections* charges him with degeneration in his sentimental aestheticization of real history (71-72). However, as Jacobus suggests, Burke's opponents actually share with him similar fears and anxieties: "The scary suspicion lurking behind such language is not that Burke's eloquence is impotent, but that it might prove altogether too powerful—that representation itself might change the course of history . . . Such a mode of influencing events yet to come threatens to undo our entire sense of history" (Jacobus, *Romanticism* 50).

The politics of Burke's aesthetics not only permit him to assume a certain historical role in relation to the French Revolution, they insist on making history and theater analogous. Burke argued for "the pleasing illusions" of ideology, and the necessity of making "power gentle" and "obedience liberal" (*Reflections* 171). His obsession with the metaphor of draperies, however, goes deeper than the immediate need of current politics. For him, "the decent drapery of life," and "the wardrobe of a moral imagination" are essential in the making of human history, for they not only dress up "the defects of our naked shivering nature" but dress it up in such a way as to make the dresses our second nature (*Reflections* 67). It is on this ground that Burke fears the direction of modernity, which threatens not only a social and moral order but the very touchstones of humanity: "On this scheme of things, a king is but a man; a queen is but a woman; a woman is but an animal; and an animal not of the highest order. . . . The murder of a king, or a queen, or a bishop, or a father, are only common homicide; and if the people are by any chance, or in any way gainers by it, a sort of homicide much the most pardonable and into which we ought not to make too severe a scrutiny" (*Reflections* 171). The passage demonstrates Burke's historical and political lamentation over the loss of the order of chivalry and his fear of the killing of fathers. But the threat of modern chaos is also feared here as an undiscriminating violence that might undo the very furnishings which constitute the touchstones—the being and history—of humanity. On this scheme, things and beings are related not by analogy, but by the act of stripping, a destructive social leveling, and determined by the economy of gains. What is left will be our brutal, "naked shivering nature," which is not only devoid of social and cultural distinctions but also of any signs of our very humanness—by doing away with the wardrobe of our moral imagination, we do away with ourselves as human beings.

However, Burke seems to have committed the same error as the strippers and levelers in his argument, in which the fate of kings, queens and bishops are used to stand for common humanity and in this sense not regicide and parricide but common homicide. And the argument itself may not be more than a metaphysical and historical justification of inherited social arrangements. But Burke's stress is also on human volition in the making of their history: after all, the wardrobe of the draperies of life which dress up the very essence of that life is at their disposal. As Bromwich suggests, it is a matter of the choice of inheritance: "He says again and again that the choice is ours to make; that the history of which we are composed will be written only by ourselves" (*A Choice* 46). One cannot hope to be liberated from the past, because the past humanizes. In other words, history is history in the sense it is what "become us," so far as it is shaped by acts of human play. The sublime proposition in the Burkean sublime equivocation of taste in the *Enquiry*, translated into the dramatization of revolution and history in the *Reflections*, can be summarized in Bromwich's interpretation of the Burkean idiom "prejudice renders a man's virtue his habit . . . To justify the conventions by which we act, and to teach them some day to others, we have to come to know ourselves through the history that is our nature" (*A Choice* 53). The Burkean history, in this sense, is a sublime drama. The concept of choice registers both the aspiration for a relative constant and the desire for limitlessness and disruptive play in his structure and appeal to history. This is one important way to understand the sense of immediacy and fervor in the desires and terror of the *Enquiry*, and the dramatic appeal to history against revolutionary metaphysics in the *Reflections*. The Burkean sublime thus configured is a historically burdened aesthetics that equivocates the world and the stage, life and death, things and human feelings. And by such equivocation, it reestablishes the relation and correspondences between them and the possibilities for new choices and new direction. The Burkean practice itself, in this sense, is a choice of inheritance. It restructures the Longinian sublimity into a reciprocal play between figurative language and sublimity as affect, a theatrical sketch as enactment and as a process of transference. If the Kantian sublime is a masterful recuperation of reason, Burke's dramatic sublime obscurity is that of relocating and restaging modernity as an historical problem. Burke's historical aestheticism is in this sense a sublime offering that casts the aesthete-philosopher-poet as the expert audience, critic, and potential director of history. And it offers a sublime cultural restructuring, as Jean-Luc Nancy formulates it in his study "The Sublime Offering," of the motif of the sublime in relation to the genealogy of art and philosophy in Europe, that crosses the limits of its own historical condition (25-44).

Chapter Three

Wordsworth's Poetic *Prelude* to Modern History

Wordsworth's poetics of literary modernity

The sublime desire for poetic limitlessness and historical redirection also features prominently in Wordsworth's modern poetics. It is a poetics that emphatically demonstrates a historical hyperbolization of literary agency and a longing for a cultural avant-garde as well as a legislative function for a new kind of poetry. In this chapter I explore Wordsworth's repeated attempts to figure a modern poetic beginning as an emblematic construction of the Romantic sublime. The said construction represents poetic practice as a hyperbolized cultural avant-guardism, which has since characterized modern European literature. I examine Wordsworth's multiple poetic beginnings as epitaph, as a search for origins, and as constructions for historical tendencies for his times. I reread the *Prelude* with its Romantic and post-Romantic commentaries as a poem of beginnings.

Like Burke's historical-aesthetical inquiry, Wordsworth's commencement poetics also derive directly from his sense of crisis. It is a poetic mechanism that aims to address how one begins a different kind of poetry that is discontinuous from its precedent but nonetheless historically grounded, and can thus initiate through cultural imagination new historical beginnings. The movement of Wordsworth's poetic modernity, in this sense, is predated by the reconstructive genealogy of the sublime of the eighteenth century, which begins with the historical recovery of the integral originality of Longinus. According to Michel Deguy, the sublime in its modern variation is rescued and revived with the chance and precariousness that mark its history, and with "the values of fragility, contingency, and perishability" (6). In Deguy's reading, Longinus, in his time, is deprived of gods, but on familiar terms with Homer. And because of this, "the question of the *sublime* was doubtless first of all an attempt to measure the decline of the Orient, to measure the author's distance from the time of gods and heroes when nature had still been a temple of living heroic pillars" (6). It is therefore a historical question. But even then the sublime is not an aesthetics of nostalgia. Longinus has expressed the wistful longing to remain at least capable of gauging the elevation of the sources. In this sense, he "is not so much an author who enviously respects the gods of Homer while dissimulating his disbelief, he is rather one who looks at the past in order to reestablish through his own discourse some hope of a truly exalted discourse, precisely for the generation that follows him." For, to begin with, "the Treatise *Of the High* is a letter to young Terentianus" (7).

If we follow Deguy's delineation, we can conclude that the Longinian sublime is a commencement aesthetics, one that begins things and is therefore future oriented. In Longinus's treatise, one of the definitions of the sublime is that it consists in the feeling of ravishment that makes one pass on, that it is a movement of being carried away. The sublime is perceived simultaneously as a process of traversal, of disruption, uplift, and transport (Longinus 7.2-9.2). For Longinus to be carried away is to begin at an ending and remain capable of gauging the sources. And to be ravished is to exceed. This is what Longinus offers his modern heirs in the eighteenth-century revival of the sublime, and what underwrites this aesthetic movement's historical aspiration.

In his reading of Wordsworth's "Nutting" as a poem about beginnings, which he defines as "suspension and decision," Jonathan Arac suggests that part of Wordsworth's modern literary project is also a matter of excessive commencement. That is, Wordsworth begins by poetically reestablishing "our" relation to "things." As a poem that proposes to read "indifferent things," the action of "Nutting," which "fights the fear of the vacancy that things take on in their indifference," falls on "dragging to earth with crash" (Arac 43). In Wordsworth's enactment, "all things" might be "indifferent," but "through our action upon them" the unknown can be pointed out, feelings restructured, and relationships reestablished: "The otherness of things, their 'quiet being' . . . revealed through our action upon them, becomes a positive value against solipsistic doubts and the literarization of the world. This action, then, restored the otherness of things and rescued the boy from fiction. It was an act of modernity; it stripped away old clothes; restored us 'to earth' like the giant Antaeus whom Hazlitt took as a figure for true poetry" (Arac 43).

To understand "Nutting" as the germinating poem in Wordsworth's attempt to craft a "true" modern poetry is to highlight his act of modernity as one of stripping, "dragging to earth with crash." It is a violence that restores the otherness of things, as "quiet being," just as it is upon the restored otherness of things and their "quiet being" that the boy in the poem is rescued from fiction and "we" are restored to "earth." In the poem, the "mutilated bower" left over by the excessive act of stripping and restoration is then the ground upon which a new poetics, and through which a new human history—as relations between each other and that of the world—is established. This "mutilated bower," in turn, becomes the defining legacy of Wordsworth's initial act of poetic-cultural modernity. For example, Geoffrey H. Hartman has spotted in this left-over bower the emblem of "the emergence of a modern imagination" (73), whereas Arac locates in it Wordsworth's historicity—the act in the poem is his part in the "beginning of English literature" at the "end of English poetry . . . the modernity of his poetic act forms a parenthesis, a suspension within tradition, like the fictional action of 'Nutting,' suspended within the address to the maiden" (47). By resituating Wordsworth's beginning therefore redefining his legacy, this reading also helps understanding the other two monuments in Wordsworth's project of modern English poetry, that is, the Preface to *Lyrical Ballads* and *The Prelude*, which I elaborate on below.

Wordsworth's beginning poetic act, thus, can be understood as a poetical-historical suspension, and a cultural (stripping) violence that simultaneously restores and engenders. It is also a sublime ruse, which Jacobus calls a striptease. But it is a striptease with consequence. The poetic mutilation is carried upon a social transaction—the consigning of the otherness of things and the "dearest maiden" to gentleness. And the "gentle" mutilation begins "English literature" at the "end of English poetry," a beginning at the ending that restored history. Like the Longinian movement of the sublime it is a moment of ravishment that exceeds. And by this excessive act both the poet and history are carried forward in a new cultural imagination.

Wordsworth's literary modernity, like the Burkean sublime, is thus structured as a process of transference. The movement between beginnings and ends, poetic origins and historical directions, "gently mutilated" other places and things and the present moment of the poet's place and time, is what predicates his commencement poetics and gives impetus to the rush of poetic numbers in his lifelong writing of *The Prelude*. It is also what underwrites his formulae of the modern poet as translator and "knots" (Arac 39) together his poetic modernity. Wordsworth's acts of literary modernity, in this sense, are not confined to stripping off old clothes. In a letter written to Lady Beaumont on 21 May 1807, immediately after the publication of his *Poems in Two Volumes*, Wordsworth proposes: "Every great and original writer, in proportion as he is great or original, must himself create the taste by which he is to be relished; he must teach the art by which he is to be seen" (*Poetical Works* 150). This proposal echoes Pope's exultation of the sublime Longinus, whose end in creating the sublime taste by which he is not only himself relished but also passed on, is an ethico-political one. With he "is himself the great sublime he draws," Pope's commentary refers not merely to how Longinus has maximized his great laws with his grand style, but to his achievement of a legislative and representative function. Wordsworth's assertion that the poetic act of modernity has to begin with the creation and teaching of its accommodating taste testifies to an aspiration to the same (mis)fortune of Longinus—to "be taken as a metonymy of their culture" (Ferguson 38). Or in Burkean terms, it is to redress that culture with draperies newly woven from the mutilated wardrobe of inheritance. This is probably why the commencement poetry and poetics of Wordsworth are not only concerned with "dragging to earth with crash" but also to bury the dead properly. Besides the "Essays upon Epitaphs," Wordsworth composed several poems with epitaphic motifs. "A Poet's Epitaph" (1798-1799), purporting to be a gravestone inscription upon an unnamed rural poet, seems to be one of his earlier attempts at the sublime task he later proposes to Lady Beaumont. Its intensity lies in the responses of the living rather than the memorial to the dead. The dead are buried for the education of the potential gravestone readers. However, Wordsworth is wary of the immensity of the task. A proper reader is hard to come by in the modern world. Thus, the first nine stanzas of the poem are actually a poetic expulsion of improper readers: men of the severed modernity, "unable or unwilling to appreciate the deceased" (Scodel 388). The last six stanzas, however, move to enlist an ideal but solitary figure as the potentially qualified reader:

> But who is He, with modest looks,
> And clad in homely russet brown?
> He murmurs near the running brooks
> A music sweeter than their own.
>
> He is retired as noontide dew,
> Or fountain in a noon-day grove;
> And you must love him, ere to you
> He will seem worthy of your love. . . .
>
> In common things that round us lie
> Some random truths he can impart, —
>
> . . . But he is weak; both Man and Boy,
> Hath been an idler in the land; . . .
>
> Come hither in thy hour of strength;
> Come, weak as is a breaking wave!
> Here stretch thy body at full length;
> Or build thy house upon this grave. (*Lyrical Ballads* lines 37-60)

The description of the figure as modest, homely, rustic, and retired is to establish bonds—first with the deceased, then with the readers of the poem. It is an act different from the boy's dragging and reengendering in "Nutting" but similar in the perceived ends, that is, to reestablish the relation between things and being from the primeval ground. Since we know nothing about the deceased except that he is a nameless rural poet buried in the humble country graveyard, and the rustic figure is the only one capable of being in communion with him, we must assume the latter is his "living embodiment" (Scodel 390). In turn, if we want to reestablish our severed ties with the deceased, thus restore our own humanity, we must love the homely rustic and his sweet murmurs unconditionally. Reason is irrelevant in establishing ties of love, and we must suspend our judgment, because we must "First learn to love one living man; / Then may'st thou think upon the dead" (3-4). Love, as a primary human bond, is evoked to heal the cut inflicted by history that severed modernity from its roots. The demand on the readers is therefore sublime, in that they must surrender their modernity (one must remember that the man is an idler, as against the business of the day), suspend their interests and judgments, and submit to the seizure, the ravishment of love that will carry them away and pass them on to a newly rerooted humanity. At this juncture, Wordsworth's sublime demand is similar to the Burkean appeal to "the moral constitution of the heart" (*Reflections* 176).

The final stanza entreats the rustic not to mourn for the actual dead, but continue "In common things that round us lie" (49), to use his privileged, unsevered connection to the deceased: "Here stretch thy body at full length; / Or build thy house upon this grave" (59-60). By stretching his body full length or building his house upon the grave, the rustic (poet?) literally dwells upon and extends the memory of the dead. He and his house becomes the living gravestone that both buries the dead and connects him with the living world. The act reestablishes the correspondence between the living and the dead, the beginning of all "human" relationships. The legacy of the gravestones here is different from what is left over in the "mutilated bower." Wordsworth's commencement modus operandi seems much less violent here. In this case the Wordsworthian rustic, as the one potential builder of new houses upon the grave, has to be weak (53). The action begins with a breaking up of self and the existing relations between him, the dead, and the world. It is a disruption of the self, not other things and beings as in "Nutting," that reengenders both a new self and the correspondences of the world. However, even though the rustic figure seems to embody Wordsworth's prerequisites for an ideal executioner of his project to redirect history, Wordsworth himself is removed from the homely country graveyard of life and death. As always, he is elsewhere. Wordsworth is not the figure that stretches his body in a deathlike posture upon the grave. His pose as the epitaphic poet is more like that of the critic—the expert reader and potential director. His place, like the Burkean director, is off-stage, away from the country graveyard.

Wordsworth begins his erection of the epitaph—his own house upon the grave—by reconstructing the ground. "It need scarcely be said," but he nonetheless says it, as the emphatic opening of his three long essays, "that an Epitaph presupposes a Monument, upon which it is to be engraven. . . . This custom proceeded obviously from a twofold desire; first, to guard the remains of the deceased from irreverent approach or from savage violation: and, secondly, to preserve their memory" ("Essays upon Epitaphs" 49). The custom of gravestone inscription may have proceeded from the desire to guard the remains of the dead and to preserve their memory, but its significance comes from its presupposition of a historical monument, a monument that is the visible ruin of ancient customs but cannot be presupposed or upheld simply by the precedents of historical practice. The desires that ground the reerection of the monumental ruins have to be traced to their deeper burial. "And, verily, without the consciousness of a principle of immortality in the human soul, Man could never have had awakened in him the desire to live in the remembrance of his fellows: mere love, or the yearning of kind towards kind, could not have produced it" (50). The principle of immortality as the originary ground of human ties has to rest upon the a priori of being. But it can only be located in its humanity, for it is not mere love or kindred feeling. It is "a necessary consequence of this conjunction" of "the principle of love which exists in the inferior animals" and "the faculty of reason which exists in Man alone" (50). Yet it is a necessary consequence, not a direct result, of such a conjunction, "but only to be come at through an intermediate thought, viz. that of an intimation or assurance within us, that some part of our nature is imperishable"

(50). The principle of immortality, then, upon which all other human monuments are structured and made subsequent, begins as a consequence of a complexly interwoven network of primeval desires, human reason, and a divine or other a priori assurance. And as a consequence, it begins with human history: "If we look back upon the days of childhood, we shall find that the time is not in remembrance when, with respect to our own individual Being, the mind was without this assurance; whereas, the wish to be remembered by our friends or kindred after death, or even in absence, is, as we shall discover, a sensation that does not form itself till the *social* feelings have been developed, and the Reason has connected itself with a wide range of objects" (50). The establishment of this principle and its subsequent monuments originates, somehow, as human development and social transaction. And like the typical Wordsworthian move of backward looking, the search for origins turns out to be the search for tendencies: "Never did a child stand by the side of a running stream, pondering within himself what power was the feeder of the perpetual current, from what never-wearied sources the body of water was supplied, but he must have been inevitably propelled to follow this question by another: 'Towards what abyss is it in progress? What receptacle can contain the mighty influx?' And the spirit of the answer must have been . . . *as* inevitably,—a receptacle without bounds or dimensions;—nothing less than infinity" (51).

The backward look establishes not only the never-wearying sources of a perpetual current, but also its mighty influx—a movement without bounds. The never-wearying sources and infinity as necessary endings are the "monuments" that the epitaph presupposes and is concerned with. The inscription is erected upon the grave that not only buries but also perpetuates. Setting off upon such grounds, the essays upon epitaphs, like other Wordsworthian epitaphic compositions, are concerned with the living rather than the dead. And this is probably why the essays are actually about the setting up of judgments and tastes and the education of the readers. Close connection with the bodily remains of the deceased may be the very sign of our humanness in any civilization, for "it may be said that a sepulchral monument is a tribute to a man as a human being . . . and for the common benefit of the living" (Wordsworth, "Essays upon Epitaphs" 53). But a good epitaph, properly written, read and located, aspires to something more: it is as if one then "has mounted to the sources of things—penetrated the dark cavern from which the River that murmurs in every one's ear has flowed from generation to generation" (79). The erection of the epitaph upon the grave is a boundary-crossing pose that mounts the sources and redirects the flow. It is a sublime construction that crosses over both life and death. If breaking like a wave to join the sea is the destiny of the weak rustic who is the necessary actor in Wordsworth's project of poetic modernity and who accomplishes his assignment by a passive, deathlike gesture, Wordsworth the epitaphic poet, "as the metonymy of his culture," builds his own monument by relocating and defining the sources. This is a masterly movement that refigures both the origins of being and human, social transaction, and reestablishes the correspondence between them. The Wordsworthian gesture is a sublime attempt, which hyperbolizes its own agency in its address to the trauma of modern history from a resurrected primordial ground:

> was it for this
> That one, the fairest of all rivers, loved
> To blend his murmurs with my nurse's song,
> And from his alder shades and rocky falls,
> And from his fords and shallows, sent a voice
> To intertwine my dreams? For this didst thou, O Derwent, travelling over
>   the green plains
> Near my sweet birthplace, didst thou, beauteous stream,
> Give ceaseless music to the night and day, Which with its steady cadence
>   tempering
> Our human waywardness, composed my thoughts
>
> To more than infant softness, giving me
> Amid the fretful tenements of man
> A knowledge, a dim earnest, of the calm
> That Nature breathes among her woodland h[aunts]?
> Was it for this—. (Wordsworth, "MS. Drafts and Fragments 1798-1804"
>   lines 1-16)

The query to River Derwent, a connected sequence of 150 lines drafted by Wordsworth in October-November 1798 is the "seminal poem" of the various versions of *The Prelude* (J. Wordsworth, "Revision as Making" 485-90), the poet's ever expanding preamble to his crowning philosophical epic *The Recluse*. The opening of the seminal lines is a question that leaps in medias res—"was it for this?" It is not only a beginning in mid-line, but also in lower case, "and requires an antecedent to 'this' that is never supplied" (J. Wordsworth, "Revision as Making" 486). The beginning with a question in lower case in the middle of things not only demonstrates a poetic *humilitas* that Wordsworth adroitly sets up in his Preface to *Lyrical Ballads* as requisite to modern poetry. It also shows an uncertainty, a poetical and procedural hesitation, while the lack of antecedent furthers the sense of doubt but promises an infinitude of redefinitions. It suggests other possible beginnings and endings to the poem—"was it for this"—that the poet's beloved river would blend its murmurs with his song and send a voice to intertwine with his dreams? The interrogation is both about the intention of the river and the nature of the poet's present undertaking. The poet wants the music of his "beauteous stream" to temper "Our human waywardness," soften and compose his thoughts, and give him "A knowledge, a dim earnest, of the calm" that is one with Nature. But he is not sure of his end either as personal or poetical possibility. For he is about to "speak of things / That have been, and that are, no gentle dreams / . . . / The time of unrememberable being" (16-19). He is all too aware that his is not the song of innocence, and with a memory "Amid the fretful tenements of man," Nature's guidance seems much needed but tantalizingly "dim."

The childhood memory of himself as a "rover" in nature is a memory of being suspended dangerously: "While on the perilous edge I hung alone" (43), "But ill sustained, and almost, as it seemed, / Suspended by the wind which blew amain / Against the naked cragg" (38-42). He is hesitant about his path, therefore questions the river's winding flow, although after 94 lines, he reassures himself and launches out again with a new sense of purpose: "Nor while, though doubting yet not lost, I tread / The mazes of this argument" (98-99). Wordsworth's anxiety about the "seminal" point of the poem points to his anxiety about its end. And that is the end, the limit, and the direction of an English literary modernity. *The Prelude* is, after all, preoccupied with the motif of beginnings and has replaced its end—*The Recluse* is never written. Therefore the question of beginnings is the lasting question of the poem. Its end as a Romantic aesthetic prelude to renewed modern history seems to depend on its poetic passages—the direction of the rush of poetic numbers. However, while the 1799 *Prelude* is an expansion of the seminal lines, in the 1850 revision, the question is put off until the middle of book 1. The poet begins instead as the returning prodigal son: "O there is blessing in this gentle breeze, / A visitant that while it fans my cheek / Doth seem half-conscious of the joy it brings / From the green fields, and from yon azure sky. / What'er his mission, the soft breeze can come / To none more grateful than to me; escaped / From the vast city, where I long had pined // A discontented sojourner: now free, / Free as a bird to settle where I will" (*Prelude* 1850 1.1-9). The journey is set out as an escape. The poet has finally set himself free from the vast city, where he had dwelt unhappily. He is sure of his welcome, for the word "sojourner" marks a temporal duration, and establishes his origin as the rightful son of Nature who was momentarily led astray amid the fretful tenements of man, but returning repentant and grateful. Thus, "What'er his mission," nature will not begrudge its blessing for the homecoming prodigal. In these revised seminal lines, the poet assumes the loving guidance of nature, for in his refiguration, nature's love not only manifests itself as a "gentle breeze" from the "green fields" and "azure sky," but "Doth seem half-conscious of the joy it brings." Thus the poet wanders on with confidence, as he is "now free, / Free as a bird to settle where I will." The subsequent question "and what clear stream / Shall with its murmur lull me into rest" (1.10-13) becomes simply rhetorical. The choice is in his hands, for "The earth is all before me," and he only needs to look about: "and should the chosen guide / Be nothing better than a wandering cloud, / I cannot miss my way" (1.16-18).

But this new seminal confidence is deceiving. The question of direction in the new beginning is delayed, displaced, but not removed. Hartman thinks "*The Prelude* opens with a success immediately followed by a failure" (33-69). Following and anticipating the new freedom, "poetic numbers came / Spontaneously to clothe in priestly robe / A renovated spirit" (1.51-53). Spontaneous poetic lines rush out because the poet "felt within / A correspondent breeze," that first "gently moved / With quickening virtue, but is now become / A tempest, a redundant energy, / Vexing its own creation" (1.34-38). This famous corresponding breeze brings the poet hope of "service high" and "Matins and vespers, of harmonious verse!" (1.44-45). But the breeze as tempest also vexes: "but the harp / Was soon defrauded, and the banded host / Of harmony dispersed in straggling sounds, / And lastly utter silence! "Be it so, / Why think of any thing but present good?" (1.96-100). After the initial exultation, Wordsworth seems perplexed by and tries to offset the opposition between the present good and the poetic outburst by a "reversal of mood." Such a "reversal of mood," suggests Hartman, has redeemed Wordsworth's usurpation of Nature, contoured in his declaration of total freedom of choice, to transcendence, through a return to nature (Hartman 35). It is a transcendence structured with ingenuity. In this way Hartman both points out and absolves Wordsworth's problematic beginning in relation to his end. Wordsworth's failure, for him, begins when as a poet he places "the cart before the horse, Poetry before Nature" (35). In the poet's over-anxious seminal rush, the ideal process of "Nature proposes but the poet disposes" becomes one in which "A *personal* agent replaces that of nature: 'I paced on . . . down I sate . . . slackening my thoughts by choice' (1.60)" (Hartman 35). For Hartman, however, this process which begins as a failure only foregrounds the sense of "double agency," the "reciprocity" that is at the heart of all Wordsworth's poetry. It testifies to his continuous anticipation of "a movement of transcendence." As a first experience, it is a "subtle bravado" which is symptomatic of Wordsworth's "creative difficulties" that resulted in an "indeterminacy" of the poem's purpose (Hartman 36-38). This vital "indeterminacy," this seminal "restlessness" is perceived not only to belong to Wordsworth's means but also to his end. In the rush of his verse, the direction of the "growth of a poet's mind" seems uncertain. The poem that begins with a whole long roundabout story of the growth of the poet's mind becomes an ever-expanding appeal to Nature for proof that it had indeed intended him to be a poet. But in Hartman's final analysis, Wordsworth is none the worse for it. His "failure vis-à-vis nature (or its failure vis-à-vis him) is doubly redeemed" (Hartman 40). For the poet has learned his present faith that self-renewal is possible without the violence of an apocalypse, in a continuous "movement of transcendence" that turns paradoxes into reciprocities. It is a movement that charts out "the progress of a soul by way of a '*naturaliter negativa*'" (Hartman 33).

I linger on Hartman because his reading of Wordsworth's poetic choice as transcendental is fundamental in establishing the poet's Romantic project as historically escapist. It is a reading that recuperates Wordsworth's compositional difficulties into dialectical (divine-inspired) necessities to an end, that is, poetry's coming-to-be for itself, a process by which both Romanticism and poetry are rid of their historical burdens. On the other hand, Hartman is also the foremost interpreter of Wordsworth's seminal restlessness, which, I want to stress, is crucial in understanding the latter's project of a modern poetic beginning. For, indeed, the "rush," hesitation, and roundabout movement of the "poetic numbers" in *The Prelude* are central to understanding the purpose and interest of Wordsworth's longest poem. Was it for "*this*" that the poet's beloved river murmurs along to join his present song? The question, deferred and replaced after an elaborate enumeration of his "best and favourite" aspirations, possible beginnings and subsequent repudiations, of his contrary yearnings for "those lofty hopes" and the "humbler industry" (1.133-34), becomes resonantly more emphatic. Thus the confidence: "and should the chosen guide / Be nothing better than a wandering cloud, / I cannot miss my way. I breathe again!" (1.16-18) is more of a wish, a blind hope. In the actual listing, the poet senses the danger of putting immediate thoughts and passions into songs and tries to temper the unruliness of things and feelings by deliberate choice and distancing. Anxiety and an almost overwhelming desire to precipitate headlong into a "proper" poetic undertaking become the predominant note and threaten to lead the poet astray: "Sometimes the ambitious Power of choice, mistaking / Proud spring-tide swellings for a regular sea" (1.166-67). Wordsworth cannot even ask the resourceful river until after he labors elaborately to list all the wrong undertakings. By the time he moves close to wonder about "was it for this," the "this" has to be read rather emphatically. Was it for this? The doubt becomes hyperbolic. It is made real and prolonged. This is why I do not follow Hartman's transcendental-metaphysical absolution of the contrary tendencies in the poem. In fact, neither the aesthetical nor the cultural historical path for *The Prelude* is settled. The poem, as a poem, hangs suspended between the epic and the pastoral. And its necessary end, the "philosophical song" of *The Recluse*, is never written. To overcome such incompletion in constructing a Wordsworthian "whole," critics have tried to "collect and resolve the contrary qualities" by finding a center of "higher realization," just as M.H. Abrams has discerned that "all its parts are centered in love" (Arac 57-59). Thus in their redirection *The Prelude* has achieved a "circular shape" "centered in love," which, according to Arac's paraphrase of Abrams, is "a romantic version of Christian and Neoplatonic commonplaces that figured the progress of the soul as a journey leading through a circuitous path to home" (Arac 60). It is against such a desire for a harmonious resolution, such satisfying, compensatory circuits that Hartman insists on the dark "indeterminacies," and the fierce self-conflicting struggle of the poet. But in the end, Hartman is also "inclined to fall back on the nearest steadying commonplace" (Hartman 66) as is the fate of the critic he himself contoured, by settling for the redemption of a Hegelian movement of transcendence.

In his reconsideration of Wordsworth's sense of history, Alan Liu, like Hartman, also focuses on the "trafficking" of the poetic passage in *The Prelude*. But instead of continuing with the transcendentally metaphysical "life as a journey" motif, he rewrites Wordsworth's Romantic journey into a "tour." Liu examines the variable concerns of *The Prelude*: history, revolution, nature, imagination, poetry and the role of the poet, all in its framing structure—on how it organizes its tour. In his discovery, history, in the midst of Wordsworth's poetic trafficking, is an essential source that is not in the tour, but a ghost presence, by being elsewhere, points to the otherness of the tour (see A. Liu). Not unlike other Romantic criticisms, though, the interest of Liu's theory also seems to be elsewhere: by looking at the "sense of history" in Romantic poetics, he takes up "the challenge" to redefine history as referential truth, as an "evacuated ontology," "*elsewhere* than in the phenomena," and literature as "second-order negation" (A. Liu 39). Although I do not agree with Liu's conclusion that *The Prelude* manifests "a poetics of denial" and that Wordsworth, by denying history, unwittingly realizes it (35-40), I take up his illuminating charting of the poet's "Romantic" and "subliminal" "tour," and expand on his registry of the "marked breaks" and "shaped absences" (A. Liu 46) in a structure of what he calls the elsewhereness of Wordsworth's poetic trafficking. In Liu's definition, a tour is something "designed only to make sense of passage, not of a goal . . . From a viewpoint within a tour, therefore, any sense of completion posited at the terminus can only appear a gap, an absence" (4). Thus in this renewed tour model which emphatically reinstates Wordsworth's poetic trafficking with worldly concerns, "literary texts" and "historical contexts" are reposited in a "dynamic" structure of "marked breaks" and "shaped absences." Wordsworth's *Prelude*, emblematic of the Romantic, hence emphatically literary text, is shaped by "the history *not* there" (A. Liu 46).

The end of *The Prelude*—the shaping of a modern poetics as a means to reimagine history after traumatic revolution—indeed seems to depend on the structure of its poetic traffic. In its fifty years of writing and revision, the haunting question of the ever-expanding poem remains from beginning to end a question of direction. Foremost among its many interests, *The Prelude* is an extended poetic preamble on the possibilities of a poetics of modernity and the role of the poet amid his new "worldly concerns." I would like to extend and rework Liu's trope of the "marked breaks" and "shaped absences" here with the aim to further explore the construction of the poem and its end to restore history, but rid it of the implication of a Hegelian "beyond" and "the ghost presence" of historical reference. I emphasize that as "marked" and "shaped" ruptures, these breaks and absences in the Romantic journey delineated in the poem are intended moments of suspension. They are part of a deliberate poetic structure whose aim is cultural and political rather than unwitting, dark, indeterminate lacks of a metaphysical whole. In this sense they are not only perceivable gaps in the movement of the poem but also points of crossing over, like the figures of "the supplement" (Derrida 141-64). In his reading of Rousseau, Derrida suggests that the concept of the supplement "harbors within itself two significations." First, "the supplement adds itself, it is a surplus, a plenitude enriching another plenitude, the *fullest measure* of presence." Second, "but the supplement supplements. It adds only to replace. It intervenes or insinuates itself *in-the-place-of* . . . Compensatory [suppleant] and vicarious, the supplement is an adjunct, a subaltern instance which *takes-(the)-place* [*tient-lieu*]. As substitute, it is not simply added to the positivity of a presence, . . . its place is assigned in the structure by the mark of an emptiness" (144-45). What Alan Liu charts as the "marked breaks" and "shaped absences" of a prototypical Romantic tour, are the surplus and replacement in a peculiarly structured poetic relation of supplementarity, in which the punctured gaps "insinuate" themselves "in-the-place-of," and "take-(the)-place" of the journey proper and reset its direction. As long as they are "supplements," they are limited, because their place is "assigned." But they are also positive interventions since they are "compensatory" and "vicarious"; they take place in the substitution. The "marked breaks" and "shaped absences" in Wordsworth's Romantic journey in this sense are the vital moments of cultural poetical excess, rather than uncovered dark recesses of "indeterminacy." They become the "plenitude enriching another plenitude." In this sense they make up the journey, poetic as well as historical. These moments of excess—what Wordsworth himself designates as the "spots of time" (1850 5.444, 10.58)—are also moments harboring what might be called the spectral sublime (an important component in Wordsworth's modern poetics to which I will return in a later section).

Similarly concerned with the breaks and absences, the "truncations" of Wordsworth's journey, Arac stresses the mutual replacing and displacing in the relation of supplementation in his rethinking of *The Prelude* and its poetic, critical directions. "*The Prelude* offered 'several frames of things, . . . They may be 'mutually indebted' or instead 'half lost / Each in the other's blaze" (8.481-84). The process may transform from a totalizing 'swallowing up of lesser things in great' to a disruptive 'change of them into their contraries' (11.179-80)" (Arac 70). He picks up the trope of the journey only to find discrepancies, crevices, and interruptions, and sees in the "circular shape" of the Romantic path both the consoling promise of a "compensatory return" and the figuring of a lack or excess. Arac suggests that the "lack" or "excess" in the Wordsworth circle is the deferral of its end, which actually expands the end into "something ever more about to be," and Wordsworth recuperates the end through interruption and reward from discrepancy. The movement of *The Prelude*, seen in such light, is a movement to integrate "spots of time" into a consecutive history of a "life" project, but "Wordsworth's feeling is represented as always strangely elsewhere." The movement or truncation between the elsewhereness and the consecutive history is the "typical spotting and knotting," a "doubling back" movement that tries to "single out moments that can be joined each to each to define a direction for the present" (Arac 61).

The movement from Hartman to Liu and to Arac marks the shift in Anglo-American Romantic criticism from the discrimination of indeterminate discrepancies in the Romantic structure to the effort to abandon the Romantic principle—the spiral pursuit of metaphysical redemption—in the critical enterprise altogether. Arac has actually chosen to be "against" the "literary symbol and philosophical dialectic" of the Romantic principles that inscribe part into whole, that Coleridgean ideal of "a redemptive process in operation" that "reconciled all the anomalies and promised future glory and restoration" (Arac 57). In this way the emphasis in reading *The Prelude* is returned to the contingent structure of its poetic direction, which is visibly an emphatic part of Wordsworth's original proceedings and hesitations. This will also be my point of entry in reading the poem as the text that not only exemplifies Wordsworth's attempts to reconcile a poetic modernity, but also is emblematic of a Romantic poetics that aims to imaginatively reengage modern history.

Attempting to capture Wordsworth's original, read historical, proceedings and hesitations, I propose that the key moments—the most notable jumping blocks in Wordsworth's longest poetic traversal from event to event and meaning to meaning—are the well-known "spots of time." These "spots"—momentary glimpses into the meaning of life and history at particular spatial and temporal junctures—should be understood vis-à-vis Walter Benjamin's definition of history in his "Thesis on the Philosophy of History." That is, to "articulate the past historically" one has to "seize hold of a memory as it flashes at us at a moment of danger" (*Illuminations* 255). A major part of the poetical-historical action in *The Prelude* is the construction of gazes at past moments, often reremembered, to make sense of the present. But often, when the gaze doubles back, much that is retrieved seems uncanny—they make neither poetic nor historical sense. On the sweet and green shores of Esthwaite's Lake, confronted with "a spectre shape of terror," the poet as a boy is remembered to have had his initial "spots of time" experience:

> The succeeding day,
> Those unclaimed garments telling a plain tale
> Drew to the spot an anxious crowd; some looked
> In passive expectation from the shore,
> While from a boat others hung o'er the deep,
> Sounding with grappling irons and long poles.
> At last, the dead man, 'mid that beauteous scene
> Of trees and hills and water, bolt upright
> Rose, with his ghastly face, a spectre shape
> Of terror; yet no soul-debasing fear,
> Young as I was, a child not nine years old,
> Possessed me, for my inner eye had seen
> Such sights before, among the shining streams
> Of faery land, the forest of romance.
> Their spirit hallowed the sad spectacle
> With decoration of ideal grace;
> A dignity, a smoothness, like the works
> Of Grecian art, and purest poesy. (*The Prelude* 1850 5.442-59)

In moving from a spectacle of terror to moments of "seeing," much depends on the poet-child's turning to sources elsewhere. Amid the beauteous scene of the boy's beloved nature, the dead man rose "bolt upright." But even as a boy, the poet's feeling at the sight of the "ghastly" dead man was not a "soul-debasing fear" but "A dignity, a smoothness, like the works / Of Grecian art, and purest poesy." Because he had read romances and knew the ideal grace of poetry, so "Their spirit hallowed the sad spectacle." This is poetry that translates possible "fear" into real "dignity." Here culture has to compensate for nature to make a terrible moment sublime. Later in a comparable moment in the "revolutionary" books, at the scene of the Paris Massacre, the poet again gazes aghast:

> I crossed the square (an empty area then!)
> Of the Carrousel, where so late had lain
> The dead, upon the dying heaped, and gazed
> On this and other spots, as doth a man
> Upon a volume whose contents he knows

Are memorable, but from him locked up,
Being written in a tongue he cannot read,
So that he questions the mute leaves with pain,
And half upbraids their silence. (*The Prelude* 1850 10.55-64)

The pain is genuine. But at the spot, the poet-spectator could not even feel the terror, let alone the subsequent sublimation at "the dead, upon the dying heaped." The historical sight then has to be compared to a volume, the content of which he might have had glimpses of elsewhere to know it to be "memorable" but not enough to make sense. The spot is one that refuses to be knotted, the reremembered scene yields no meaning until the poet appeals further afield. The poet finally experiences and vaguely comprehends the terror and anxiety presented by the aftermath of the revolutionary massacre by "scattering" himself and the "mute," painful "volume" into "tragic fictions or true history, / Remembrances and dim admonishments" (10.76-77). The experience on the spot can only be vaguely experienced elsewhere in a "volume." Or, rather, the experience becomes experience, memorable hence meaningful, only through its analogous existence in the volume, which in turn has to be scattered by the poet, with himself, into either "tragic fictions" or "true history," "remembrances," and "dim admonishments" elsewhere. The spectacle of the massacre is turned into the spot of experiencing terror, memory, and meaning. And by such spotting and knotting—a doubling back movement of mutual transference—the poet also reconstructs other historical cultural sources. Tragic fiction, true history, and memory all become necessary elsewheres for the sublime experience. Wordsworth's hesitation, his inability to read the Revolutionary terror on the "spot" as a meaningful volume reflects his poetical-historical dilemmas, which are the necessity and difficulty of mutual transference. And the simultaneous effort to construct a resourceful elsewhere can prove too strenuous. The experience of Revolution can remain baffling; and terror sometimes excessive. The structure of turning amongst different things and sources seems both the only way out in the poetic supplementation that takes place at the historical impasse and a precarious one. This, a necessary but unreliable structure of transference, is what I believe led to Wordsworth's formulation later of the poet as translator, and his reliance on the "shadowy things"—the poetic moments and images that manifest the uncanny or spectral sublimity—in the emphatically evoked elsewheres. One might even argue that in Wordsworth's attempt, the aesthetic revival of history depends on managing the spectral sublime and the act of translation.

Managing the spectral sublime

"I saw before me stretched a boundless plain / Of sandy wilderness, all black and void, / And as I looked around, distress and fear / Came creeping over me, when at my side, / Close at my side, an uncouth shape appeared / Upon a dromedary, mounted high. / He seemed an Arab of the Bedouin tribes" (*The Prelude* 1850 5.71-77). This "uncouth shape" appears in the "educational" book 5. The prospect (and guilt?) of plunging into the "black and void" "sandy wilderness" of a self-education conditioned by the early deaths of both father and mother for the poet is necessary but "destitute." It begins with distress and creeping fear. And it is at this moment that the Arab appears, "mounted high," as "an uncouth shape." As we have learned earlier in the poem, this is actually the result of a dream conceived by the poet's seaside reading of Cervantes's "famous history of the errant knight." In it, the supposed "Arab of the Bedouin tribes," as guide and traveler, like Cervantes's knight errant, is onto his own strange quest. The poet wants to "cleave unto this man" and "share his enterprise," an enterprise as "disturbed" as "his countenance," after which the poet hankers but is mercilessly left behind. However, by turning "this Arab phantom" into "this semi-Quixote," "I to him have given / A substance" (5.143-44). In the moment after, meaning—that subsequent poetic substance—is made not in the celebrated symbol of the stone and shell the phantom guide holds in his hands, but in the disturbed and disturbing identity of him as the Arabian knight. By representing the Arab phantom as a semi-Quixote, the poet maintains his distance from the silly chivalric romance while salvaging the quest from burlesque. The memory left over from his imperfect childhood reading of the Arabian tales transforms the haunt of the knight errant into "a living man, / A gentle dweller in the desert, crazed / By love and feeling, and internal thought / Protracted among endless solitude; / Having shaped him wandering upon this quest!" (5.144-48) The ghost of Quixote, by way of the gentle dweller of the desert, is both pursued and reshaped into the Romantic sojourner. Meanwhile, like the maiden in "Nutting," the Arab of the Bedouin tribes is consigned to gentleness, and like Margaret crazed by love and feeling. The stories of the Arabian Nights, from the poet's boyhood fragmentary reading and repeated telling, in his adult-poetic dream become subsumed in Cervantes' records and Wordsworth's "natural lore." And these Arabian phantoms revive Wordsworth's otherwise quixotic quest. By subsuming "the Arabian tales" in Cervantes' records, the excess of the phantasm is domesticated into an insane but recognizable, therefore sympathetic, motif: the quest of a (mock) Romantic hero, be it knight errant or self-hatching poet. Scheherazade, the "original" conjurer elsewhere vanishes long before the knotting of the margins of Wordsworth's new plot.

One should not forget that the Arab Quixote is the apparition of the poet's epistemological and educational dream-play. A dream, like the well known "actual" dream of Descartes, "is usually read in terms of its own rereading, the interpretation supplied by Descartes himself," in which the picture of "a visionary pitting himself against overwhelming odds" covers "its inconsequential dream-play with vanishing books and lost texts" (Jacobus, *Romanticism* 119). Wordsworth's vision is built upon the dream-play that makes books vanish and loses texts, but a very consequential one. By turning into dreams other people's words elsewhere and revisioning them, Wordsworth attains his literary modernity by traversing the dangerous but invigorating other places and times and makes them "new" and "common-place." Such traversal is not only a matter of masking the anxiety of influence or making "manageable a larger and more inescapable anxiety: that our texts have always been written before, that the loud prophetic blast of harmony is pentecostal and speaks with many voices" (Jacobus, *Romanticism* 124). It is also an attempt to acquire primordial authority by domesticating cultures elsewhere as natural native grounds. As Wordsworth himself characterizes it in the "Essays upon Epitaphs," it is as if one had "mounted to the sources of things" (79). Wordsworth "mounts" the "dark" "sources" that he by act of stealth remakes along the way. He then renders them "commonplace" things of life so that both the difference of things and the one "loud prophetic blast of harmony" (*The Prelude* 1805 5.96) can be made out of the many voices. Whereas the "otherness" of things is consigned to gentleness or allowed to vanish so that natural lore can be woven out of the cultural given (learned). Wordsworth's book of education is about the self-nurturing of the boy-poet where the hands of nature are made out of his stealthy readings of cultures elsewhere, and by the same twist knots his own difference upon them. This, the precariously knotted twist, is the texture of Wordsworth's and the Romantic hinterland. And though neither the self-nurturing boy-poet nor the reader is told "why hath not the Mind / Some element to stamp her image on / In nature somewhat nearer to her own?" we all learn that there are these other places where "Visionary power / Attends the motions of the viewless winds, / Embodied in the mystery of words: / There, darkness makes abode, and all the host / Of shadowy things work endless changes,—there" (*The Prelude* 1850 5.597-601). It is this nurturing elsewhere where "shadowy things work endless changes" from which Wordsworth crafts his Romantic poetics, and where he severs and bridges the "beginning of English literature" from the "end of English poetry."

However, Wordsworth's relation with the "shadowy things" of his endless elsewheres is not always one of stealthy objectification. The Arab phantom, like the Hawkshead shepherd in book 8, is the important "solitary object and sublime" (*The Prelude*, 1850 8.407), essential not only in the poet's earlier education but also to the worldly end of the movement of the poem. The poet's encounters with the gigantic human forms (the shepherds) and the "mountain high" "uncouth shape" (the Arab phantom) are underwritten by his play of "the politics of the sublime" (Harrison 57-78). In fact, the episode of the Arab knight has been read as the most sublime moment in the poem. Its sublimity comes from the disturbing but overwhelming image of the Arab phantom, as harbinger of the news of apocalyptic destruction and guide of "unerring skill" to the poet's quest, and from the incomprehension, the half-terror, half-delight of the poet. In Burke's *Enquiry*, the sublime is defined in terms of the spectator's experience of being subjected to powers beyond his control. It is always accompanied by terror—the spectator must be threatened by a superior, often destructive power in order to feel the sublime. This "politics of the sublime," as Harrison points out, also "enables in part the transference of power between spectator and spectacle" (Harrison 73). This formulation of the transference of power helps us understand the interest and purpose of the apparition of the Arab knight, as "in Wordsworth's poem, however, the inversion of this relationship between spectator and spectacle invests the apparently powerless with an alarming power" (Harrison 74). In his dreamy encounter with the Arab phantom, the poet stands in incomprehension but also in awe of the latter's spectral sublimity. Like the boy in front of the giant shepherd figures, he cannot "contain" the Arab "as an object of his cognitive grasp" (Harrison 74). I would go further to suggest, however, that beyond the power of the poet's comprehension, the spectral Arab appears as a figure to which the poet submits not only "in a moment of cognitive erasure" (Harrison 74), but also in a moment of willing suspension. In front of this spectral figure, he suspends his faculties of doubt and judgment, as well as the direction of his very poetical and historical course. "At the sight / Much I rejoiced, not doubting but a guide / Was present, one who with unerring skill / Would through the desert lead me" (5.80-83), "I wondered not, . . . / Nor doubted once ..., / Having a perfect faith in all that passed. / Far stronger, now, grew the desire I felt / To cleave unto this man" (5.111-16), while "he hurried on / Reckless of me" (5.117-18). The poet's encounter with the commanding Arab phantom is figured as suspension, submission, halted in its headlong precipitation only by the object's reckless desertion—"In chase of him; whereat I waked in terror" (5.138). It is subsequently compensated "in soberness" as a "spot" of sublimity, which testifies to the necessary state of "obscurity" that constitutes the Burkean sublime. It is a state in which the spectator is "vulgarized": "It is our ignorance of things that causes all our admiration, and chiefly excites our passions. Knowledge and acquaintance make the most striking causes affect but little. It is thus with the vulgar, and all men are as the vulgar in what they do not understand" (Burke, *Enquiry* 61). The emphasis on the necessity of "obscurity" and its association with the vulgar not only blurs the boundaries between the aesthetic subject and object, but also anticipates their possible inversion in the obscurity. It also associates the sublime aesthetic-poetical course in the moment of obscurity with the worldly course of "all men." It levels the poet down to the fate of the vulgar in front of that which he does not understand and reestablishes correspondence between his function as a poet and the passions or understandings of "all men."

The poetic direction of *The Prelude,* with its worldly concerns of history and revolution, then, becomes "a matter of managing sublimity" (Bourke 240-56) and is predicated on the function of the poet. In Bourke's delineation, managing the sublime "comes to consist in the rehabilitation of the terrible, the effective resolution of complexity and awe. And the poet becomes the apparent agent of this resolve." To read the typical Wordsworthian "spotting" and "knotting" as the "managing" of sublimity is to conceive the agency of the poet as that which "relieve[s] us from prostration, to lift us up when fallen" (Bourke 240). This is why for Bourke, the impulse of the Romantic sublime is inevitably to regularize and unify—"but as a project of coordination and harmonization, the Wordsworthian sublime, in its aggressively destabilizing aspect, becomes a mute hypothesis: for it is always on the way to being something else; it has already been enlisted as a constituent element in the project of consolidation" (Bourke 240-41). I agree with Bourke that the Wordsworthian sublime here relies very much on the rehabilitation of the terrible, but do not see the consequential project of *The Prelude*, or also necessarily, the Romantic poetics, as a project of consolidation. Bourke's critique of the Wordsworthian sublime as the portent of consolidation in this sense is like Eagleton's exposure of the Burkean ruse of sublimity, in that they both commit the fallacy of presupposing the stability of meaning and boundary of Wordsworth's and Burke's aesthetic categories. In Bourke's reading of Eagleton's reading of Burke, "The instincts of fear and self-preservation which sublimity excites are the occasion of the principle of generation . . . so the sublime had been posited as the motive for containment" (241). Eagleton's mistake is to read the principle of generation as containment; it is a "mis-take" of beginnings for the end. While the Burkean sublime disrupts to regenerate, the Burkean beautiful is not only a harmonizing sociability, but also one of beguiling threat, as "the smell of flowers disposes people to drowsiness," and "that this quality, where it is highest, in the female sex, almost always carries with it an idea of weakness and imperfection. Women are very sensible of this; for which reason, they learn to lisp, to totter in their walk, to counterfeit weaknesses, and even sickness" (Burke, *Enquiry* 297, 203-04). This trickery of the beautiful in the scheme of the sublime is vindicated later by the early twentieth-century Chinese critic Liang Zhongdai. In his cross-cultural discussion "Lun chonggao" ("On the Sublime" 1934), he takes the perceived Kantian sublime sacrifice of the sensory in the assertion of reason to task by expanding the Burkean unease with the beguiling threat of the feminine. Liang redefines the sublime as the aesthetic category that exults in an unbound and anarchistic abandon of libidinal energy, but which resides rather more often in the terror of the feminine. By that he means that the sublime of the feminine comes from the sudden collapse of our normal perceptual standards, which can potentially exceed the harness of any cultural program and political purpose. In this sense, the beautiful and sublime differ only in degree, not in kind.

Bourke also insists on the possibility of movement between the sublime and the beautiful by pointing to the end of the Wordsworthian sublime as "the figuring of a beautiful community." His reading of the recuperation is built on the anteriority of the sublime to the beautiful. Such anteriority grants beauty as "the privileged moment of sublimity." The sublime, in its perceptual anteriority, is posited only "in the context of its subsequent beautification" (Bourke 224). However, this understanding not only presupposes the relative stability of the categories of the sublime and the beautiful when they are on their own, it also misconstrues their simultaneous, supplementary relation as a temporal progression. In Wordsworth's own trajectory, in the "archaeology" of the *Guide through the Lake District*, the sublime does occupy the place of anteriority and the beautiful, the very *telos* of Nature: "Sublimity is the result of Nature's first great dealings with the superficies of the earth; but the general tendency of her subsequent operations is toward the production of beauty, by a multiplicity of symmetrical parts uniting in a consistent whole" (*A Guide* 181). The sublime, as Wordsworth found engraved in the world, is the primary instance of Nature, as its "first great dealings," even though "the general tendency of her subsequent operations is toward the production of beauty," toward the ideal of the whole. However, as "origin and tendency" are "notions inseparably co-relative" (51), they may be "mutually indebted" or instead "half lost / Each in the other's blaze"

(*The Prelude* 1850 8.486-87). Their movement may transform from a totalizing "swallowing up of lesser things in great" to a disruptive "change of them into their contraries" (11.179-80). Also as it appears in the prose fragment "The Sublime and the Beautiful," "the same object may be both sublime & beautiful," and a "'healthy state' of mind depends upon its being affected by both 'exaltation or awe' *and* 'love & gentleness'" (349). Thus the observation that the sublime "always precedes the beautiful in making us conscious of its presence" (350) should not be read as pointing to a lineal temporal sequence of before and after, but to a matter of precedence, of commanding presence, or of a primal interruptive leverage in our consciousness that affects our perceptions. The slippage in Bourke's critique of the Wordsworthian sublime is his fixation on the *telos* of *The Prelude*'s poetical movement and its "retroactively forged" "political destiny." To presuppose its *telos* is to precipitate oneself, against the warnings of the poet and the poem's deliberate structure of endless elsewhereness, to its end that is always already deferred, and in the end replaced. For in the poetic movements of *The Prelude*, as epitomized in the not infrequent "spots of time," the sublime with its attending terror almost always crops up in medias res of the beautiful moments in nature. It is amid the "beauteous scene" that the apparition of the potential sublime, masquerading as the drowned schoolmaster or "the dead, upon the dying heaped," either as the result of natural calamity or the aftermath of revolution, is projected, not as the "preordination" of beauty but as moments of rupture, of suspension, and as structures of crossing over. For after all, Wordsworth's sublime is "aggressively destabilizing."

Figuring the poet as translator

The figuration of the poet as agent of this historical-aesthetic resolve, and the figuring of himself as a modern poet is Wordsworth's recurrent concern. In *A Poet's Epitaph*, Wordsworth identifies simultaneously with the liminal figure of the rustic stretched full length upon the grave, and distances himself as the epitaphic poet who occupies a "midway-point" between the lines elsewhere. In the Preface to *Lyrical Ballads*, he further defines the role of the poet as translator. The task for the poet contoured in the Preface is a certain cultural and social responsibility to counteract the corruptions of history, to reestablish communal "primary laws of human nature" against the "combined forces" of the times. But Wordsworth also notes that the poet's "employment is in some degree mechanical" (Preface to *Lyrical Ballads* 138), and thus itself part of the fallen modern condition. Thomas Pfau reads these paradoxical statements as Wordsworth's acknowledgment of a "principal challenge" to his "desired, universal homogeneity of the affective," and such a challenge is "mounted neither by the historical shifts of poetry's social field of reference nor by the calcified 'phraseology' of 'poetic diction.' Rather, it is the inevitably supplementary status of the poetic sign, always in an arbitrary and asymmetrical relation . . . to 'feeling,' which constitutes the most tenacious impediment to Wordsworth's theoretical vision of a socially and culturally efficient poetic technique" (137). This has warranted Wordsworth's move to centralize the "event of figuration" in the poetics professed and his substitutive introduction of the concept of translation. The locus of Wordsworth's culturally and socially burdened poetics in the act of figuration and the poet as translator, in this sense, is an unsettling but unwitting substitute itself, a structural ruse that simultaneously problematizes and effectuates his theoretical prospect.

The implication of Wordsworth's "translation," thus understood, falls on its status as technical apparatus, its concern for faithfulness, which "effectively distracts from its functional status," namely, the deduction from the essential homogeneity of "feeling" the social exigency of a cultural value of "sympathy" and community itself (Pfau 137). In such a recasting, the cultural ambition of the Preface appears to be the aftermath of its structural poetics indeed. Wordsworth's own apology seems to warrant such an understanding—"I may have sometimes written upon unworthy subjects; but I am less apprehensive on this account, than that my language may frequently have suffered from those arbitrary connections of feelings and ideas with particular words and phrases, from which no man can altogether protect himself" (Preface to *Lyrical Ballads* 153). The poet, by presenting himself as the casualty of the "arbitrary connections of feelings and ideas with particular words and phrases," minimizes its threat. After all, they are accidental slips the poet occasionally suffers from. However, to present the accidents as inescapable, as that which are truly apprehensive, and "from which no man can altogether protect himself," one should notice that Wordsworth also establishes the essential centrality of "those arbitrary connections." Just as in his assiduous (chronic) writing and rewriting, prefixing, and suffixing, the preface to a series of experimental poems has become a systematic defense of a poetry of modernity. The event of figuration is characterized by a supplementary structure of translation. And in its act of substituting, displacing, and replacing, it becomes the overriding structure that simultaneously figures the "dark caverns" of origin, upon which the arguments of Wordsworth's new culturally and socially burdened poetics are predicated. What may seem the "progressive totalization of the affective" (Pfau 137) in the Preface actually is an overriding structure of substitution. It is punctuated by shifts from "the subjects and aim of these Poems . . . to their style" (Preface to *Lyrical Ballads* 131), from "essential passions" to "elemental feelings," to "regular feelings," to "moral feelings," to "general sympathy," to "general passions and thoughts and feelings," and to "the great and universal passions of men." These movements are not only the important but unwitting accidental affective shifts, but also the fundamental principle of Wordsworth's experimental poetics whose cultural ambition is supplemented in its structure of elsewhereness.

In outlining the situation and the poetic attributes of the new experimental poet, Wordsworth observes that the poet possesses, among other things: "a disposition to be affected more than other men by absent things as if they were present; an ability of conjuring up in himself passions, which are indeed far from being the same as those produced by real events, yet (especially in those parts of the general sympathy which are pleasing and delightful) do more nearly resemble the passions produced by real events, than anything which, from the motions of their own minds merely, other men are accustomed to feel in themselves" (Preface to *Lyrical Ballads* 138). His observation highlights the peculiar relation of supplementarity in the affective structure as an interplay between the absences and presences. It is a function that falls on the act of "conjuring up." The poet, in this sense, above all things and distinguished from "other men," is a conjurer by proximity. The act of conjuring emphasizes the sense of insinuation, the surplus that takes-(the)-place in the structure of supplementation, and the sense of making good by filling in the void. But the poet as conjurer does not conjure up "passions" out of nothing. His conjuring trick is the turning of "absent things" into present ones and present things into absent ones. Thus the "conjuring up in himself passions" is a process of translation, and the conjuring poet the translator: "As it is impossible for the Poet to produce upon all occasions language as exquisitely fitted for the passion as that which the real passion itself suggests, it is proper that he should consider himself as in the situation of a translator, who does not scruple to substitute excellencies of another kind for those which are unattainable by him" (Preface to *Lyrical Ballads* 139). The definition of the poet as translator establishes the centrality of the structure of elsewhereness in Wordsworth's schema of a poetic modernity, in which poetry begins as substitution. And the very make-up of the poet as translator is his ability to substitute between excellencies of kinds. In such a definition, the "great and universal passions of men," as the regenerative, primeval ground of Wordsworth's revolutionary poetics, indeed only denote an interest, not an essence. They can only appear in figural forms. The poet's attempt at reconstructing a communal culture and historical direction, as expressed in the Preface, depends on the very "metaphors" and "figure" that conjure up both the "essential passions" and his corresponding, sublime poetic end. Here Wordsworth recapitulates the relation of translation in the construction of his poetics and its cultural impulse. As a response to the unhumanizing calamities of the "combined forces" of the times ("Letter to Charles Fox" 202), Wordsworth stresses the urgent need for the reconstruction of a communal culture—a national character through the transformative power of natural sublimity and beauty upon human passions—through the conjuring tricks of a new poetry. In the proposition, the transformative end of Wordsworth's professed poetics depends on the translatability between natural images, the essential human passions, and a "general sympathy": "Now it is manifest that no human being can be so besotted and debased by oppression, penury, or any other evil which unhumanises man as to be utterly insensible to the colours, forms, or smell of flowers . . . they must have been not the nourishers merely, but often the fathers of their passions. There cannot be a doubt that in tracts of country where images of danger, melancholy and grandeur, or loveliness, softness, and ease prevail, that they will make themselves felt powerfully in forming the characters of the people, so as to produce an uniformity or national character" ("Letter to John Wilson" 350). This is the sublime goal of Wordsworth's poetics of translation, which appears much less a picture of harmonizing totality than a willful imposition of the translatability between kinds. It is this overriding structure of translatability between the poet's social and cultural interest and a restrictive, formal poetics that enables the correspondence between the discursive, poetic, and cultural transactions. As Benjamin illuminates for us in his meditation on *The Task of the Translator*, translation not only points to the self-difference of the original, but is a "liberation" that is mutual and reciprocal between the "original" and its "translation." It expresses above all things "the great longing for linguistic complementation" (Benjamin 79). In other words, translation is a process of supplementation that emphasizes reciprocity, mutual complements, excessive beginnings, and a process of replacement.

In book 12, near the end of *The Prelude*, after endless detours and "fresh starts," Wordsworth emphatically restates his *ars poetica* and his being as poet:

> that meanwhile the forms
> Of Nature have a passion in themselves,
> That intermingles with those works of man
> To which she summons him; although the works
> Be mean, have nothing lofty of their own;
> And that the Genius of the Poet hence
> May boldly take his way among mankind
> Wherever nature leads; that he hath stood
> By Nature's side among the men of old,
> And so shall stand forever. Dearest Friend!
> If thou partake the animating faith
> That Poets, even as Prophets, each with each
> Connected in a mighty scheme of truth,
> Have each his own peculiar faculty,
> Heaven's gift, a sense that fits him to perceive
> Objects unseen before, thou wilt not blame
> The humblest of this band who dares to hope
> That unto him hath also been vouchsafed
> An insight that in some sort he possesses,
> A privilege whereby a work of his,
> Proceeding from a source of untaught things
> Creative and enduring, may become
> A power like one of Nature's. (*The Prelude* 1850 13.290-312)

The poet is implicated both in the scheme of Nature and the works of men, works that are "mean" and may have nothing lofty in themselves. Thus he is simultaneously elevated to the great designs of the passionate and leading Nature and recast back into his origin of *humilitas* in relation with the common "mankind." His place as the ordained modern prophet is "that he hath stood / By Nature's side among the men of old," that he is both cultured and in communion with nature, that he links the past, present and future, "And so shall stand for ever." The poet's role, in such a "mighty scheme of truth," is, indeed, the reprieve of history. And in his reprieve, the relationship between the poet's poetic power, the mighty scheme of Nature, and the "mean" and low works of men, is not one of precedence and follow up, of totality and accompaniment, nor is it realized in Hartman's reciprocity. It is figured instead as a translation. The poet, summoned forth by the "intermingl[ing]" of natural schema and the needs of "mankind," connected "each with each," even "The humblest of his band who dares to hope," translates "Heaven's gift," "An insight" that is vouchsafed in him, into poetry and the works of man and vice versa. And only so, he "shall stand for ever," retrieving, refiguring history "By nature's side among the men of old." And it is only in such relation of translation that he rebuilds the sense of the sublimity of poetic power and the preordination of his poetic career as agent of history.

The poetic imperative of historical redirection

The Simplon Pass episode in book 6 is often read as the emblematic height of the Romantic journey. This height as well as its sublime propensity to be on the way to being something else, dramatizes the structure of supplementary in the "knotting" of the "spots" of excessive beginnings and redirections in the poem. It begins where the poet has to cross the Alps:

> When from the Vallais we had turned, and clomb
> Along the Simplon's steep and rugged road,
> Following a band of muleteers, we reached
> A halting-place, where all together took
> Their noon-tide meal. Hastily rose our guide,
> Leaving us at the board; awhile we lingered,
> Then paced the beaten downward way that led
> Right to a rough stream's edge, and there broke off;
> The only track now visible was one
> That from the torrent's further brink held forth
> Conspicuous invitation to ascend
> A lofty mountain. After brief delay
> Crossing the unbridged stream, that road we took
> And clomb with eagerness, till anxious fears
> Intruded, for we failed to overtake
> Our comrades gone before. By fortunate chance,
> While every moment added doubt to doubt,
> A peasant met us, from whose mouth we learned
> That to the spot which had perplexed us first
> We must descend, and there should find the road,
> . . .
> And, that our future course, all plain to sight,
> Was downwards, with the current of that stream.
> Loth to believe what we so grieved to hear,
> For still we had hopes that pointed to the clouds,
> We questioned him again, and yet again;
> But every word that from the peasant's lips
> Came in reply, translated in our feelings,
> Ended in this,—that we had crossed the Alps. (*The Prelude* 1850 6.562-92)

In the crossing, the ascending has hardly begun when it comes to a halt. In fact it starts from a "halting-place," where "hastily rose" their guide and deserted them, and "awhile we lingered, / Then paced the beaten downward way." The journey begins as halting, desertion, lingering suspension and descent, and then, lured by the deceiving but "Conspicuous invitation to ascend / A lofty mountain," the poet and his friend "clomb with eagerness, till anxious fears / Intruded . . . While every moment added doubt to doubt," a peasant told them they have missed their way and have to return to their earlier halting "spot." Despite persistent "hopes that pointed to the clouds," the poet and his companion have to believe what they are "loth to believe," that the peasant's words, "translated by our feelings," come to mean "that we had crossed the Alps" in the most disappointing way. And what is worse, the right path, if they were to retrieve it, as pointed out by the knowing peasant, shows "that our future course, all plain to sight, / Was downwards" (6.585-86). Wordsworth is incredulous, he is "grieved," but again he lets go.

Whether one sees "a humane liberation" (Arac 66) or a poetic ploy in the letting go, there certainly is reward: the promise of "something evermore about to be." While the one emphasizes the hesitation, the semi-impotence and subsequent consolation in the process, the other stresses the making good of a promise, a deliberate backward move forward (Romantic in the Coleridgean sense), in order to stage emphatically "something evermore about to be." After all, the poet prefers "the budding rose above the rose full blown" (*The Prelude* 1850 11.121). Wordsworth does recall having had a distant glimpse of Mount Blanc early on, "That very day, / From a bare ridge we also first beheld / Unveiled the summit of Mount Blanc, and grieved / To have a soulless image on the eye / That had usurped upon a living thought / That never more could be" (*The Prelude* 1850 6.524-29) The danger is not so much that the end will be too flimsy, that one may not get there, but rather once one does see it, "That never more could be." The promise of the end—that "living thought"—is usurped upon because the "something evermore" is no longer "about to be." The summit unveiled becomes "soulless," the glimpses of the end do not live up to the expectation. If Mount Blanc does not look like Mount Blanc, not only "the hope to 'reach a chosen point' is repeatedly frustrated" (Arac 67), but also the origin of that hope, of that "chosen point" becomes dubious. Neither can promise anything "to be." However, Wordsworth always has his elsewheres to turn to: if the sight of Mount Blanc disappoints, there is "The wondrous Vale / Of Chamouny stretched far below, and soon / With its dumb cataracts and streams of ice, / . . . made rich amends, / And reconciled us to realities" (*The Prelude* 1850 6.529-34) But there is nothing to reconcile him with the same beguiling and betraying "realities" when he fails to experience the crossing of the Alps. Thus, after some brief interval in the narrative sequence, literally a blank space between the lines, the poet exclaims:

> Imagination—here the Power so called
> Through sad incompetence of human speech,
> That awful power rose from the mind's abyss

> Like an unfathered vapour that enwraps,
> At once, some lonely traveller. I was lost;
> Halted without an effort to break through;
> But to my conscious soul I now can say —
> "I recognize thy glory": in such strength
> Of usurpation, when the light of sense
> Goes out, but with a flash that has revealed
> The invisible world, doth greatness make abode,
> There harbours; whether we be young or old.
> Our destiny, our being's heart and home,
> Is with infinitude, and only there;
> With hope it is, hope that can never die,
> Effort, and expectation, and desire,
> And something evermore about to be.
> Under such banners militant, the soul
> Seeks for no trophies, struggles for no spoils
> That may attest her prowess, blest in thoughts
> That are their own perfection and reward.... (*The Prelude* 1850 6.592-612)

Imagination becomes necessary only because of the "sad incompetence of human speech." Even though it is "an unfathered vapour" that "rose from the mind's abyss," it is still an "awful power" that soothingly "enwraps" the "lonely traveller" and uplifts unattainable "experiences" and makes them possible to experience. This time, in its balmy encircling, the poet "Halted without an effort to break through," suspended willingly for the possibilities of the sublime "spot." The sublime moment indeed follows, as the poet's concession, a conscious submission proclaimed as recognition of "thy glory." If sublimity is not experienced in the actual crossing, it is relived in the "moment after," a moment made real in the willing suspension of comprehension on the part of the poet. And it is indeed a sublime moment—disruptive, enclosing, threatening, and promising at once, where expectation and desire are given full play. "And something evermore about to be"—it comes to be and fathers into being the poet's possibility of experience through a movement that disrupts and exceeds. Imagination, as the absently present source of the poet's sublime experience, becomes the "banners militant" which both figure and "attest" to the Soul's, if not nature's, "prowess."

Pursuing the question of poetical-historical direction and the poem's structure of elsewhereness, Gayatri Chakravorty Spivak, in her reading of the 1805 *Prelude*, book 9 to book 13, has submitted three theses, two of which are: 1) Wordsworth coped with the experience of the French Revolution by transforming it into an iconic text that he could write and read and 2) he suggested that poetry was a better cure for the oppression of mankind than political economy or revolution and that his own life had the preordained purpose of teaching mankind this lesson: "Many passages in these later books bring the French Revolution under control by declaring it to be a *felix culpa,* a necessary means toward Wordsworth's growth as a poet" (Spivak 52).

Spivak understands the "always elsewhere" of the Wordsworthian text as a gesture of displacement, as the purging of experiences that leave history as mere traces of personal memory. Thus in Wordsworth's effort to seek control of "the heterogeneity of the revolution through literary-historical and then iconic textuality" (52), the following lines become pivotal: "Behold me then / Once more in Nature's presence, thus restored / Or otherwise, and strengthened once again / (With memory left of what had escaped) / To habits of devoutest sympathy" (*The Prelude* 1805 11.393-97). In such a typical moment of the poet's restoration to "habits of devoutest sympathy" in nature, history, in the schema of the natural and the poetic, does seem to reside in the "left-over memory in parenthesis" indeed. Wordsworth's *ars poetica*, seen as such, is "a subjective theory of human value" through which he affects an inward turning, and "poetry, disclosing man's inner sources, is the only way." Of this turn, Spivak of course cannot but doubt: "Suffice it to say that I am deliberately wondering if indeed poetry can get away *a posteriori* with a narrative of political investigation when it never in fact 'irreducibly intends' anything but its own 'constitution'" (73). In the last instance she almost echoes Abrams: in some final sense, the end of *The Prelude* is about the discovery of its own *ars poetica*. Spivak's thesis emphasizes the mutual displacement of textuality and history, the poetic-literary and sociopolitical, the personal and public. They suggest relational irreconcilability in their supplementation. Poetry and literature seem to be the emptying out of life and escape from history. The end of the development of the poet's mind seems suspicious indeed. However, I propose a different reading of such relations of supplementarity in the poet's schema of revolution, nature, and poetry. I suggest this as a way to conclude the discussion on Wordsworth's modern poetic beginnings whose aim is to redirect history. Thus we return to the rhetoric of placement and reread the lines in book 9 where Spivak thinks Wordsworth turns to seek "alternative literary-historical cases" instead of a "substantializing chronicle of the power structure of the French Revolution":

> I was unprepared
> With needful knowledge, had abruptly pass'd
> Into a theatre, of which the stage
> Was busy with an action far advanced.
> Like others I had read, and eagerly
> Sometimes, the master Pamphlets of the day;
> Nor wanted such half-insight as grew wild
> Upon the meagre soil, help'd out by Talk
> And public News; but having never chanced
> To see a regular Chronicle which might shew,
> (If any such indeed existed then)
> Whence the main Organs of the public power
> Had sprung, their transmigrations when and how
> Accomplish'd, giving thus unto events
> A form and body . . . (*The Prelude* 1805 9.91-106)

Here the poet stands at an impasse. The problem outlined in the opening lines is a problem of incomprehension—the poet is at a loss as to the history and meaning of the "transmigrations" of "the main Organs of the public power." It is an incomprehension that results from a lack—the lack of "a regular Chronicle" that can account for what Spivak calls "the power structure of the French Revolution," and a "chronicle" whose structuring and implications can give "a form and body" "unto events" (9.105-06). In other words, Wordsworth is indeed at an historical impasse, the "Organs of public Power" with their grotesque "transmigrations" seem to have sprung from nowhere. The events—"The dead, upon the dying heaped," "have no form and body," therefore no meaning and history. The lack is the lack of history. There is no elsewhere to trace the traces of the action, hence no possibilities of history. Spivak has earlier defined history as a trace structure that structures its own traces elsewhere, in its effort to seek origins and ends (Spivak 46). Wordsworth's dilemma at the scene of the revolution-turned-violent is that the events cannot be traced, and there is no true "Chronicle" to hold on to besides the "Pamphlets of the day." History, at such a traumatic moment of traceless "transmigrations," seems to have come to a halt. The problem here then is not so much one of displacement, since there is no "regular Chronicle" to begin with. It is rather one of searching for exits and reentries when halted at an impasse. In the face of the lack of history, Wordsworth resorts to its replacement. One should not forget that the revolution and its horrors are "recorded" here as spectacle, as the staging of something the poet has yet to know. Thus the problem of history is very much the problem of staging—the making of chronicles. When Wordsworth turns to "alternate literary-historical cases" and the writing of poetry, he is alternating—in the sense of "making good"—when there is an insufficiency or lack. By declaring and trying to trace the elsewheres of history, he rewrites it excessively.

In this sense *The Prelude* is "a poem which incorporates the discovery of its own *ars poetica*" (Abrams, *Natural Supernaturalism* 78) but not one that "never in fact 'irreducibly intends' anything but its own 'constitution'" (Spivak 75). The *ars poetica* it is discovering is the excessive promise of the redemptive sublimity of poetic power and its endless suspension and supplementation, trapped and made possible by its translations between "history," "nature," "revolution," and "poetry." In the poet's lifelong translation of the sublime (sometimes spectral) moments into "consecutive history" and vice versa, the tracing act becomes the very history it attempts to trace:

> . . . we have traced the stream
> From the blind cavern whence is faintly heard
> Its natal murmur; followed it to light
> And open day; accompanied its course
> Among the ways of Nature, for a time
> Lost sight of it bewildered and engulphed:
> Then given it greeting as it rose once more
> In strength, reflecting from its placid breast

The works of man and face of human life;
And lastly, from its progress have we drawn
Faith in life endless, the sustaining thought
Of human Being, Eternity, and God. (*The Prelude* 1850 14.194-205)

After we lost sight of it "bewildered and engulphed," history nonetheless "rose once more" abruptly and unemphatically in mid-line, because of "The works of man." Human intervention (poetry?), however haltingly and unconvincingly, has given it "body and form." We have traced its natal murmurs in the blind cavern of its origins and may thereby foretell its tendencies. It is continued and made progressive, and from this "progress" life is again redeemed "endless," the "thought / Of human Being, Eternity, and God" sustained, although more in the poet's proclamation, which seems poetically necessitated (to put a stop to the on-going poem) than "historically" or "naturally sequential."

The rise of history is both the result and constituting part of the "spotting and knotting" of Wordsworth's literary modernity. The relation between its possibility and the redemptive sublimity of poetic power is one of transmigration, of translation from moments to consecutivity, from beginnings to ends and vise versa. All this depends on the structure of the poem as a structure of replacement, a reconstitution between the elsewheres and the present moment, past and future, history and poetry. *The Prelude*, in its ever-expanding suspension and beginnings, in this sense, has taken place of its end: it transforms a poetry that restages life and history as its own original poetics. Like the Longinian sublime, it is a process that scatters and lifts up. And this is what predicates Wordsworth's attempt to negotiate a poetic modernity and his role as the original translator-poet.

Chapter Four

The Construction of the Sublime as an Aesthetic Movement across Time and Place

The modern sublime as a capacious aesthetic property

From the preceding chapters, one can argue that as demonstrated in Burke's and Wordsworth's (pre-)Romantic figurations, the sublime in its modern variation is always invoked with the sense of a historical destiny. It is formulated as something more than a self-referential aesthetic figure. What seem to begin as intra-aesthetic debates often turn out to involve a reformulation of the historical situation and destination of those aesthetic configurations. In fact, the protocol of the sublime, with its wide-ranging ethical, political, and epistemological implications, has also figured prominently as a focal point for conceptualizing the nature and direction of modernity itself. The sublime aesthetics in its movement becomes important because of its burden of cultural and historical ambition. Jean-Luc Nancy concludes that what is offered with the modern figuration of the sublime is often the act of aesthetic offering itself as the destiny of art, of philosophy, of culture, and of history: "In this sense, the sublime forms a fashion that has persisted uninterruptedly into our own time from the beginnings of modernity, a fashion at once continuous and discontinuous, monotonous and spasmodic" (Nancy 25). He defines the sublime movement as a fashion because it has always been concerned with a break within or from aesthetics, a necessary defiance. Nancy's characterization of the modern sublime, however, does not seem to take its modernity seriously enough. While it emphasizes this aesthetic figuration's accompanying sense of destiny, his own trajectory of its movement and interest is delineated more categorically in philosophical-aesthetical rather than historical terms. In other words, unlike his work on German (Jena) Romanticism, this is a delineation within the confines of the discourse of modern aesthetics. And this treatment of the modern sublime, that is, of disruption as necessity, like de Man's analysis of the dilemma of literary modernity as a wish to escape history, "treats as universal what may itself be historicized, not as the essence of literature but as the conditions of a certain kind of writing at a certain time, under certain circumstances" (Arac 37). Yet, Nancy's aesthetical-philosophical argument does point to the insights one attains by pushing the limits of the structural modus operandi of the modern sublime. Both Burke's inquiry and Wordsworth's poetic experiment demonstrate the dependence of this aesthetic figuration's historical promise on its process of structuration. According to Nancy, since the consideration of the modern sublime is a matter of necessity, "the motif of the sublime, then, announces the necessity of what happens to art in or as its modern destiny" (Nancy 26). The sublime aesthetics, in this sense, becomes "that which is offering us our destiny or deranging our history" (26). The motif of destiny thus ties the sublime in some essential way to the sense of an ending, and it is often presented as its own destination, its *telos*. In Kant, for example, it is nothing less than the sublime destination of reason itself: freedom.

Nancy develops his genealogy of the modern sublime in the familiar gray area between art and philosophy. According to his genealogy, far from being a subordinate kind of aesthetic, the sublime constitutes a decisive moment in the thought of art. It not only transforms the aesthetics of the beautiful, which was once defined as "the splendor of truth" but now "the self-enjoyment of reason." But, more significantly, it changes the entire philosophical motif of presentation (Nancy 32-34). By this Nancy argues that if form or contour is understood as limitation (in presentation), the unlimited is the concern of the sublime. However, though the unlimited maintains the closest relations with the infinite: "in the sublime, it is not a matter of the presentation or nonpresentation of the infinite, placed beside the presentation of the finite and construed in accordance with an analogous model. Rather, it is a matter—and this is something completely different—of the movement of the unlimited, or more exactly, of "the unlimitation" (*die Unbegrenztheit*) that takes place on the border of the limit, and thus on the border of presentation" (Nancy 35). What Nancy elaborates in rather abstract and speculative terms can be translated to mean that the sublime in this sense is a matter of aesthetical-historical grounding and a structure of cultural beginnings. Like Longinus's "thunderbolt" (*On the Sublime* 3), "the unlimited as such is that which sets itself off on the border of the limit, that which detaches itself and subtracts itself from limitation by an unlimitation that is coextensive with the external border of limitation" (Nancy 35). Although Nancy's configuration of the sublime lies nonetheless alongside the philosophical motif of presentation, the sublime refigured by his arduous argument is removed from its usual metaphysical transcendental end to a structural movement of unlimitation, highlighting the act of grounding. And though such a formulation is derived from a critical interpretation of Kant's philosophy of the aesthetic judgment, it sheds light in a more general sense on the figuration of the sublime as an aesthetics of modernity. This is because Nancy's formulation, "*un enlèvement*" (35), directs attention to the emergence and structure of the modern sublime as a dramatic movement that takes place on the border of the limit. It pinpoints the concern of the sublime aesthetics as a question of figuring its own aesthetic and historical ground. The "*enlèvement*" in this sense is the vested interest of the modern sublime, as well as the task of aesthetic-literary modernity. Nancy's insights tell us that the modern reverie of the sublime is an ambitious movement of the unlimited that figures in its act of unlimitation an endless possibility of beginnings. The sublime, then, in its modern figuration is simultaneously a regrounding and a beginning: "The unlimited begins on the external border of the limit: and it does nothing but begin, never to finish . . . Rather, the unlimited engenders and engages itself in the very tracing of the limit: it retraces and carries off, so to speak, 'unto the ground' what this tracing cuts out on the edge of the figure as its contour" (Nancy 35-36) In this sense the sublime will always be an aesthetics of movement. This movement of unlimitation is not concerned with a potential infinity as a "numerical concept," or of a progression without end. It is an act that signals new formations: "it is an unlimitation, a dissipation of the border on the border itself—an unbordering or overbordering, or overboarding" (Nancy 37).

This historical-aesthetical gesture, as Nancy displays it philosophically, and as both Kant and Burke characterize it in their respective sublime constructions, is a striving movement, and an act of suspension, or a supplementation. It is a cognitive as well as an affective effort in relation to the sense of limit. The sublime in this sense can be understood as the sentiment of the limit. The sublime gesture offers up this sentiment of the limit as the beginning of continuous striving. It offers itself as the supplementation that suspends and retraces and carries off "unto the ground." And by the same gesture engenders new beginnings. For Kant, the sublime offering is the act of freedom in thought. For Burke, it is the motion of possibilities for refiguring both the distinction and correspondence between things, human beings, and feelings, hence the possibilities of history. And for Wordsworth, it helps "history" to "rise once more" imaginatively and poetically. Thus, the modus operandi of the modern sublime is an historical one, although Nancy analyzes it here mainly in post-Kantian terms as a motif with self-generating and self-vexing properties within the vicissitudes of modern European aesthetical philosophy. As the central property in the building up of a cultural modernity from late eighteenth- into mid-nineteenth-century Europe, the sublime in its simultaneous celebration of and desire to guard the disruptive, the "flash" that scatters and lifts up, typifies the historical direction of the aesthetic turn of its leading theorists. Their modern aesthetical projects, for all the conceptual and methodological differences, have nevertheless espoused the kind of cultural avant-guardism that Schiller spells out for historical redirection. The sublime, as the aesthetic property that preoccupies them in their encounter with a distraught modernity, is indeed a movement of unlimitation that sets up its own legislative function in the act of crossing over and passing on.

One can argue, then, that the modern sublime in its eighteenth- and early nineteenth-century European preoccupation is favored and elaborated upon because of its aesthetical-structural possibilities. They are seen as the cornerstones of a new cultural imagination. This Romantic construction of the sublime is also stressed as a capacious aesthetic property that can lend itself to redress the modern cultural and historical crisis. It is simultaneously an aesthetics of disruption and a regrounding movement by which historically ambitious cultural practitioners can come face to face with the terrors of modern history: from colonial to revolutionary violence and to the radical reordering of human society and perception. In the sections that follow, I will demonstrate that the sublime is also transformed as the timely spirit of a new Chinese poetics because of its promise as a disruptive and at the same time exemplary aesthetics. Its choice in early twentieth-century China highlights the nature of cultural translation as the "making of hypothetical equivalences" (L. Liu 16). The emphasis here, I suggest, should be laid on the term "hypothetical" in using Lydia Liu's formulation, because then it foregrounds the sense of choice and precondition in the translation act. This act of making transcultural equivalences involves not only "coauthorship" and reinvention. More emphatically it consists in foregrounding comparable historical anxieties and needs. It is an act performed at a related but differently configured modern moment.

The Romantic sublime in its passage as timely spirit of a terrible but necessary Chinese cultural modernity is preferred and refigured because it captures the affective and perceptual ferocity of modern history; and because it offers promises of beginnings in its propensity for excess. The revelry of the sublime in the modern Chinese poetic revolution owes as much to its aesthetic protocol, with attendant ethical and political implications, as to the terrible modernity (at least in the eyes of the aesthete-poets) as its historical grounding. With these preconditions, the sublime is refigured as a passage that allows both disruption and continuity with the dread of, as well as fascination with, terror and destruction at its center. Its very choice disrupts the perception that the Chinese cultural modernity is at best emulative of its "Western origin." The transformation and practice of a Romantic poetics of the sublime in early twentieth-century China begins with a "crash" that aims to "drag to earth" not only its own tradition but also the crisis-ridden modern world. It also consigns "the otherness of things" in the original of the cultural translation into "quiet being" (Wordsworth, *Nutting* 43-48) through processes of historically motivated eclectic appropriation and reinvention.

The question of a modern Chinese literary beginning

In 1842, the Opium War between Great Britain and China ended with China's shattering military defeat by the British, and the signing of the Nanking Treaty with Great Britain forced the formal opening of China to the Western powers. In 1858, English and French troops advanced on Peking; within two years Anglo-French military forces had invaded Tientsin, captured the Capital city of Peking, and compelled China to sign another treaty. Before the founding of the Republic of China in 1912, China endured yet another major loss at the culmination of the Sino-Japanese War (1894-1895). Reviewing the events of this stormy era on the eve of revolution in 1911, one witnesses a succession of humiliating defeats suffered by a rapidly declining dynasty at the hands of foreign powers whose military and technological dominance posed a serious threat to the very existence of the nation itself.

China was shocked out of its complacency to face the painful realization of its national weaknesses and backwardness. What followed was a period of seething activity in translating Western works—philosophical, scientific, political, and literary. This activity was to exert an important influence on the emerging literature in subsequent decades. (Lin 18-20)

Often, narratives about the beginning of modern Chinese literature like this link historical events and literary formulations in unequivocal and causal terms. In these accounts, the onslaught of history is delineated as a series of catastrophic events set in clear, memorable dates, highlighting the threat and dominance by "foreign powers" and "painful realizations" on the part of the Chinese in the process, ending with the emergence of a different literature as a direct response. The problem of accounting for the modern Chinese cultural beginning in this way is that there are contending narratives that extend the emergence of modern Chinese culture into previous centuries (see D. Wang; H. Wang; Kowallis). And this kind of story also oversimplifies the traversal of literary influence and cultural translation: as if alien concepts and influences followed directly on the heels of the foreign troops. However, these narratives do highlight China's massive modern encounter with the West as a shock, as historical and epistemological violence, out of which a new Chinese literature emerges as aftermath, as part of the "traumatic choices" made out of "painful realizations" (see Levenson 156-63) Thus they emphasize that the literary-aesthetic in its modern Chinese formation is simultaneously sociopolitical. And it is a cultural formation inseminated in China's entanglement with the catastrophes of history. Here I revisit these commencement narratives of Chinese cultural modernity critically to show their contested nature, as they are the founding narrations that shaped the vision of the new poets and in turn perpetuated by them. I also demonstrate that while modern Chinese literature is shocked into existence, influences, as they were, did not march in like foreign troops. The troops, as central metaphors in the project of modern Chinese cultural translation, are like the dark shadowy terror at the heart of the modern sublime, the transformation of which is both its challenge and target resolution. What emerged out of the project of cultural translation are newly hypothesized—differently historically motivated—equivalences, to an originally reformulated and capacious aesthetic agency of other places and times. Thus one can say that Chinese cultural modernity literally began as a rupture.

As part of the "traumatic choices," there was "a period of seething activity in translating Western works." It is common knowledge that while Fu Yan interpreted and translated Thomas Huxley's *Evolution and Ethics* (1898), Shu Lin (1852-1924) made popular his rather liberal renderings of over a hundred foreign fictions in classical Chinese. In poetry, Manshu Su (1884-1918) translated nineteenth-century English Romantic poetry into the familiar classical verse forms. In this sense, though Julia Lin's account of the beginning of modern Chinese poetry oversimplifies the historical complexity that led to such a drastic cultural change, it foregrounds the role of translation in the inception of a different kind of literature which comes to be known as modern Chinese. It also links translation, particularly the translation of nineteenth-century English Romantic poetry, to one of the most significant, if traumatic, revolutions of twentieth-century China: the revolution of Chinese language from *wenyan* (the classical) to *baihua* (the vernacular). Since the modern Chinese intellectual tradition literally institutes itself with translation (read adaptation, appropriation, reformation, and re-creation) and what Lydia Liu terms other translingual practices, it seems inevitable that any inquiry into the former should commence with the latter's place and implications. For instance, David Wang's study of late-Qing translations is entitled "Translating Modernity," in which he has noted that the Qing translators' witting and unwitting misinterpretations of the originals generated spontaneous alternative versions of the modern (Pollard 303-29). But although Lin's delineation echoes the tales that the self-consciously modern Chinese writers tell themselves about their choices (or the lack thereof) of beginnings, like many others, it mistakes historical linkages and choices for inevitable historical necessity. For her, the series of catastrophic events, the choice of particular translations, and the emergence of a new literature is a causal progression. It thus fails to account for the actual conditions and terms within which a Chinese cultural modernity is wrought into being.

Similarly trapped is the other familiar model of the opposition between tradition and modernity. Such opposition rarely illuminates the actual aesthetic choices or historical situation of any given cultural transformation. This is amply demonstrated by Lin's reading of some of the most illustrative modern Chinese poems, and by Michelle Yeh's study of modern Chinese poetry since 1917. They both point out that in most of these compositions it is exceedingly difficult to tell where tradition ends and modernity begins (Yeh, *Modern Chinese Poetry*). Thus, instead of continuing with the impact—response or the tradition—modernity models, a discourse on Chinese cultural modernity should begin with questions such as "What is so 'modern' about modern Chinese history and literature?" and "In what ways did the May Fourth generation, and their predecessors, attempt to define their difference from the past and articulate a new range of sensibilities which they would consider 'modern'?" (O. Lee, "In Search" 110)

The literary revolution of early twentieth-century China, usually marked by the 1919 May Fourth Movement (see Chow) as the moment that initiated Chinese cultural modernity, is noted in various versions of modern Chinese literary history (Y. Wang; *Zhongguo*) for its antipathy to tradition and passion for revolution, which underwrote the feverish activities of translingual practices. Many of the writers and cultural critics of the period, sometimes called the New Culturalists, were themselves translators (interpreters, adapters, and borrowers) before or while they turned to creative or critical writing. Both the collective and individual desires for translation stem obviously, among other things, from a shared sense of belatedness on an international scene on the part of the translators as New Culturalists. The anxiety of being too late and the overwhelming fear of being culturally subsumed better account for the Chinese intellectuals' headlong rush to bring a self-chosen modernity into being than any history of the inner dynamics between the new and the old, or of tradition and modernity. The sense of belatedness, I suggest, is in this sense already a translation. It is a translation of spatial difference into temporal sequence, an equivocation that makes relational unequal things. What is generated as a result of the modus operandi of translation—the introduction of new words, the transformation of literary forms, changes in ways of perception and representation, the emergence of new genres and ideas—is cultural sea change. It is a change that accounts for and amounts to the shifting and transformation of cultural meanings. Translation in the modern Chinese New Culture Movement is accounted for by many contemporary intellectuals as the search for that which is useful and translatable elsewhere in the building up of a modern Chinese culture-nation. The making of modern Chinese poetry, because of the continuing ambivalence of its historical and cultural status and the peculiarly difficult process of its coming into being, is a particularly telling instance.

Along this trajectory, the making of a sublime modern poetics in the New Poetry Movement by its leading poets in early twentieth-century China can be understood as a project of cultural rejuvenation through translation—translation defined as timely but ambivalent hypothetical equivocation between things and events both long ago and faraway. It is a reference to the trans-spatial as well as the trans-temporal movement—the poet's evocation and refiguration of aesthetic tenets and ideals of both the modern West and his own ancient tradition. As such it is reevoked with the Benjaminian sense of translation as the issuing of its afterlife from the original (Benjamin 71), not only with longed-for possibilities but also attendant anxieties. This sense of translation also echoes the Burkean and Wordsworthian sublime establishment of correspondence, of substitution that takes place. By probing into the attempt to translate both the "West" and "tradition" into an origin of modern Chinese poetry, I hope to draw attention to the complicated and often difficult process of the beginning of Chinese cultural modernity, to the New Poetry Movement's intricate relation to European Romanticism as an aesthetics of modernity, and to the process of what might be called its creative transformation in the Chinese refiguration. In other words, by beginning with translation I end with creative formations. For what came as the result of the creative refiguration is the Wordsworthian "rush" of new "poetic numbers" and the original modern Chinese poet, its problems and ambivalences notwithstanding. And this effectively unsettles the picture of the New Poetry Movement as iconoclastic or derivative. Next, I concentrate on Guo Moruo and his attempt to write a new sublime Chinese poetry as the prime example of such a transformative process.

The sublime as timely spirit in the New Poetry Movement

Before turning to Guo's poetic theory and practice as a prime example of the transformative-creative process, I elaborate more on the passage of the Romantic sublime and its figuration as the timely spirit for modern Chinese poetry and culture. If the project of modern Chinese literature is envisioned to wrest whatever is literary and cultural from its age-old cocoon, poetry is seen as the last to be disentangled from its traditional bondage. Many literary historians have noted that to sever themselves from the past, a handful of pioneering modern Chinese poets eagerly experimented with a wide range of Western forms, from free verse to the sonnet. But "not withstanding this dedication to modernity, tradition persisted. Consciously or not, the pioneers intermittently harked back to the familiar modes of the past. Echoes of earlier masters reverberate through their lines; colloquialism sits uneasily beside traditional motifs" (Lin 31) This, however, is usually attributed less to the (lack of) individual talent on the part of the poets and more to the tradition of which they tried to wrestle themselves free. The early modern Chinese poets are said to have been weighed down by "the great legacy of the traditional poets" (Lin 31), especially its thousand years of refinement. Tradition looms doubly ominous for the aspiring modern poets, both as an overwhelming heritage and as a lack. For "one must bear in mind that the new poetry was not built directly upon the old, as were modern Chinese fiction and drama, both of which had a long and remarkable vernacular tradition in their favor" (Lin 31). The new poetic rebellion had to be groundbreaking in rejecting not only *wenyan* as its poetic medium, but also all the conventional verse forms and prosodic rules. It also had to master *baihua*, the vernacular, before it could "elevate" it to the status of the only acceptable medium for the new verse and create its own new prosody. The modern Chinese poetic revolution thus cannot be understood simply as a poetic revolt against the antiquated and worn. Nor is it a regenerative cycle between the new and the old. This is probably why influence studies in poetic form and prosody, no matter how eruditely and intricately accomplished, can at best explicate the particular aesthetic choices of the poets and their implications, cultural and formal, with a perhaps (Gálik, "Comparative Aspects" 177-90). What is often missing in the otherwise excellent prosodic and formalist studies, in the careful tracing of influences and inventions, is their historicity. For the New Culturalists and modern Chinese poets, emphatically and passionately, the question is formal as well as cultural, but above all timely.

As I have elaborated in earlier chapters, Bourke describes English Romantic discourse in its relation to political modernity as the advent of a modern aesthetics that attempts to inaugurate "an era which disowns the historical inheritance that defines it" (199). That is, it is a historical disjunction but nonetheless burdened with history's precedents. This may partly explain the modern Chinese poets' fascination with the Romantic as both subject and form, and their preoccupation with the figuration of a timely spirit. Similarly afflicted with the anxieties of a traumatic modernity, they imagined their cultural aspirations and practices as aesthetic reactions against the onslaught of history, and in this sense aesthetic regeneration as historical redirection. The ambition of the New Cuturalists, like that of their European Romantic counterparts, at least as it is defined by Lacoue-Labarthe and Nancy, is concerned as much with the invention of genres and the erection of aesthetic doctrines as it is with the possibility "for an entirely new social function for the writer . . . and consequently for a different society" (5). And beginning with such concerns, its point of departure similarly entails the deliberate hyperbolization of literary agency as the first move of historical redress.

In his preface to the opening issue of *Chuangzao jikan* (The Creation Quarterly), published in July 1921, and in canonical images of the Romantic sublime, Guo declares that "'The Creator—I' will call upon the might of the 'erupting volcano' and the '*Sturm und Drang* of the Universe' to 'create a bright world'" ("Xu" 1-2). This statement is regarded as the manifesto of not only the Creation Society, which Guo cofounded, but also of a Chinese Romanticism. The Chinese Romanticists emphasized inspiration, emotion, and imagination in poetic composition. In their poetic theory, they stressed the need to exercise "absolute freedom" in poetic form. They also translated the works of Byron, Shelley, Keats, Heine, Goethe, Whitman, Wordsworth, and many others, setting them up as references for their own composition. The exaltation of Romanticism as the most properly modern aesthetic ideal, poetic subject, style, and sentiment, as I mentioned above, is by no means accidental or simply idiosyncratic on the part of the few interested poets. In the history of modern Chinese literature, it has always been exalted or derided as the spirit of the times.

The New Poetry Movement began as a revolution of language and poetic form, which though necessary was then deemed insufficient. Because it seemed to lack the bearing and scope that could match the sweeping tempo of the New Culture Movement. The New Chinese poetry, once it had established its chosen language and medium—the switch to vernacular and abolition of regulated forms—seemed to need a new spirit. That is, it needs not only new subject matter but also new moods and sentiments as well as new ways of expression, to substantiate it. As Congwen Shen writes in 1931, the Romantic poets of the Creation Society, "with their exaggerated, heroic, crude, and fearless momentum, pushed open a new frontier for Chinese literature" (qtd. in Long 91). The content, sensibility, and expressions of Romanticism seem indeed to have brought new ideals and possibilities to the New Chinese poetry. In line with the demand of the times, its exaggerated passions and crude heroism, especially as an embodiment of a youthful hope after destruction, have not only reshaped Chinese poetic composition but also the structure and modes of feelings of an entire generation. In this sense it is seen as aesthetically and historically necessary as part of the volcanic eruption of the sweeping cultural revolution. *Sturm und Drang* had become the slogan of the day among the cultured youth. And as Ou-fan Lee demonstrates in his study, *The Romantic Generation of Modern Chinese Writers* (1976), it had shaped the psychocultural tempo of modern Chinese literary movements as well as individual authorial choices.

To inaugurate an era that disowns the historical inheritance that defines it is a sublime task. It is no wonder then that sentiments and ideas like the sublime hover at the center of the new Chinese cultural movement. To re-create a Chinese sublime seemed to be the demand and spirit of the times. Early on, when the pioneer of modern Chinese aestheticism, Guowei Wang (1877-1927), expounded on the relation between the aesthetic, the innermost psyche, and emotional depth, he was addressing "specific social maladies. He considered the aesthetic—aesthetic education and experience of art—to be a cure for an emotionally depressed and morally degenerate society" (B. Wang 24). The innermost psyche and emotional depth he was concerned with were no other than the psychic and affective ills caused by the trauma of the violent modernity. Thus his exposition of the sublime in obvious Kantian and Schopenhauerian terms could also be associated with Burke's historical aestheticism: "When an object hostile to our will confronts us and violently tears up our will and dissolves it, so that our cognitive faculty assumes independence and we penetrate deep into the thing itself, we call this object 'sublime' and the feeling that of sublimity'" (G. Wang 1635). In Wang's reconstruction of the sublime object and feeling of sublimity, the violence of terror and destruction are requisite and overwhelming. It "tears up our will." The subsequent ascendance of cognitive faculty and its "penetration" to the essence of things is at most a post facto understanding, not even a Kantian mastery of judgment. Wang was so caught up with the sublime's function to tear us away from the anxieties and tensions of a traumatic modern Chinese life that the ultimate moment in his feeling of sublimity is the moment of death. This is why Ban Wang has described Guowei Wang's venture into a historical-aesthetic redemption as "sublimation unto death" (B. Wang 17-54). From Guowei Wang to the May Fourth Romanticists, of course, the pursuit of the sublime had undergone considerable changes; it was pursued with a different "spirit" of the times. As champions or ardent followers of a raging cultural revolution that was set to redeem a failing social and political modernization, the New Culturalists struggled with a sublime discourse less hesitant, more ferociously heroic and destructive, and marked with unbound defiance and unabashed yearnings for greatness. However, as I will elaborate later, it nonetheless carried on the preoccupation with death initiated by the earlier melancholic Guwei Wang. In terms of poetics, the search for a modern Chinese sublime is defined as matters of both structure and sentiment, congregating on the grandness of scope and loftiness of feelings which in turn constitute the greatness of the poet. In a letter to GuoMoruo in 1920, while editing and publishing his earliest poems, the aesthete and critic Baihua Zong wrote: "Your poems tend to be conceptually lofty and forceful; it shows that you should be good at writing big poems, the sublime kind ... There are very few people who are capable of doing this in China. It will prove your greatness" (Tian, Zong, and Guo 27). A new Chinese poetry of "the sublime kind," which constitutes the new "great" poet, should be conceptually "lofty" and "forceful," structurally "big," and often heroic or at least defiant in subject matter. Zong's call for poetic composition and sentiments of a different kind seems to echo the Romantic construction of the expressive a priori of artistic manifestations. It also echoes that construction's aspiration towards the sublime as well as its insistence on the correspondence between the poetic quality and the greatness (or the lack of it) of the poetic mind, as Abrams sets out in *The Mirror and the Lamp* (21-25, 97-102). And the demand here is not only presented as an aesthetic one, but it is also seen, definitely and more emphatically, as a demand of the times, as something necessitated by the spirit of the age.

The spirit of the age, in fact, is so pervasive that not only is modern Chinese literature conceived as its direct embodiment, but it has also become an ongoing, prolific discourse in itself. If the lasting preoccupation with the timely spirit readily lends itself to a reading of early modern Chinese literature as the beginning writing of a "national allegory" (Jameson, "Third-World Literature" 65), the proliferating discourse testifies to its contention and dissension. For the contemporary May Fourth culturalists as well as later critics and historians, how to understand and define the timely spirit becomes synonymous with understanding the quintessence of the cultural revolution and its historical implications. In its contentious definition and redefinition, it has become a necessary preamble in the discourse of modern Chinese literature. The preoccupation with the spirit of the age attests, of course, to the New Culturalists' Romantic entanglement as well as the prevalent sense of the present as a moment of crisis. As James K. Chandler shows it in his study of Romantic historicism, *England in 1819*, the term spirit of the age was "one of the most self-consciously novel and distinctive coinages of that (Romantic) period," and had been coined "precisely to identify its own novelty and distinction" (105-14). Its novelty is in the fact that it marked the beginning of "the epochs of the concept of the epoch" (105), and established the legitimacy of the "preoccupation with contemporaneity" (106). Highlighting one's own "contemporaneity" as a distinction, as a difference from previous moments, is definitely one of modernity's efforts to legitimize itself, even when it is set up as a reaction. As Chandler shows, what is established by the numerous Romantic writings on the "spirit of our times" is precisely the importance and difference of "our age." John Stuart Mill, in his famous series of articles on the subject, put it most clearly: "The idea of comparing one's own age with former ages, or with our notion of those which are yet to come, had occurred to philosophers; but it never before was itself the dominant idea of any age" (qtd. in Chandler 107). The dominant idea of comparing one's own age with the former and those yet to come is an attempt to both set apart and reconnect the past, the present, and the future. By locating the present as beginning and emphatically placing the past in its place and as past, it sets up the sense of urgency of the present moment and is future oriented. The aesthetic movement of the sublime, as a movement of passage that first drags the past "unto the ground" and then sets it off again, seems an exemplary embodiment of such timely spirit.

The evocation and easy transposition of the spirit of the age by modern Chinese writers and critics as a "dominant idea" certainly derives from their sense of their very own historical situation. It puts into focus their feeling of crisis. "Modernity" called forth as such acquires an unequivocal sense of urgency, as something tantamount to ultimate difference. The New Culturalists' exultant obsession with the spirit of the times also testifies to their uneasy relation with both modernity as that which looms obscure and overwhelming, and tradition as something they know defines them but from which they desire nothing less than complete disentanglement, at least rhetorically. The discourse on the timely spirit, highlighting the notion of contemporaneity, seems to offer them that sense of distinction and the inevitability of change. The contention on its definition is thus emblematic of the struggle in the construction of modern Chinese cultural history.

Yiduo Wen (1899-1946), Guo's famous contemporary poet and poetry critic, has summarized the spirit of his age in five cardinal points: the spirit of movement, the spirit of rebellion, the spirit of science, the spirit of *datong* (universal equity), and the frustration of youth (Wen 3). Wen's construction privileges the spirit of movement and rebellion as much as the frustration of youth. For the later inheritors and explicators of the May Fourth tradition, though, these early summonses of the spirit are too ambivalent and do not live up to its requisite radicalism. Thus, the post-Revolution critic Qifang He (1912-1977) tries to clarify and rehistoricize the spirit when he joins the effort to redefine the timeliness of the *The Goddess*, the earliest poetry collection of Guo Morou, decades later:

> The timely spirit of the *Goddess* lies mainly in this: it has expressed, emphatically, the hopes and aspirations of the Chinese people, in particular of the young Chinese intellectuals, for the regeneration of their homeland; it has expressed their revolutionary spirit and their optimism. It writes about their discontents and curses towards the old China, but more significantly it portrays the dreams, prophecies and acclamations for a future new China. Of course it has betrayed the frustrations of some of the young intellectuals at the time, but what it demonstrates mostly is a sense of longing for the light, of acclamations for the new things, of beliefs in the strength and confidence of the people, and of a love of life and nature. All these can be said to be the manifestations of the spirit of May Fourth and its optimism. (442-43)

If in Wen's earlier delineation of the spirit of the times, the pathos of the day is parallel to the movement of defiance, He's postreconstruction subsumes the longings, frustrations, and struggles of the May Fourth New Culturalists into a grand evolutionary narrative of a Chinese revolutionary nation building. It recasts the timely aesthetics of *The Goddess* as a sublime ruse, in which the end, as he appendixes it anachronistically, swallows up the lesser things. What is missing in his, as in many other post-Revolution presentations, is the spirit of the age, both in its formal constructions and its cultural underpinnings. This is probably why the more or less revisionist critics of the later generations prefer to hark back to the pre-Revolution definitions and criticisms, definitions such as Yang Zhou's, which stress the specificity of the May Fourth spirit and describe it as bordering on an almost irascible ferocity. Zhou's exegesis also highlights the simultaneity, or rather, the peculiar symbiosis of the formal with the cultural: "in its content, it emphasizes self-expression, proclaims individualism, and works towards the realization of a 'self-consciousness;' while formally it strives to shake off the shackles of the prosodic limitations of classical poetry and moves toward free verse. These are the demands of the times to new poetry, and these are the literary manifestations of the May Fourth spirit" (Zhou).

The spirit of the May Fourth, often identifiable as the Romantic sublime in the figuration of the New Chinese poets and which has come to stand for the beginning of a modern Chinese cultural tradition, is thus best described as a spirit of destruction as well as creation. In the retrospective representations of it, though, literary historians tend to downplay the shared sense of anxiety, desperation, pain, and anger which sometimes turn into a vigorous protest or melancholia that attends the historical trauma and is prevalent in the writings and moods of the young intellectuals. This is emphatically so in their desire to construct a triumphant narrative of historical progress, even when they do discern the petulance, the frustrated ferocity bordering on savagery in the raging of the age. In fact, pain and anxiety, which are central in the construction of the modern sublime, seem as much the feelings and spirits of the age as the longings and hopes for a different future. Zhou's delineation of the timely spirit seems to stress the striving towards "self-realization" on the part of the modern Chinese subject, at least as it pertains to the new literati and intelligentsia, while Huang-dong Yan more vividly and more specifically narrows it down to the progress of the new poet. In his revision, which faintly echoes Carlyle or Fichte, as well as what is found in the self-image and imagination of the New Culturalist poets themselves, the poet is the first seer that awakens to the new world. But what does he see?

> An ugly, cold world without light, without warmth, without freedom and without happiness! He sees around him Hell and prison houses, oppression and deception, crimes and suffering. Thus he suffers and weeps. Then his suffering turns to hatred, his weeping anger, and when they became uncontainable, he bursts forth into a most fierce protest, and begins a violently passionate struggle that culminates into an ultimate "No." He not only wants to break away from the old world, but also wants to tear it apart, crumble it and crush it to pieces! His anger burns like fire, his protest turns into a storm, and he strikes at the whole old world, old system, like a thunder. (Yan 275)

Although Yan's portrayal of the poet's progress as the coming-to-be of the modern Chinese subject champions what has become known as positive Romanticism in its revolutionary fervor, it nonetheless foregrounds the feelings of pain and anger. It highlights anxious desperation as the underwriting affective structure of the modern Chinese aesthetics and the grounding passion for the spirit of the age. What is perceived as the old China, as well as that which looms dark and large from the impinging West, which together constitute the menacing present for the young Chinese intellectuals, is akin to the idea of the terrible in the construction of the modern sublime. It reminds one of Burke's formulation of the latter as redress to the wounds of modern history when he similarly felt such history's encroachment in late eighteenth-century England. These wounds and threats are dark and obscure, like the era that defines them, and the desire and passion to disown them are passions that belong to self-preservation. This is the departure as well as the crowning gesture of the sublime. The modern Chinese aesthetics, as seen pioneered and embodied by the May Fourth spirit, can thus be summarized similarly in the way Furniss describes the eighteenth- and early nineteenth-century European sublime, that is, it "typically celebrate[s] the energetic, the obscure, the disruptive, the unlimited, the powerful, and the terrible as a new set of positive aesthetic terms" (Furniss 20). Or it can be understood in the way Guo describes his two volcanic years of poetic eruption immediately after May Fourth: "Whitman's poetic spirit which seeks to do away with everything old and restrictive is especially suitable for the *Sturm und Drang* of May Fourth, I am completely shaken by his majestic and unconstrained tone. Under his influence, and spurred on by *Baihua* (*Zong*), I composed 'Yelling on the Edge of the Earth,' 'Earth, My Mother,' 'Ode to the Bandit,' 'Good Morning,' 'Nirvana of the Phoenix,' 'Heavenly Dog,' 'Lamp of the Heart,' 'Coal in the Furnace,' 'Lesson of the Cannon,' and so on, poems of masculine savagery" (Guo, *Guo Moruo lun chuangzuo* 204).

This perception of a violently disruptive but unlimited sublime as the only possible cultural reaction against the terror of modernity explains, at least partly, why the search for the sublime, or the great, the lofty, the powerful, and the excessive, is perceived to embody the spirit of the times. This way of delineating modern Chinese literary history along two affective-aesthetic lines runs through modern Chinese critical practice. For example, while Jaroslav Prusek proposes to read modern Chinese literature along the lines between the lyrical and the epic, Xiaobing Tang has delineated its contours in a dialectic unity of the heroic and the quotidian. As cultural configuration as well as formal construction, this search represents a vital component of the early modern Chinese cultural scene. Such an understanding of the aesthetic reprieve also demonstrates that the modern Chinese sublime, at its earlier poetic inception, which coincided with the roaring furor of the New Culture Movement, is invoked and refigured predominantly with the sense of the defiant, the savage, and the terrible. It is not so much (at least not yet) a struggle for moral perfection through a transfiguration of the Kantian transcendental, as later (from the 1930s onward) developed in the aesthetic theories of Zehou Li. Li's ongoing project went from the 1950s to the 1980s (Li, *Zhongguo*), which is in turn developed through a critique of his "idealist" predecessor Guangqian Zhu (see W. Ban 155-93). Moreover, in the quest for the sublime, two other things have become clear: 1) with the introduction of "moral pathos" defined by Prusek as a "feeling for the tragedy of existence" (3) as its central tenet, Chinese literature has taken an affective turn. Or, as Guo proclaims for the modern Chinese literary institution, "the essence of literature derives from feelings and ends in them" (Guo, "Geming yu wenxue" 312). The modern aesthetic turn for those in quest of a sublime poetics is definitely an affective construction that is predicated on feelings and passions, its end the building up of the social function of the writer and a new society through its aesthetic and moral affect; and 2) in the figuration of the poet's progress as the coming-to-be of a modern Chinese subject, the writers and critics have also figured themselves both as harbingers of its death and the vanguard of its redemption. Like the searchers of the modern sublime in Europe, they have also shown an aspiration to the condition of a great sublime, who, in their figuring, is as much an individual genius as an epic culture hero. It is in this aspiration to be taken as a metonymy for their culture, to refigure a Chinese epic culture hero, that we can probably muster an understanding of the lurking persistence of tradition in the almost savage celebration of the disruptive, and the uncanny resemblance to continuity in a radical revolution, which is a phenomenon so far only accounted for by the unwitting tenacity of old cultural memories and odd incongruities in the progression of the spirit of the age. There are exceptions to this kind of delineation (see Denton). For example, Yeh demonstrated the complex and intricate interweaving of tradition and modernity in some of the best modern Chinese poetry. She also characterized these relations as "innovative continuity," "literary influence as predisposition and mutual reinforcement" (Yeh, *Modern Chinese Poetry* 114, 118).

The passage of the sublime as the spirit of the times across different temporal and spatial locations is consequential upon projects of cultural translation, as demonstrated in the case of its poetic refiguration in the Chinese New Poetry Movement. Cultural translation here is understood as a disruptive and innovative continuity, or mutual "mutilation" as well as reinforcement, not only in terms of translingual practices but also in its willful refiguration of instances from its own tradition. The sublime is transformed in this sense both because of its intra-aesthetic propensity, not universally determined but always historically reformulated with timely motivations, and its extra-aesthetic burdens. The latter is understood as its specific social cultural situations and worldly ends by which its agency and capacity are envisioned and figured. The sublime's passage as a spirit of *Sturm and Drang*, which celebrates the disruptive, is evoked first at the moment of Europe's headlong plunge into a massive and unknown (Wordsworth cannot read it) modernity, and later, at the moment when this modernity's encroachment is felt as the dark shadows of marching foreign troops in China. This passage highlights the fact that both this aesthetics' original formulation and subsequent transformation are burdened by a shared though asymmetrical history. In both cases it is concerned with the desire to erect new cultural monuments upon the ruins of modern destruction. And this concern explains why the fear of and the desire to counteract terror are at the center of modern sublime's invocation and passage. In this sense Burke's fear of the colonial terror in Ireland, which laid the foundation for his later fear of English colonization of India shown in his political treatises, is not all that different from the Chinese New Culturalists' dread and furor at the marching foreign troops. It also foreshadows that, with terror at its center, the formulation and refiguration of the modern sublime at different historical junctures are too often too "aggressively destabilizing" to resolve the "flashed up" fears and disruptions to achieve its historically envisioned ends. The "sublime humanity" that Schiller fancies (38), as well as the historical ends and modern poetic beginnings both Wordsworth and the Chinese new poets aspire to, are often momentarily patched up as forced poetic closures.

Chapter Five

Guo Moruo and the Reformation of Modern Chinese Poetry in a Sublime Poetics

Setting an example for a modern Chinese poetics

The search for the sublime, both in content and form, seemed to be the demand of the times and hence, indeed, one of the pervasive concerns of the early twentieth-century Chinese literary revolution. This is manifested sometimes in the aesthetic longing for the great, but more often in the willful poetic abandon in the savagely disruptive. The modern poetic revolution is at the forefront of this quest. And its process is most symptomatic of such a quest's cultural and aesthetic ambition.

The new *baihua* (vernacular) poetry movement of this period differed from the late Qing poetic reform in that this was a concerted, self-conscious movement with stated principles and goals and clear guidelines; and it aimed at nothing less than a groundbreaking revolution of Chinese poetry both in sentiment and form, as well as its medium of composition. Its end was the establishment of a new kind of Chinese poetry to replace the orthodoxy of the classic; of a poetic ideal that celebrated the new, the different, and the great instead of the familiar, the overwrought, and the refined. But the experiments of the pioneering new poets were considered at best a partial success by the time of the New Culture Movement, ironically because of their very revolutionary status—the lack of any prototype for creative emulation or critical comparison. The establishment of modern Chinese poetry is often believed to be "carried on, extended and at times completed with considerable success" (Lin 75) only in the later decades, during and after the storms of May Fourth (1919). Of the better-known inheritors of the poetic experimentation are the Romantic Formalist poets, for example Yiduo Wen and Zhimo Xu, so called in modern Chinese literary history because their composition and theory are seen to have helped the maturation of a modern Chinese poetic form. Their considerable success, however, is interestingly attributed not to their revolutionary zeal but to the fact that "with their excellent classical background and their knowledge of Western poetry they were able to profit from both Western tradition and their own heritage . . . As a whole, the Formalists' poetry reveals a gradual mastery of the vernacular medium, a more felicitous exploration of complex themes and imagery, and a romantic lyricism expressing themes of human significance" (Lin 75). Whereas the Symbolists such as Wangsu Dai and Jinfa Li, another small group of modern poets who had won certain critical acclaim and popular success, "sought to penetrate to the mystery of beauty and existence by way of symbols, strove to capture elusive moods by means of Charles Baudelaire's theory of *correspondences* between the senses" (Lin 75). This account, rather than clarifying matters, points instead to the vital ambiguity in the relationship between the struggling modern Chinese poets and the sources of their creativity, both Western and traditional. The choices of the individual poets demonstrate, for instance, that the popularity of European Romanticism and early modernism as a major corpus of translation and cultural-aesthetical influence may be seen to be favored rather for their reaction against modernity. Or, simply, modern Chinese poets found in them analogous sensibilities to those found in their familiar therefore comforting traditional Chinese nature poets and the Lyricists. However, neither the Formalists with their propensity for "romantic lyricism" and clearer pronouncements on form both in theory and practice nor the Symbolists' search for "elusive moods" in the Baudelairean sense were considered the mainstays of the poetic spirit of the age by their contemporaries. Guo, who has "Romantically" defined modern poetry writing as the Wordsworthian spontaneous overflow of feelings (Guo used the phrase rather freely, it is difficult to determine if the reference is direct or the result of more general cross-cultural, trans-lingual practices)—"as the recording of powerful passions" "whose function is in the expression of sentiments" (Guo, "Guanyu shide wenti" 106; "Lunshi sanzha" 211; all translations are mine unless otherwise noted)—divides poems into two kinds by comparing them to the waves of the ocean. In his categorization, "the mighty torrents of the tidal waves are like the poetry of the powerful and resounding; they are Qu Yuan's *Lisao*, Chai Wenji's *Hujia Shibapai*, the Songs of Li Bai and Du Fu, Dante's *Divine Comedy*, Milton's *Paradise Lost*, and Goethe's *Faustus*. The gentle ripples are the poems of the elusive and exquisite, like *Guo Feng* of the Chou era, Wang Wei's four-line seven-character *jueshi*, the classical Japanese poet Saigyo's lyrics on bananas, Tagore's *New Moon*" (Guo, "Lunshi sanzha" 205-06).

By his own standards, and that of the poets and critics around and after him, Guo should be "the" modern Chinese poet. This is because first he is "the only major poet whose career has spanned the entire historical development in mainland China of the new verse, from its nascent state to the present" (Lin 197). And his poetic "explosion" seems to best embody the spirit of the age, an "explosion" that is seen to bring a fresh approach and new modes of feelings that are "dynamically contemporary," though many have noted or lamented the loss when he is later perceived to turn from an earlier Romantic individualism to collective proletarianism (see Lin 197; Gálik, "Kuo Mo-jo" 28-62). The dynamic contemporaneity of Guo's poetic eruption seems to rest with its very emblematic representation of the affective turn, in its expression of the might of feelings. And it is these qualities, according to Baihua Zong, that have enabled him to write poems of the sublime kind. Yang Zhou characterized it some twenty years later in similar torrential terms, linking unequivocally personal poetic qualities with the "spirit of the times." He claims that in the expression of powerful emotions, Guo "is the brightest, where many writers pale in comparison" (Zhou). In the composition of other poets, "that meandering personality waiting to be liberated from oppression is but an enclosed small river aimlessly struggling before the dam. Only when it reached him, did the water gather momentum and expand into the limitless roaring waves of the Pacific which rushed to tumble the world" (Zhou).

Guo's career seems so tied up with the question of Chinese cultural modernity that the prototype of the modern Chinese poet's progress is literally predicated on it. This portrait of Guo is collaborated by Xiaoming Chen's recent intellectual-personal biography of him in English, which also charts Guo's political as well as career path as prototypical of the modern Chinese intellectual quest (Chen, *From the May Fourth Movement*). As his fellow New Culturalist Yiduo Wen remarked, Guo is the only truly modern poet "who has grasped the spirit of the time" (Wen, *Wen Yiduo Quanji* 185). Han Tian, another fellow poet-dramatist, puts it in more "dynamically contemporary" terms: "This is my critique of your poems—if it is said that your are a poet, I'd rather believe that you have the soul of poetry; because every single composition of yours is your blood, your tears, your autobiography, and your 'Confessions'" (79). Guo's poetic becoming is almost univocally described in various accounts of the New Cultural Movement as the process of awakening, weeping, bursting forth, and thundering strike, and most discussions of the spirit of the times begin with his first poetry collection *Nüshen* (The Goddess), which typically celebrates the energetic, the disruptive, the unlimited, the terrible, and the sublime. It seems appropriate then, to explore the aspirations and trappings of the New Culturalists "to be taken as metonymy of their culture," which Guo passionately enacts and shares with his fellow poets and critics, on his terms and by his example. In particular, I attempt to elucidate the historical and aesthetic implications of these efforts to refigure a sublime Chinese cultural modernity through analysis of the exemplary compositions from Guo's *The Goddess* and the later historical-poetic drama *Qu Yuan*, which is regarded by many as the most sublime poetic-dramatic composition in modern Chinese literary history.

The search for the great in sensibility and form

Critic Achilles Fang is known to have pronounced something contradictory but "true" about Guo and his poetry: "Humorless sincerity, death-seriousness, even deadly dullness—traits one seldom finds in traditional Chinese poetry—mark Kuo Mo-jo's poetry . . . the emergence of Kuo Mo-jo on the Chinese poetic scene was almost miraculous; it marked the end of tradition" (186). One might take exception to Fang's aesthetic judgment, except when applied to Guo's literary activities in the post-Revolution period. But Fang has certainly made clear the link between Guo's poetry and poetic career with the question of tradition and modernity. Although as Lin points out, Guo's very emergence may have injected a much needed vitality into the new verse, it had hardly brought down the curtain on tradition. It had indeed, however, established "traits" that have dramatically, if for some traumatically, changed Chinese poetry, in both sentiment and form, medium of composition, and aesthetic, cultural function. Although he has also composed numerous "gentle ripple" "lyrical" poems, Guo is known and remembered in Chinese poetic history as a major "tidal wave." Some critics have simply put his compositions as the search for and embodiment of the "big." On reading the first edition of *The Goddess*, fellow poet Baiqing Kong exclaimed that "The brushstrokes of Guo Moruo's poetry are vigorous and bold; they are not restricted to the trifling skill and ornamentation of a scribbler. He is indeed a great natural and unaffected poet" (qtd. in Pu 35-36). Xiang Zhu, another contemporary fellow poet, suggested on the other hand that Guo's obsession with the "big," together with his one-dimensional imagination and monotonous poetic structure, made the reader nervous (365). Whereas Xingcun Qian puts the jubilant execution of *The Goddess* back into the timely pursuit of the Romantic and the sublime, as he sees it, the poetry collection is marked by "exuberant feelings," "robust moods," and "ferocious expressions" and "contains tremendous force" (qtd. in Pu 35-36). Guo's own elaboration on his philosophical-aesthetic enterprise seems to confirm his friends' impressions: "Where then do we look for this 'greatness'? It is impossible to find it in our mortality; it is impossible to find it in the small human world. Only the cosmos is the greatest. We can only find the biggest in the cosmic universe. We must fuse with the sun, the moon, the stars, the majestic mountains, the River and the ocean, light, darkness, life, death and all other eternal phenomena, we must fuse into them, into this 'greatness,' only then, thus subsumed and attached to the cosmic greatness, will our this worldly life become eternal. And this is called the great in the small, the eternal in the moment, and these are the beginnings of pantheism" (X. Zhu 222-23). This has been well known as Guo's expression of pantheism, but it equally emphatically demonstrates his invocation of the Romantic sublime.

In the rush to eulogize Guo's vital exuberance, his dynamic bursting forth (one cannot fail to notice the "organic" phrasing), however, both his contemporary poets and later critics seem to have forgotten that his prolific composition, his vast range of poetic subjects, his stylistic virtuosity and inventiveness were part of a deliberate, concerted, passionately launched, and staunchly guarded program. His tremendous energy that paved "a new avenue for poetry at once affirmative, exciting, dynamic, and contemporary" (Lin 198) is part of a revolutionary program not only of poetry writing, but also of the new province of literature in relation to the traumas of modernity. It is a creative and regulative process marked by pain, desperate seeking, and hesitation as well as outbursts rather than an organic bursting forth. Like the sublime poetics it seeks to transpose and reconfigure, it is a process that begins at the limits. Baihua Zong, the first editor of Guo's experimental poems and an avowed modern Chinese aesthete, however, has understood the implications of Guo's new poems much better than his other contemporaries. For him, Guo's search and experimentation is much less the bursting forth of exuberant individual talent than a pursuit emblematic of the quest of *baihua* poetry itself. It highlights both the possibilities and limitations of the new poetic experiment and is thus designative of its direction. "Your song of the Phoenix"—this refers to Guo's "Fenghuang Niepan (The Nirvana of the Phoenix)," first published in 1920 and then included in *The Goddess* in 1921— "is nothing less than sublime; the backbone of your poems is of a unique profoundness so that the poems' overtones are difficult to exhaust, unlike most of the new poetry today which is conceptually weak and of no tonal implications, and which can hardly bear a single reading. It shows that *baihua* poetry should pay particular attention to its conceptual underpinnings and search for sincere emotions because it seeks to be without the accessory of ornate diction" (Tian, Zong, and Guo 25).

Like many of his contemporary New Culturalists, Guo's budding forth on the literary scene was first as a translator with a different cultural and social vision. His translation of Goethe has earned him the title of a Chinese Goethe (L. Liu 191). His rendering of *The Sorrow of Young Werther* into the modern vernacular Chinese was a bestseller among urban youth, alongside his translations and introductions of Heine, Shelley, Byron, Whitman, and many more Romantic and other European (as well as Japanese and Indian) poets. Guo's translations come with his search for and attempt to refigure in China a new literature whose function and end is its moral pathos: "Art is capable of unifying people's sentiments and of mobilizing them to work for a common goal. There is ample evidence to show that this is indeed the case, although I can't possibly cite every single instance here: take Italy before the Unification. It was owing to Dante's *Divine Comedy* that the Unification movement was able to prevail. The same can be said of the impact that the works of Voltaire and Rousseau had on France before the French Revolution. According to Treitschke, Goethe's influence was not the least bit inferior to that of Bismarck on what was to be born as the German empire. And we all know that the great Russian Revolution was also pioneered by the devoted efforts of some men of letters" (Guo, "Wenyi zhi shehui shiming" 83). This passage is from Guo's public lecture entitled "The Social Task of Literature and Art" and delivered at Shanghai University in 1925. If one can disregard the naiveté of his unheeding confidence, considering the tremendous enthusiasm of the age, what emerges is a clear vision of the province of a modern Chinese literature and society. It is worth noting here that Xun Lu (1881-1936), another mainstay of modern Chinese culture, has made similar remarks on the greater moral affect of literature in healing the national wounds of modern history when he explained why he gave up the study of medicine to become a writer (Lu, *Nahan*). Strikingly reminiscent of Wordsworth's Preface to *Lyrical Ballads*, Guo's new mapping wills and marks simultaneously the affective turn—the stress of moral pathos in Chinese literature "called on artists and writers to forge sublime sentiments among the people and mobilize them for a greater cause" (L. Liu 191). This stress on the affective in literature, especially in the sublime, is echoed by Baihua Zong, who expounds with equal passion: "The literature of a nation in times of construction and revival is almost always optimistic and forward looking. Because there is Whitman's unprecedented sublime jubilation, there is also the American spirit of youthful and fearless construction. The French literature of decadence will not suffice to revive the national spirit of France, but Romain Rolland's writings of optimism will influence a future France, a future Europe. This is why I pray privately but fervently for the appearance of many jubilant and magnificent poems, to lead our poor nation mired in muddy depth to an uplifting aura of happy exuberance" (Zong, "Letter to Guo Moruo" 106). Guo and Zong's vision—comparatist in the fashion of the time—also foregrounds the historical situation of Chinese modernity in its cultural reference to Europe. In their use of the examples of the moral affect of literary culture, from Dante to Rousseau to Goethe and the revolutionary Russian men of letters, they have made clear that the end of "the feverish activity of translation" is the forging of a modern Chinese culture and the shaping of modern Chinese subjects. Both Guo's and Zong's comparativist models also prove that their relation to their Western sources of comparison are not determined by the semicolonial Chinese situation, as Shih suggests in her study of Republican Chinese modernism (see Shih). For example, as we see in their choice and comparison, not all French (Western) writers are the same or similarly emulatable (the French writers of decadence are different from the French Romanticists and so on), and the decision is undoubtedly upon the desired Chinese course in its vision of an ideal modernity. The sense of historically burdened but nonetheless self-willed choice in Guo's "supranationalism" is also demonstrated in the multiplicity of his sources. The names of European authors Guo has mentioned in his translations and introductions, as well as those traced as major influences on him by his critics, are numerous and diverse. They include Kant, Nietzsche, Freud, Bergson, Goethe, Heine, Wordsworth, Shelley, Coleridge, Baudelaire, and Whitman. Furthermore, Guo seems more a comparativist than an "influenced" writer. As his own references show, in his thinking about a modern Chinese culture, the cultures and cultural histories of the West are sources and comparable examples of his point of departure. Also, Guo's inspirations and references are not restricted to those of the West. Besides his reliance on the legends and legendary poetic sources of his native cultural history, and the so-called Chinese classics, despite his desire to revolutionize them, he also constantly refers to Tagore, Saigyo, Shonin, and many other "Eastern" sources.

Transforming a sublime vision for new literary function

Guo's poetic revolution, especially his embodiment of the sublime affective turn, should thus be understood in terms of his historical and cultural vision. And this is the only way to comprehend the implications of his difference from the earlier New Poets, and hence the very meaning of the emergence of a modern Chinese poetry. As "the first outstanding positive Romantic poet and literary theorist of the New Chinese Literature Movement" (Yan 173), Guo Moruo's thinking on literature has extended to reflections on the origin of artistic expression, the role of the author, and the social function of literary and artistic activities. As a true "Romanticist," he has always maintained that literature is the "self-expression" of the author: "Literature and art are like the flowers and grass that bud forth in spring, they are the culmination of the inner wisdom of the artists" (Guo, "Wenyi zhi shehui shiming" 83), and "The nature of literature is subjective, expressive, not impersonal or imitative" (Guo, "Wenxue de benzhi" 221). Guo's insistence on inspired human subjectivity as the origin of literary and artistic expression, from the very beginning, runs counter to the more dominant strain—the Social Realist tradition—in the New Culturalist (later the Socialist) movement. Thus it is no wonder that his poetic theory and practice, especially from the earlier oeuvre, are often considered subjective idealist or are perceived as a passing phase in his career, as well as in the modern Chinese literary movement, wrought by the undue influence of European Romanticism and the theory of "art for art's sake" (until he came to his own under more revolutionary persuasions). Only in recent studies of Guo, a few critics like Huang-dong Yan begin to show that Guo's concept of "inspiration," of "self-expression," and of literature as naked representation of human nature is more complicated than customarily presumed. His introduction of "creation" into Chinese literary thinking is a refiguration rather than an "application" of the Romantic notion.

What does Guo mean by "expression?" In an essay entitled "Yinxiang yu biaoxian (Impression and Expression)," he explains: "Things and objects of the universe touch us through our senses, impress upon our consciousness, and these are impressions. The artist brews over such impressions in his soul, synthesizes them according to their own principles, and re-presents out of it a whole new world. And this is expression" (195-96). As Yan argues, Guo's definition of "expression" here can as well be described as materialist. His "expression" or "self-expression" do not completely belong to the realm of the subjective, they are not cut off from the world of things or social life; the subjective and objective are linked and work upon each other through the functioning of "impressions." And, likewise, the inner world of the artist is "touched" with "things and objects of the universe." Thus in Guo's delineation, the realization of artistic creation—"the re-presentation of a whole new world," is by no means the culmination of detached subjective activities, but a process of re-creation of accumulated impressions of things and beings that have touched us in the world. In Yan's words, it is the dialectic unity of the subjective and objective. However, contrary to such "dialectical materialist" reading, Guo seems much less interested in the end of dialectic unity than in the process of "creation." That is how he distinguishes the act of "expression" from manifestations of the a priori and from the imitation of the external. Guo's definition of "expression" as process emphasizes rather the crafting in artistic activity, and the performance of the artist. It does resemble the Romantic aggrandizement of the author, as well as its hyperbolization of literary agency. But like the earlier Romantic movement in Europe, the hyperbolization of both author function and the institution of literature is not so much the reflection of a desire for self-aggrandizement of individual talents, but rather seen as the demands of history. It is for the refiguration of artists and men of letters as "epic culture heroes" who can be taken as a "metonymy of their culture." Guo has further elaborated his theory of the process of "expression" in corporeal terms:

> The creation of art is a natural process that happens within. Its insemination is from the intercourse between the internal and the external, the communion between nature and the soul. Its nourishment is also supplied by the world outside, but it is not a copy of its external raw material. Just like the silkworms that gnaw and digest mulberry leaves, and spit out silk threads. The silk threads though came from the fiber of the leaves; they are not the leaves anymore. . . . A person from conception to birth has to reside inside his mother's womb for nine months. During the nine months he is nourished by the body of his mother, who in turn consumes food from outside sources to sustain herself and the embryo? But the baby she gives birth to bears no resemblance to anything she has swallowed, only to greater or lesser degrees to herself. (Guo, "Wenyi de shengchan guocheng" 97-98)

Guo's natural metaphors stress the complicated laboring process of artistic creation. Although with no self-conscious or declared propensity for the maternal, his choice of the silkworm and pregnancy-birth-motherhood as comparable idioms for artistic expression shows that his formulation of literary production is predicated on labor, conversance, and correspondence, rather than the inspired feat of "genius." His "self-expression," "a natural process that happens within," is not a movement of detachment from the social or "objective" life. Rather it is the result of "intercourse" between them. Moreover, the correspondence between Guo's artistic embryo and the outside world does not rest with the moment of inception; its complicated rearing process also depends on the nourishment from the external. This is interpreted by Guo's Marxist defenders as his departure from the traps of subjective aestheticism and his linkage of the origin of art to human society and the objective world, thus rescuing his theory, at least on the fundamental questions, from idealism to materialism. Such an argumentation notwithstanding, Guo's theory of "expression" indeed falls on the relation of correspondence between "things and objects of the universe" and human consciousness. At the same time, his emphasis on the process, on the labor of creation, is formulated against the notions of "reflection," "imitation," and "representation," which already begin to take hold of and later culminate into the dominant trend of modern Chinese literary and artistic expression for more than fifty years. Though Guo's theory locates the origin of art in "natural" and social life, it simultaneously highlights its difference. What emerges from the "creative" process is nothing less than "a whole new world." Guo's idea of "creation," unlike his European Romantic predecessors', is much less Godly, or Godlike. It is rather one of being touched, of crafting and laboring. The metaphors of impregnation, formation, and shaping into being, of swallowing, spitting, and weaving, while emphasizing the act of literary production and the agency of the artist, foreground the specific process of artistic and literary realization. They delineate it as a movement of turning, of traversing from things and objects to feelings and consciousness, or vice versa;

of making things into being. The role of the artist, in such a feat, is to shape things into being by deriving from and engendering their correspondence. In this sense it is comparable to the task of the translator, whose function is to establish "hypothetical equivalencies" between different things. And the poet is like the Wordsworthian translator. In the same vein, Guo has further elaborated on the relationship between art and nature and the artist's place in it: "The relationship between nature and the artist is like that between the woods and the carpenter. Nature is the source that supplies raw material to the artist, but to coalesce these materials into a new life, a whole new world, this depends largely on the exalted self of the artist! We don't need to follow Kant in declaring that the whole world is nothing but our own creation, but the world of art should be our occasioning" (Guo, "Yinxiang yu biaoxian" 200). Guo's portrait of the artist and his place in relation to the world of things clearly indicates the traces of his part in the "translingual activities." The disavowal of the Kantian legacy is simultaneously an evocation. It attests to Guo's attempt at translating and refiguring, if a bit awkwardly, his cultural legacies from the West, which typify not only his literary activities but also those of the many New Culturalists. It figures Guo as *the* Chinese Romanticist, as well as the visionary reformer of a new Chinese literary tradition.

Given his vision on the moral affect of literature and his stress on correspondence as the quintessence of artistic realization, how does Guo define the actual process of literary "creation"? In a letter to Zong Baihua, which to all intents seems his manifesto on poetry, Guo is unequivocally Romantic in evoking and laying stress on "inspiration" and "imagination:"

> In my view, any poetry that is the sincere expression of the poetic feeling and inspiration in our heart, that is the Strain [in English in the original] flowing from the sources of life, that is the Melody [English in original] played on our hearts' string, that is the tremblings of life, and the crying of the soul, then it is real poetry, good poetry, it is the source of our human joy. ... Poems are not "made" but "written." I think the poet's state of mind is like a bay of clear water, when there is no wind, it is as still as a quiet bright mirror, all impressions from the universe, immense or minute, accumulate their reflections in it; but when the wind blows, seething waves toss and roll, and the impressions of the universe tumble in it. The wind is what is usually called intuitive initiation or inspiration; the tumbling storms heightened sensibilities. The impressions that rock and roll are imaginations in captivity. These, I believe, are the thing-in-itself of poetry, and once they are written, they simultaneously acquire body and form. (Guo, "Guo Moruo lun chuangzuo" 137)

The conjunction between Guo's "Strain flowing from the sources of life" and the Romantic spontaneous overflow of feelings is unmistakable. And predictably, Guo has also stressed the role of imagination in poetic creation. However, one should note that in his reflection on the process of poetry writing, the moment of "spontaneous overflow" is only a *moment* of bursting forth after a long rearing process, in which he again accentuates correspondence and reciprocity. For him, inspiration is but the wind of natural and social human life, which touches upon and brings havoc to the poet's state of mind; imagination the accumulated, restless, and stirring impressions. To make matters clearer, he again resorts to corporeal idioms to further his ideas on such process: "I often think that artists are like the work bees. They gather nectar from whichever flowers they come across. And the gathered and processed nectar from thousands of flowers becomes honey, an original re-creation. The product of an artist is also like that" (*Guo Moruo lun chuangzuo* 609). His delineation of the necessary steps in poetic creation also includes the "cultivation of the artist, such as the accretion of impressions and the learning of forms and technique" (609). Guo's emphasis on both simultaneity and the working process of poetry writing, no matter whether dialectically resolved or simply contradictory is first and foremost historical, as has been argued by critics from opposite sides of the spectrum. It is a double-edged sword wielded to carve the difference of, and a different place for, the New Poetry, and consequentially a new literary culture, from both the "old" orthodoxy of classical literature and the "new" mechanical, nonaesthetic tendencies of some of his fellow modern artists. Guo's passion for "the spontaneous overflow of feelings" is in line with what he perceives to be the end of the modern poetic revolution—the replacement of the rigid, over-wrought, decadent and degenerate artifice by sincere life, simple feelings, and immediate expression. And for him and his fellow New Culturalists, this is not only a question of expression or form, but also involves redefinitions of the very "life" and "nature" of art. It is dependent upon the fundamental difference between a new literature that aims to forge sublime sentiments among the "people" and the old culture (cultivation) of the scholar-official (*shidafu*) class. Poetry "that comes from the spontaneous overflow of feelings is the finest. If it is merely feigned artifice, it is but the potted *bonsai* good enough only for the pleasure of the rich and leisured," Guo observes in his "Lunshi sanzha (Three Letters on Poetry)" (210-11). And in the same vein he further defines the "life" of New Poetry: "The burgeoning of a poem is like the growth of things in nature, it has to come out without any affectation. I believe the life of New Poetry lies exactly in this" (210-11). Guo's adherence to spontaneity and overflow of feelings, which to many betrays his Romantic legacy, is also a part of the spirit of the age. It is part of the revolutionary statement of the May Fourth intellectuals against that which is "old," "overwrought," and "degenerate" and thus at odds with the "modern." It embodies the very aspirations of the New Cultural Movement which aims at the democratization of both form and content of a modern Chinese culture, and as such foregrounds the question of the relationship between necessary formal revolution and revisions of the cultural function of poetry.

Guo's espousal of the sincerity of poetic form and spirit, his quest for expressions of unhindered overflow of feelings, is thus closely associated with the search by himself and his contemporary writers and critics for meaning and place for a new kind of literary culture in modern China. Guo's own vision of the function of literature and artistic expression is controversial from the very beginning. In asserting that "the spirit of art is non-utilitarian" he seems to aver that the departing point of his formulation is precisely the Kantian purposiveness without purpose, whereas the utilitarian motives in literary creation is a sign of degeneration, "far removed from the spirit of literature itself." And "utilitarian" intention for him means Schopenhauer's "pure objectivity" (Yan 182). Obviously, Guo takes seriously German "idealist" philosophy and the ideas of other European Romanticists. But the "influences" did not stop here, or rather he has gone far beyond the "influences." The refrain of purposiveness without purpose is, after all, only the departure of his argument, not its end. In "Wenyi zhi shehui shiming (The Social Task of Literature and Art)," as soon as he declares that "literature and art in itself are without purpose," he hastens to add:

> However, the occurrence of every social phenomenon affects everything around it, just like throwing a stone into a still pond—no matter how small the stone is, the water ripples, and spreads throughout the pond. Art and literature are one kind of social phenomenon; it certainly will affect the whole society.... Some say literature has a purpose, that this is a necessary fact after its occurrence. Everybody knows the famous debate between the school of art for art's sake, and the school of art for life's sake. Actually this is only a question about art in itself and its affect. In this sense it is like a tree. The tree itself is not grown so that people can make things out of it, but we can use it to make anything we deem suitable. (84-85).

As has been pointed out by many, Guo's elucidation on the role of art and literature separates art in itself from its social function. It differentiates the intention of the author from the affect of the text: a differentiation that has led some to pronounce his theory dialectically contradictory. And his figuring of art as social phenomenon in organic metaphors certainly betrays his "idealist-Romantic" legacies. But for all the differentiation and figurative renderings, the conclusion of Guo's exposition is the emphatic social function of literature. The differentiation has shifted the highlight from individuated intentionality to the historical social affect of the text. The purposiveness of artistic creation, in this sense, is not only because of, but also despite its "originary" purpose. Guo's theory, in this light, is unresolved or even contradictory. And it is a contradiction that both betrays and circumvents his "Romantic" entanglement. As someone who is intent on the refiguration of a new Chinese epic culture hero—the poet as "metonymy of their culture"—the move to affect as consequence rather than intent of art seems a move away from, or at least a distraction from, the very intent. Nevertheless, Guo's move is towards the social function of literature. It is an embrace of the affective turn championed by the European Romanticists and chosen by the Chinese "New Culturalists." It is a historical choice that not only brings into focus, but also hyperbolizes the literary agency. After all, Guo's public lecture is entitled "The Social Task of Literature and Art," in which he has gone on at great length to elaborate the agency of literary and artistic expressions: "The contribution of art to human civilization is immeasurable," he declares, and epitomizes it in two ways: "Art works to integrate people's feelings, and lead them to act towards a set goal . . . art can raise our spirit, and sublimate us by working within our hearts." Such was the case when the King of Chu was besieged, it was Zhangliang's flute that finally scattered his soldiers and dealt him the final blow, and this proves the immense power of music" (84-85). Guo's eulogy of the moral pathos of artistic affect is unabashedly hyperbolic. But it is saved from "propaganda" by his simultaneous insistence on art's "in itself": "I believe the salvation of China is impossible without artistic and literary movements . . . This does not mean that we hope every artist will become a propaganda artist. We only hope that he can expand his life, to fully experience the demands of social reality, and thus acquire the self-consciousness to redeem the people and the nation. Art that emerges from such self-consciousness retains its independence, but its affect is limitless to China's future" (88). Guo's conviction of the power of art is based on its affective properties, which in turn are produced from the "self-consciousness" of the artist. Guo's self-consciousness, however, derives not from the ontological a priori, but rather the process of reciprocity between "life" and the artist's mind. It is a self-consciousness that came from fully experienced "demands of social reality." The emergence of artistic expression from such self-consciousness is thus neither utilitarian nor transcendental. It is a bursting forth after the process of reciprocation between the demand of the times and the sincerity of life and feeling on the part of the artist. The task of the artist, in this sense, is that of the translator, who turns "life," "social reality," or the demands of the times into consciousness and feelings and reciprocates them into a new *being*—"Strain from the sources of life and Melody from the bottom of our heart."

Nüshen (The Goddess) and poetry of a sublime modernity

The making of a new Chinese poetry is thus the making over of both "form" and "content" and of its medium of composition and "sensibilities," predicated on the revision of its affective agency. In other words, the revolution of form, which has come to stand for the modern Chinese poetic revolution, is as much a revolution of "feelings" and "affects." Although the advocacy, experiment, and practice of *baihua* as the only poetic medium quickly held sway despite fierce opposition, the goal of the pioneering *baihua* poets—the great revolution of form—by many accounts ended rather far from it. The first of the cardinal points in Shi Hu and many other pioneering new poets' quest was the abolition of *wenyan* and its replacement with *baihua*—"the living language"—in poetry writing, so that the composition "can be both read and heard," "that are expressive as well as graceful" (Hu, *Bishang liangshan* 200-05). And the second is a new harmony of "natural" rhythms, which should come from the casting off the clichés of classical prosody and the creation of a modern rhythm. Hu's great revolution of form is simply and unequivocally described as: the dismantling of all the bondage and shackles of tradition:;say whatever you want to say, and write exactly the way you speak. (Hu, "*Zixu*" 380-83).

The purpose of Hu and his friends seems to be the greater freedom of both "expression" and "ideas." The emergence of "real *baihua* poetry" depends not only on how one says and writes it, but also on what one has to say. From its nascent stage to its still controversial practice and discussion at present, the "point" of modern Chinese poetry lies as much in its formal revolution as in its shift of poetic subject and object. Dismantling the shackles of tradition necessarily means certain democratization of "spirit" and form. And it is not coincidental that the pioneers of *baihua* poetry were also the forerunners of the New Cultural Movement. One of the most common themes of early *baihua* poems was simply voices of hatred and rebellion against "feudalism" and the defunct ruling order, or expressions of longing for "light" and freedom. Its shift of poetic subject is also marked by a new worldliness. For the first time in Chinese cultural history, poetry is brought face to face with what Dun Mao called "the question of life and social phenomenon." It has moved from capturing the elusive moods and refined sentiments of the aristocracy-gentry to the immediate expressions of the life and sufferings of the multitude (see, e.g., Yan 267).

However, despite the audacity of the declarations, the sincerity of their manifested aspirations, and the momentum of the times, the revolution of the early *baihua* poets, by subsequent acquiescence, had stopped rather short of its aim. At their best, their compositions are considered commendable but circumscribed experiments. The reasons attributed to this are historical: that as experimental, literally groundbreaking works, there were no comparable prototypes to emulate or identifiable references to refer to. And there is an irresolvable paradox in the revolt against tradition by those who were at least partially reared—nurtured to maturity—by that very tradition. The undoing of tradition from both within and without proved often too formidable a task. They could not simply shrug off their very own cultivation. This is seen both in their attempt at the formal restructuring and the revolution in poetic sensibility. The earlier poets were unable to shake off either the influence of classical prosody (or their composition simply drift into prose), or the sentiments of the *shidafu* class (Yan 268-70). The irony of this is best captured in Shi Hu's poem "Oath," which he composed as a pledge to the cause of New Poetry when he decided to begin his *baihua* experiment, and in which revolutionary passions are arranged in strictly classical prosodic lines—the poem was composed in "*Xinyan's* Spring" song form. This is probably why the ambition of poetic epoch-making aspired to by Hu and other pioneering new poets is seen to have been fulfilled only with the appearance of Guo's *Nüshen*. Whatever its reception, poetic, critical, historical, then and now, it is regarded unequivocally as the first though experimental but "realized" poetry collection of the New Literature Movement, and as the culmination of the longings and aspirations of a whole generation of heroic quest (Bian 152-57). The appearance of *Nüshen* is as much an advent as a fulfillment. It is in this sense an historical event, marking the arrival of the Chinese poetic and cultural "modernity."

What is so different about Guo's *Nüshen* that it is hailed as an historical monument, and what is so "modern" about it that discussions of the spirit of the times are literally predicated on it? As Guo's first poetry collection, it consists of his poems composed during the period 1919-1921: one poetic prologue, fifty-three "free style" verses that vary in subject and formal structure, and three verse dramas. One of the most noticeable features of the volume is that almost all its consequential works are composed at the height of the May Fourth Revolution, the "hurricane" (Guo) period of the New Culture Movement. The coincidence of Guo's poetic outbursts with the raging waves of the times made him the poet of the age, and his poems the very embodiment of the "modernity" that he passionately championed. Although Guo is credited as the first *baihua* poet who had truly achieved the poetic freedom that the movement set out to attain—his composition marks the emergence of a Chinese "free verse" and verse drama—he is not lauded mainly for his stylistic and generic innovations. Above all things, he is remembered as the vanguard *par excellence* of modern Chinese literature and his poems the metonymy for "new poetry." Even in 1923, only two years after the collection's publication by Shanghai Taidong Book House, it was already eulogized by fellow poet and critic Yiduo Wen as the very embodiment of the spirit of the age: "If we talk about the New Poetry, only Mr Guo Moruo's compositions can be called by such a name. This is not only because formally and stylistically his poems are the most remote from the old poetry, what is most important is that the spirit of his poetic work is the spirit of the times—the very spirit of the twentieth century. Someone said that literary works are products of the times, and *The Goddess* is unabashedly its prodigal son" (Wen, "Tade jingshen" 432). And Wen's comment has since become the standard in Guo criticism (see Yan 272-73).

Nüshen, or more exactly its spirit and timely birth, is indeed the prodigal son of its age. Its rearing process encompasses the "hurricane" and raging waves of early modern Chinese history, and it is born out of the modern trauma as its redress. Guo has repeatedly described the deluges and torrents of this particular period of Chinese history as his poetic inspiration, an "influence" that is felt and remembered in almost bodily terms: "During the months between the end of 1919 and the beginning of 1920, I was almost immersed in poetry every day. And every onslaught of poetic influence put me in a state of high fever. I was shivering between heat and cold so hard that I could hardly hold my pen. When I said 'poems are written, not made up,' it was based on my feelings then" (Guo, "Wode zuoshi jingguo" 144). *Nüshen* in this sense is both an offspring of and a hymn to the struggles of May Fourth, and as such, the understanding of its formal revolution and poetic subject-object has become metonymic in understanding the "spirit" of Chinese modernity. *Nüshen* thus becomes synonymous with the aspirations for the "new" in form and subject of the New Poetry movement. As many have argued, it succeeded for the first time in crafting what has come to be called a Chinese free verse, a free verse form that is neither loosened lines of an otherwise classical structure nor imitations of its Western counterpart. It is also credited with having introduced the Chinese verse drama, or dramatic poems. And as embodiments of the "sentiment" of the times, the poems exemplify the very spirit of hope and longings of the age, of its passions and vitality, and an unsurpassed audacity to break away from the familiar, the conventional, and the old. It becomes one of the strongest voices of protest, rebellion, and destruction as well as "creation" during and immediately after the May Fourth period. And all this is ushered in with a ferocity bordering on savagery, with images from the self-incinerating phoenix to the dog that barks at the sun, from the blazing coal to the sun-creating goddess, which has earned Guo the title of the "tidal wave" poet. The experiments in the collection also mark a revolution of "sentiment" in Chinese poetic history, since aside from its manifested concerns about what to write and how to write it, it also symbolizes a revolution in "feelings," of what should or can be appropriate poetic "sensibilities." In the midst of the eulogies and exclamatory superlatives that laud Guo's "creative" poetic revolution of modern form and content, and the easy identification between his "revolutionary" poetic affect and the "spirit" of the age, however, strangely little is said about how the new sentiments were ushered in. What were the aesthetic underpinnings of the affective revolution? And what is the relationship between Guo's aesthetic construction and the direction of history?

The collection is predictably noted for its "positive" Romanticism. It is considered "positive" and Romantic because of its overflowing optimism and its tone of uncontrollable vehemence, its "explosive," roaring expressions and vast galloping imagination, and its extreme hyperbole and fantastic language. However, hardly any attention is paid to the fact that in Guo's experiments, for the first time in Chinese poetic practice, the sublime was ushered in as an aesthetic ideal in itself. Guo's figuration of the sublime in *Nüshen* is an original transformation of the necessary properties of the Romantic sublime. Like the European prototype, it is an historical reformulation of the excessive propensities of an aesthetic ideal centered on pain and desperation, on the disruptive and the limit of death. For example, the lasting poetic images and sequences from the collection are the self-destruction of the phoenix before her regeneration; the striving of *Nüshen* to create a new world upon the ruins of the old; Poet Yuan Qu's passionate but desperate search for liberty; Rong Nie's and Zheng Nie's self-sacrifice (the heroism in the collection is almost always suicidal). The affect of the "explosive" passions rendered through Guo's bombarding verses is often more defiant than "positive," as is often celebrated. These poetic constructions are better seen as an exclamation, a struggle for the great, and an expression of awe for the grandeur and might in nature as well as in humankind. In its strife to break away from the confines of tradition and search for freedom of form and poetic subject, Guo's compositions hover at the limit of death. The verses in the collection no longer maintain the symmetry, harmony, refinement, and poised delicacy of both form and sensibility assumed in classical Chinese poetry. Instead, they hyperbolize a stylistic and affective ferocity, ruggedness, simplicity, and the power of the great. What the collection has achieved, as many Guo critics have pointed out, is a sense of poetic audacity and vigor lacking in Chinese poetic history. But what is most striking about the different but nonetheless equally exalted and exalting verses are the traces of turbulence, of tremendous, sweeping movement. The sublime transfigured in Guo's new verses is a sublimity of the joys of destruction bordering on savagery.

The affixed rebirth of the poetic spirit

"Fenghuang niepan (The Nirvana of the Phoenix)" typifies the "spirit" of Guo's poetry collection and hence the very "spirit" of May Fourth. It is celebrated for its passions of idealism, uninhibited imagination, fantastic imagery, audacious exaggeration, grand scope, vehement tones and turbulent rhythms. And these are qualities that come to be regarded as the staples of a "Chinese" "positive" Romanticism, and which certainly seem to have established the theme of regeneration in the poem (see C. Li 8-24). However, what is most important but often unnoticed is the poem's structural and thematic attempt at epic making as well as Guo's search for new cultural icons and his effort to re-create a "modern" Chinese legend in due process. In his notes before the "Prelude," Guo tells his readers that the image of the "Phoenix" comes from the "Realm of the Beyond" (*Tian fang guo*), which is an archaic name for Arabia that often evokes associations of fantasy and legends. But the name itself is equivalent to the Chinese *fenghuang* (*feng*: male, *huang*: female) which are believed to have originated from Mount Danshe. So the poetic-epic hero is conceived as a legendary bird from the "beyond" but translatable to that which is also originary and "Chinese" and that, after five hundred years of life, burns itself with sandalwood and reincarnates from the ashes. Guo's epic begins as an elegy to the birds' impending death. The "Prelude" is a choral narrative of the preparations of the *feng* and *huang*'s self-destruction: "In the night sky of the approaching *Chuxi* (Chinese New Year's Eve), / A pair of fenghuang is hovering to and fro. / They fly away singing melancholy and low, / And with branches of sandalwood. / They flutter back atop Mount Danshe" ("Fenghuang niepan" lines 1-5).

The dirge of the narrator sets the tone for the ritual. The setting, for all its evocations of the New Year's eve, is bleak and desolate: "On the right of the mountain there are withered *wutong* (Chinese parasols), / On the left of the mountain a sweet spring drains, / In front of the mountain stands the boundless sea, / Behind the mountain lies the vast prairie, / And on the mountain is the wintry sky where a piercing wind blows" (6-10). Mount Danshe re-created is no longer full of jade and gold as it once was, though the images Guo sets up included all the commonplaces of the sublime. On the vast wintry ruins of mountain, sea, prairie, sky, trees and spring, the backdrop of the fenghuang's self-destruction is a world in proximity with death. It is a world near dusk, and like its old and tired protagonists, moribund. The "Prelude," which sets the tone for the ballad-epic, with its reoccurring refrain of the darkening night and "The *feng* has flown tired, / The *huang* has flown tired, / Their death is nigh" (13-15), successfully builds up the atmosphere of the impending end, but without any hint of beyond. The *feng* and *huang* continue their last sublime though nonetheless woeful song, while a flock of their more profane fellow beings watch vacuously: "Ah Ah! / The mournful fenghuang! / The *feng* dances, bending low but defiant! / The *huang* sings, sublime! / The *feng* dances once more, / And so sings the *huang*, / A flock of worldly birds, / Come to watch the funeral song" (29-36). In keeping with the tone set up in the "Prelude," "The Song of the *Feng*" and "The Song of the *Huang*," which make up the main body of the poem, accumulate in intensity and passion. As the swan song of the legendary birds, they build up the theme of exaltation in defiance. In face of impending terror, the *feng* and *huang* revel in the sublimity of destruction. The sense of terror divulged in the two "Songs," however, does not come so much from the birds' approaching death, which, after all, is self-chosen, a choice with hope of the beyond, but rather from their narrative. In preparing their own cremation, they soar towards the sky and circle towards earth, hover between the past and present, and roam the vast space of the poet's imagination, which is also the expansive ruins of Chinese civilization. They sing separately and in chorus, and their songs penetrate to the four corners of earth, bewailing and cursing the world of their being. The "Songs," which are their death throbs of anger and sorrow, are actually the poet's lamentation for five hundred years of (pre)modern Chinese history and the conditions of human existence. In the present "universe," in the "songs," the old world is described as the "butcher house," "prison," "graveyard," and "Hell": "You, the vast universe, as cruel as cast-iron! / You, the vast universe, as dark as black pigment! / You, the vast universe, as odorous as blood!" (39-41). The *feng* begins his mourning song as a denunciation of the world from which he and the *huang*, as symbols of the glory of Chinese civilization, are impelled to depart. But the *feng*'s indictment is not constrained to the wrongs of his immediate existence. As it is in Yuan Qu's "Lisao (Sorrows at the Departure)," the protestations and requisitions of the *feng* are directed against the whole universe, it is a reiteration of Qu's "Tian wen (Query to Heaven)." What the *feng* questions and laments are the conditions of our very human existence, and what he professes is a fundamental skepticism of the ways of being in the world, the adherence to the ultimate unchangeability which is believed to be the cause of China's lethargy: "Oh, the cosmos, / Why do you exist? / And whence do you come? / Where do you sit yourself? / Are you a limited hollow ball, / Or a boundless entity? / . . . / What other things exist beyond your perimeter?" (42-51)

Guo's query to heaven, however, is not intended to be a reflection on the nature of things and being or any a priori cosmic principle. The universal questions are posed only to lead to the rightful rage that heaven knows naught and thus cannot provide answers to human suffering and the ways of the world, especially the onslaught of the direction of modern history: "Raising my head I ask the sky, / But the sky, haughty and high, knows naught. / Bending low I ask the earth, / The earth is dead, without breath. / Stretching my neck I ask the sea, / The sea is sobbing, choked by its own tears" (58-63). "The Song of the *Feng*" is dominated by rage, a rage given vent to in bitter protest and shrill curse. Guo, through the wailings of the dying *feng*, certainly does not begrudge "high colors" of description and "vicious imagery" in an otherwise rather plain, almost colloquial ballad form. With little hint of the hope or joy of transcendence, the *feng*'s fury is vindictive: "Ah, the universe, and the world, / I will persevere to put you under my cursing-spell: / You thick-blood soiled butchery! / You sorrow infected prison! / You shrieking / ghost-filled grave! / And you Hell with dancing devils! / Why have you come to live on earth?" (68-73). If the *feng*'s despair is at the pain and terror of the world and the universe in general, "The

Song of the *Huang*" is a lamentation of the five-hundred years of Chinese history in particular. She bewails its tears and humiliations, and its present station in the vast ocean like a lonely sinking boat.

> Five-hundred years of tears pour like waterfalls.
> Five-hundred years of tears drip like the candle.
> The tears that are inexhaustible,
> The filth that is unwashable,
> The passions that are inextinguishable,
> And the shame that is inerasable.
> . . .
> Ah, Ah!
> The last stretch of our dim and floating life,
> Is like the lonely sinking boat amid the vast sea.
> . . .
> The sail is broken,
> The mast cracked,
> The oars scattered,
> The girder rotting away. (86-104)

The *huang*'s summation of recent Chinese history is not unlike its popular contemporary assessment. What it does, though, besides accreting and enumerating the pain and sorrow of the last five-hundred years, which is a "historical" period deliberately set up and aside to accentuate its abrupt and successive traumatic modern turn and the thousands of years "before," is to intensify the despair and hopelessness, the feelings of suspense rather than any sense of easy redemption. The modern Chinese sublime, as Guo figures it, is a precarious play of the dark obscurity of the terrible. It is a historical-aesthetical play different from the cathartic sublimation elaborated earlier by Guowei Wang when he traversed through Kant and Schopenhauer in his reading of the classic Chinese novel *Dream of the Red Chamber*, although both these refigurations are part of "the aesthetic search for meaning in cultural crisis" (B. Wang 17). The imagery and sentiment of the song, following and dramatizing the setting up of the "Prelude," tell a story of boundless terror and humiliated impotence which are so real that they threaten to exceed the boundaries which posit them as mere prerequisites for the sublime moment beyond: "Ah, Ah! / . . . / On the left the sea is flowing boundless and nigh, / On the right the sea is flowing boundless and nigh, / In front there is no lighthouse, / Behind the coast is nowhere to behold" (14-17). Death, in such an emphatic configuration and with such lifelike omnipresence, can no longer be read as a ruse or necessary ploy for subsequent transcendence: "Folly! Folly! Folly! / What are left are sorrow, frustration, solitude, and decay, / Those spirited corpses that surround us, / Those spirited corpses that are woven through us. / . . . Gone! Gone! Gone! / Everything is gone. / All is gone. / So will be us, / And so will you be" (39-52).

After such breathless and hyperbolic variations on death, decay, and despair, the chorus of the *feng* and *huang* finally does strike a note of defiance and heroism, at least they know they are at the limit and have no hesitation in devising a dignified end. The end they envision has no hint of the beyond, but at least has the hope of redemption. They hope to bring with them in a final act of (self-)destruction all that is unseemly and depraved from the familiar world of their origin and existence: "Ah, Ah! / The flame is up. / The fragrance arises. / Time has come! / Death is knocking on the door! / All that is in us! / All that is outside us! / All things and everything! / Please! Please!" (139-47). The legendary birds valiantly embrace their end, if not with joy, at least with nonchalance and glee: the inferno they unleash with their self-sacrifice can at least bring about the destruction of all that is dilapidated, despondent, and hideous. However, the audience of their ritual vitiates the reader's expectation of the sublime: as onlookers of the fenghuang's gesture beyond, the group of "prey of the mundane"—from the homely pigeon to the thuggish eagle—do not respond with the anticipated terror, awe, or the sense of narrow escape. They simply fail to comprehend the sublime spectacle: after witnessing the legendary birds' death chant and self-incineration, they hasten to celebrate and compete for their replacement in the feathered realm. For the unenlightened and unenlightenable birds of the world, the fenghuang's "staged" death is a foolhardy act or a capitulation to fate. Since they cannot comprehend the stagedness of the staged death and consequently its meaning. They can only gloat over the fenghuang's misfortune: "Ha ha, fenghuang! fenghuang! / You have been our feathered sovereign in vain! / So you are really dead? You are really dead? / From now on I will be the chieftain!" (148-151) sings one "vulgar" bird after another.

The failure of the "prey of the mundane" to participate metaphorically in the sublime spectacle may be the result of the very difficulties in the all too earnestly transfigured ruse. In the poet's attempt to bring the terrors of the modern world home, the fervently enumerated and authenticated wounds of history have become so real that it is difficult for the spectators to acquire that necessary distance—the possibility of differentiation which makes good affectively the spectacular show. After their emphatically repetitive construction as the main feature of Guo's ballad-epic and seemingly artless bombarding statement, the immediacy of the historical terrors and the intensity of the poet-protagonist's pain in the end overwhelm the stagedness. Because it is this stagedness that grounds the very implication of will, choice, agency and its hope of overcoming in the fenghuang's death. Failure in its perception makes the act falling short as a gesture beyond. Or this simply illustrates the very problem of transfiguring the sublime as an historical aesthetics. As redress to the modern trauma, Guo seems to have translated and refigured the very paradox of the Romantic sublime. Just as it is exemplified in the Burkean ruse and the Kantian structure of the a priori, this aesthetic construction simultaneously aspires to its verifiability by everyone (the universal) and which, by its very strenuousness, excludes the weaker subject. Guo's configuration is further compounded by his share of the Romanticists' ambition to refigure the modern epic culture-hero (he is known for his ardent admiration for Yuan Qu, Tagore, Shelley, Byron, Goethe, and so on, both poetic and personal). In his quest for a devastating heroism as the only force of redemption, he has to resort to the divine bird, which, despite the transfigured cross-cultural origins, soars far beyond the realm, hence comprehension, of the earthly multitude. In his choice of utter defiance, and at the moment of consuming rage and uncontrollable passion for total destruction and revolution, Guo, like many of his fellow radical modern Chinese cultural critics and poets, has failed to establish the sympathetic correspondence between things and beings, a failure which not only resulted in the worldly birds' inability to participate in the fenghuang's sublime play but also in the fate of modern "vernacular" Chinese poetry—a genre that has never quite resolved the paradox of its striving for stylistic and affective avant-garde and its desire for democratization, which is the very premise of its coming-into-being. The disjunction between the fenghuang's act and the home birds' response has vitiated the project of transfiguring the modern sublime as aesthetic healing of the cultural wounds of history. It attests to the conceptual and structural difficulties inherent in the strenuous affective demand of the formulations of the modern sublime and its transport. It also foregrounds the contrary impulses of the radical May Fourth intellectuals to both enlist and differentiate themselves, as defiant epic culture heroes, from the multitude. And this has proved the irresolvable dilemma of both the original and Guo's transfigured sublime cultural avant-guardism.

"The Song of Nirvana," when it does come, after the conclusive celebration by the lowly prey of the happy demise of their more heroic fellow creatures, comes more as an appendix, an epilogue rather than the poem's end. After a cock pronounces the dawn, the spring tide rises and the light that died the previous night awakens again. In chorus, the *feng* and *huang* sing forever with mounting joy, of their reincarnation, of the dewy new life of every thing and being; of freshness, cleanliness and fragrance. But above all things, they sing in and about harmony, of the oneness in being and in eternity: "We are reincarnated. / We are again alive. / One in everything, alive. / Everything in one, alive, // . . . // We are fresh, we are clean, / We are magnificent, we are fragrant. // . . . // We are sincere, we are full of love. / We are blissful, we are harmonious. // One in everything, in harmony. / Everything in one, in harmony. / Harmony is you, harmony is me. / Harmony is him, harmony is fire" (181-210). The beyond in Guo's imagination sounds strangely familiar. After all, "Nirvana" has always promised transcendence in death, as long as one practices differentiating (from the multitude) self-discipline. In Guo's idealization, the *feng* and *huang* have also aspired to bring with them regeneration of the world at large. But in the pantheistic heaven where the born again birds sing like angels, and where the "influence" of Goethe is unfailingly pointed out by a host of critics, the scene of universal bliss doggedly reminds one of the Confucian utopia of *Datong shije*—the world of universal equality, where harmony is at the center of things and being. Thus the "beyond," actualized and affixed as the end of the fenghuangs' (the poet's) sublime gesture, seems nebulous, a hyperbolic space without "content" (as opposed to the earlier songs, there is literally no imagery in the last chorus), hence highly improbable. It also threatens to resurrect with it an origin, an all too puissant cultural source the poet and his fellow modern Chinese literary practitioners vowed to do away with. Guo's phoenix, transported like this, resembles neither the Hegelian Western nor Asiatic bird (Shih 52). Its poetically affixed reincarnation complicates rather than helps the historical vision of the May Fourth New Culturalists inspired by the Hegelian spirit. It also reminds us that historical visions are not always confined in cultural manifestos. Instead, they are often redefined in poetic practices that diversify its course.

Chapter Six

Rewriting *Qu Yuan* and Towards a Sublime Denouement

Searching for origins in historical and poetic crisis

How does one account for the traces of an unwanted origin and the "echoing" of the first "murmur" of the sources (Wordsworth, "Essays upon Epitaphs" 79) in the overwhelming iconoclasm that is generally seen to typify the spirit of the times? Guo's vision of a Chinese cultural modernity involved a project of regeneration. His ambition for cultural and historical redress, which characteristically proclaimed itself with self-incineration and devastation of the world, was in the end a program of transformation. As the "true" beginner of New Poetry, his quest for directions inevitably lead him to the traces of origins. Guo repeatedly cast the origins of a new Chinese literature in a radically reinterpreted classical tradition, as well as whatever suitable foreign sources that came his way. But unlike Wordsworth, Guo was not overly concerned with burying the dead properly. His attempt to figure himself as the modern Chinese poet and a new epic culture-hero was founded upon his refiguration of new cultural monuments on the ruins of his explosive iconoclasm. Such refiguration of modern cultural monuments on the ruins of traditions involved sources from both long ago and far away. It was a transformative move that made "hypothetical equivalence" between different things and established the translatability between different origins and tendencies. This is why translation of European literature as well as the Chinese classics—Guo translated into the vernacular both the *Guofeng* from the *Book of Songs* and the complete oeuvre that had been attributed to Yuan Qu—figured so prominently in his modern poetic endeavor. This also explains Guo's preoccupation with historical-poetical figures from the very beginning of his creation of New Poetry and throughout his literary career, especially his evocation of the classical Chu poet Qu: "How do you know I am not the Yangtze River, how do you know I can only be the streams and tributaries of the Xiang and Yuan? Is it true that my might can only form the tiny Dongting Lake, but not the ocean whose limit is the sky? . . . I create the majestic mountains, and the vast sea; I create the sun, the moon and the stars; I ride the wind, the cloud, the thunder and the rain. When gathered I am only myself, but when spread I overflow into the cosmos" (Guo, *Xianglei* 18-19)

Guo's figuration of Qu as the Chinese poet sublime, as attested by this soliloquy in the earlier verse drama *Xianglei*, is undoubtedly part of the quest for the "great" of both "content" and "form" (Dafu Yu), and the "moral pathos" of his times. The project of reerecting cultural monuments, for Guo, is first and foremost a project of transposition of sources, like his refiguration of European Romanticism: Guo devoted literally half his lifetime to the translation of Qu's poetry: from 1935 to 1953, he translated the complete works of Qu from classical to colloquial Chinese. Qu's importance, reinterpreted with the concerns of Guo's times, is his historical placement, that is, his own timeliness. After all, Qu's age was also one of "great change." The time of *Chunqiu* (Spring and Autumn) is "the transition from the system of slavery to feudalism" (Guo, "*Qu Yuan* yanjiu" 411). Qu's tragedy, reframed in this way, is not only his own but also that of his times. His exile and death (he drowned himself in Miluo River) coincided with the destruction of his kingdom in a traumatic but nonetheless "irreversible" historical process. But for Guo, Qu's historicity was not limited to his role as the prototypical tragic hero in a prototypical tragic time. It was also in his revered place in subsequent Chinese cultural history as the first great Chinese poet. Qu's greatness stems from the fact that he is known as the first named Chinese poet, hence marking both a new era in Chinese poetry writing and the coming into being of the Chinese poet. Qu's appearance in Chinese poetic history is thus commemorated as a beginning, a culmination, and a departure from the old. For although he is venerated as one of the forefathers of Chinese poetry, his emergence does not seem to signal its beginning but rather its first revolution, and consequently replaces its origin as revolutionary. Qu is a noted reformer of poetic form and spirit. His invention of the "Sao style" (*sao ti*) based on Chu folk songs is seen as the first formal poetic revolution against the rigidity of the four-word lines of the older *Shijing* (Book of Songs), and it is also celebrated as the beginning of a different tradition, a sensibility or spirit, which was later interpreted as the propensity for the Romantic, for that which typically celebrates the disruptive, the fantastic, and the sublime. Guo's transformative reinterpretation of Yuan Qu is in this sense a monumental replacement:

> The "Sao style" and the classic "*zhi hu ye zhe*" prose created by Qu Yuan, is actually the vernacular (*baihua*) poetry and vernacular prose of the Spring and Autumn and Warring States periods. One can say that at the time two thousand years ago, there was also a "May Fourth" movement, and Qu Yuan was its forerunner. . . . He can indeed be crowned as the "people's poet." As a poet, he is fully conscious of the folksy and commonplace, and has made a great contribution to its spirit. He has begun single-handedly a great revolution in ancient Chinese poetic practice, a revolution in both form and content. It is Qu Yuan who introduced a "people's consciousness" into po-

etry. It is he who adopted the folk ballad form to plebianize the already rigid aristocratic ancient poetry, and bestowed upon it a new and fuller life. (Guo, "Geming shiren Qu Yuan" 46; "Renmin shiren Qu Yuan" 143)

Qu's place and his greatness in Guo's refigured genealogy is that not only is he the originary Chinese poet, but he is also the first indication of an alternative poetic voice. What he originates is a different tradition, to which Guo and his fellow cultural reformers can trace the first murmur of the wellspring of their new vision, and by which they can establish the "hypothetical equivalence" between different tendencies and revolutions, as well as the translatability between now and then, the long ago and the far away. Refigured as such, Qu's poetic revolution is not only analogous to the New Poetry movement of modern China, but also comparable to the modern configuration of the Romantic and the sublime in Europe of which Guo and his colleagues were its Chinese interpreters. Guo's transfiguration of Qu and his historicity, characteristic of the "radical" May Fourth critical tradition, are of course anachronistic. But it is a necessary anachronism that relocates origins and redirects tendencies. It has simultaneously established and replaced the beginning of Chinese poetry as one of revolution and the first Chinese poet as an epic culture-hero. Figured as such, Qu's importance in the "two thousand years" of Chinese literary history thus stands for both the coming-to-be of the Chinese poet, and the traceable origin of the particular place and function of the poet and poetry writing. It is seen to originate a cultural heroism, a poetic aspiration to be "the metonymy of their culture." What Guo establishes is not so much Qu's place and greatness in literary history, but rather the historical function of poetry. After all, Guo is not the only or first Chinese poet with epic ambitions to evoke Qu. After his political defeat and exile to Changsha, Yi Jia in the early Han period elicited Qu's example, declaring him a kindred spirit in his eulogy of the first great but defiant poet. Historian and literatus Qian Sima, on the other hand, extolled Qu's noble and unsullied spirit, affirming its light competes with the radiance of the moon and the sun (Sima 501). Sima is known not only for having written the poet's biography but also for having used him as a personal example under adverse conditions. So all-pervasive seems Yuan Qu's influence that his figure is celebrated as the very synonym of the celebration of the tragic, disruptive, heroic, and sublime. While this has obviously presented a problem for the spirit of "iconoclasm" and the desire for "radical" cultural negation on the part of some of the New Cultural critics, Qu as a historical figure and a poet has always been a topic of controversy and contention (see J. Wang; Schneider). Even Xun Lu, the most critical, least Romantic champion of revolutionary cultural modernity, in his brief fascination with the demonic in the Romantic, casts Qu as the rare embodiment of the poet sublime: "Qu Yuan alone—before he died, mind cresting with the waves of the Miluo, looking back at his native hills, lamenting their lack of a goddess—composed in sorrow a rare multifoliate work. Hostile to the muck of custom, singer of his own rare talent, complete skeptic from antiquity's origin down to details of all things living, he dared—on the shores of vastness, feeling no qualms—to give voice to what his forebears feared to say" (Lu, "Moluo shili shuo" 69). Lu draws for inspiration on *Lisao*, Qu's long autobiographical lyrical poem in which Qu figured himself as the poet on a quest and under duress. For example, he cites the poem as an epigraph for his second collection of short stories *Panghuang* (Wandering): "The way stretches long, dim and narrow, but I will quest high and low." Lu's depiction of Qu's sublimity, echoing Xie Liu, the renowned Qi-Liang (479-559) literary critic, is associated with Qu's composition of "a rare multifoliate work," as embodiment of his "own rare talent;" with his singular audacity "on the shores of vastness." Lu has also located Qu's original greatness by way of Liu Xie's conclusion that "major talent picks up its grand style" (Lu, "Moluo shili shuo" 69). In this way Lu's characterization not only coincides with Baihao Zong's call for the composition of a Chinese poem of a great and sublime kind that is conceptually lofty and stylistically grand, but it also puts into relief, uncharacteristically, the aesthetic and cultural shadows of the long ago.

Guo's poetic-dramatic figuration of Qu begins with his 1920 verse drama "Xianglei" (One of the three verse dramas published in *Nüshen*). As the first murmur from the "dark cavern of the sources of things" (Wordsworth, "Essays upon Epitaphs" 79), Qu's "Yangzi River" soliloquy manifests in every sense the spirit of the "Romantic" and the "great." It typifies the modern figuration of the classical poet as one who is too great for his age and thus an ideal tragic hero. The sublimity of the poetic affect (Guo's earlier verse dramas are most often dramatized poetic lines) comes from the tension between Qu the hero's volcanic, explosive lines and the desperation of his historical-theatrical situation. The often quoted monologue in which the hero longs to fuse with the Yangtze River, which is the "source of" all "things" Chinese, and declares his own greatness—the poet as the creator par excellence—is saved from mere grandiosity by its staging against a background of historical and personal tragedy. The iconoclasm in Qu's declaration, which echoes the aspirations of May Fourth, coupled with the terror and desperation of the situation on stage, make probable the sublime ruse and the audience's proper response.

Guo has claimed that his poetical-historical dramas are the platform where "he dons the robe of the ancients to give vent to his own speech" (Guo, "*Qu Yuan* yanjiu" 34). "Though I have never actually compared myself to Goethe, I did liken myself to Qu Yuan. What is in *Xianglei* I wrote that year, is actually 'self-expression.' What Qu Yuan voiced there are completely my own feelings," he disclosed in "Shinian chuangzuo (Ten Years of Creation)" (69). The identification has certainly established Qu as the sublime origin of Guo's creative pursuit, and it places his own composition as one that is not only about the great poet but also in his tradition. Guo has also confessed that the germination of the verse drama is derived from songs "Madam Xiang" and "Sir Xiang" from Qu's *Jiu ge* (Nine Hymns), and it begins with the actual lines from *Lisao*. It is by no means coincidental, then, that Guo begins the erection of his cultural monument with Yuan Qu, and with him as the tragic poet in historical crisis. Just as *Lisao* has always been deemed the first poem in Chinese literary history to demonstrate propensities for the Romantic, it was also one in which the figuration of a poet first appeared. Qu's poetic ideal, reinterpreted, is sublime: the first part of the poem is about his pursuit of a "beautiful polity" and the second about its fantastic disillusionment. But more importantly, it is a poem concerned with the poet's self-figuration, in which Qu has figured himself as the ideal poet under duress. Guo's *Xianglei* starts in the same vein and infuses the ideal and crisis of his poetic object with the longings and "pathology" (as Guo refers to it) of Guo's own times. However, curiously and against the grain of the much accredited timely pursuit of "positive" Romanticism, Guo seems more taken with the poet under duress and the sublime terror of his situation rather than with the poet's fantasy of "beautiful polity."

When the curtain rises, Qu is no longer the favored courtier poet. He has been betrayed and in exile, and has learnt about the destruction of his beloved kingdom of Chu. Shrouded in black and lured by the love-death song of the two Dongting fairies, he drifts on the scene on the verge of madness: "Where, and what is this place? Misty, expansive and boundless! / What are the songs? Is it Death's summons to my spirit?" (Guo, *Xianglei* 1-2). Amid the vast expanse of water (which, with a sudden leap of moods and imagination, he later calls the tiny Dongting), the exiled poet is simply lost. He seems wary though enchanted by the terror of the boundless. Like the swan song of the fenghuang, his first deliverance is a lamentation about his state of being and a protest against the way of his world, where "all is dark, obscure," maddening and bordering on death: "Qu Yuan: Sister, you cannot blame me; you can only blame the foul and befuddled world we live in! They call me mad when I am sober, just as they call the phoenix chicken and unicorn ass. I am useless and helpless. . . . I can only be mad, mad, ha ha ha ha ha, mad! And mad! . . . Ah, ah, I am tired, I am apathetic! The endless long days, they show me this foul world from dawn to dusk, and everywhere they call me insane, insane" (Guo, *Xianglei* 14-15). Unlike the fenghuang's dirge, which begins in defiance and ends in regeneration, Qu's wailing at the beginning of Guo's play simply and more directly expresses a death wish: "Oh, disillusionment! Disillusionment! Welcome! Welcome! Now that all my hope is dashed, I am standing at the gate of despair, waiting for Death to open its door. Ah, ah! Me, I am going to the abyss of the great No! (Making as if to jump)" (17). In a letter to a fellow member of the Creation Society, Guo has actually diagnosed his precursor epic culture-hero's state of mind as a kind of pathology: "The title of my verse drama is *Xianglei*. It is the result of two whole days' labor at the end of last year, derived from a kind of pathological observation I did of Qu Yuan, which is not all together satisfactory . . . in my imagination there had occurred in Qu's mind some kind of pathological association, *pathologische Assoziationen* plus certain *manische* and *stereotypische Sprache*, and this is what formed my short drama" (J. Wang 170). At the end of his historical "*Qu Yuan* yanjiu (On *Qu Yuan*)," Guo also diagnoses Qu's psycho-emotional state, as seen in some of his poetry, as pathological (Guo, "Wode zuoshi jingguo" 144). What Guo names "pathological association" in his letter alludes to Qu's confusion of himself with the father of King Yu of Xia, an earlier tragic historical figure, in his soliloquy as demonstration of a kind of transgressive megalomania. But it also casts the ancient poet's passion and outbursts as maniacal and stereotypical. Interestingly, Qu the wronged, angry, and mad figure is also commemorated along the Yangzi River as a folk-hero (see Schneider). If Qu's heroism is figured as a gesture of excess, it is an excess bordering on madness and death. His sublime poetic ravings are presented throughout the play as eruptions and explosions against the world through his sister. This latter dramatic-poetic persona, the poet's comforting and loving woman, threatens both the hero's and the play's historical and poetic integrity in her very sympathetic gentleness. Because what she represents—a "beautiful femininity"—is perceived by the hero and the poet as the very name of compromise. Thus the death wish, coupled with the threat of madness, constantly pursued by Qu in his lamentation, becomes the only defense against the fulmination of feminine compromise.

Reconciling sublime rage and beautiful tears

The central stage the threat of the feminine occupies in Guo's figuration of Qu's sublime poetic and historical-personal redemption is by no means incidental. Ban Wang's study of the century-old history of the figuration of the modern Chinese sublime demonstrates that when the modern Chinese aestheticians tried to introduce the European sublime systematically and assimilate it to the Chinese aesthetic matrix, they foregrounded the implied gender assumptions. It also points out that the traditional European aesthetic discourse is emphatically engendered. Wang finds that in the modern Chinese refiguration, "the sublime leans either toward masculine power or toward the disturbing threats of the feminine," but long ago, Longinus had also figured his sublime affect on the shattering erotic experience bordering on death when he read Sappho (B. Wang 102, 114). In Guo's play, Qu's courtship of death is his refusal of any form of concession. Of all that is dark and menacing, Qu dreads most the prospect of "whoring," an act with which he accuses his sister of enticing him, and which would place her in the ranks of the most wretched of women and all that is wretched about them. Following his avowal to adhere to the originary greatness of the Yangzi River, and his protestation against the worldly conspiracy to identify him with the small and immediate, he expostulates: "Why, why do you look down upon me? Is it that you want me to be an accommodating harlot? . . . Can it be that I am only made of rouge and powder; I can only learn to be rouge and powder, to offer myself and make up to women? Oh, why do you look down upon me? I have always blood to shed, fire to spit, no matter where and thence, my only desire is to mount and gallop beyond! . . . How is it that even you cannot offer me any understanding, ah, I am only bestowed with misfortune! I cannot believe that I have a sister like this!" (*Xianglei* 18-19). Qu's invective is of course unfounded, for his accommodating and faithful sister does show understanding of both his greatness and the magnanimity of his aspiration: "I know an endless spring that longs to gush forth like the rivers immense and majestic always flows in your heart. I know that in your heart there are always burning embers ready to be kindled and burst like the volcanic mountain. But can't you see the Rivers Xiang and Yuan when they encounter the mighty Yangtze; they also learn to bend so that they can fuse into the expansive

Dongting. Even the volcanoes cannot choose to erupt often" (Guo, *Xianglei* 17-18). Her "gentle" difference, then, is more a difference of degrees. For her, the necessity of compromise is not only an art of survival but also an art to an end: the possibility of gathering oneself—the small and immediate—into the boundless Dongting Lake.

Here, the problem of reciprocity—the communication of feelings between characters—the very predicate of human correspondence, is not the lack of sympathetic identification on the part of Qu's sister as the "weaker subject," or as the audience of her brother's sublime play, even though it seems so to the desperately heroic actor and his succeeding playwright. What impedes the correspondence between actor and audience, hence the affect of the hero's sublime longing, and prevents the translation between beings and things, degrees, and kinds, is Guo and his poetic hero's ambivalence towards the category of the beautiful feminine. Critics invariably note the two strings in Guo's verse drama, that is, the propensity for both the sublime and the beautiful. Stylistically, Guo's verse drama is typically described as encompassing the opposite aesthetic ideals of "powerfully imposing (*xionghun*)," "fiercely passionate (*jilie*)" as well as "elusively suggestive (*hanxu*)" and "gracefully restrained (*wanyue*)." The fusion of the tragically sublime and the alluringly beautiful, the masculine and the feminine, is habitually hailed as what has created the layers of aesthetic complexity that constitute the success of the play's poetic and dramatic effect (see Long, *Zhongguo* 218-385). What the critics acclaim as successful and Guo himself deems "not all together satisfactory" about the play's aesthetic resolution may well stem from the interlacing and overlapping of two different legends in the play. If the appearance of Nüxu, Qu's misunderstanding and misunderstood sister, and her misplaced sympathy is simply a foil for Qu's despairing but nonetheless sublime presence, then the singing of Ehuang and Nüying, the two fairy lovers of King Shun, who followed him and drowned in the River Xiang and since became its goddesses, is its ambiguous but necessary structuring backdrop.

The play opens with the two fairies singing. Their song is full of sorrow and longing for their lover's return. Qu hears the song as a siren call, as the beckoning of Death, luring his soul on its homeward journey. Throughout the play, the plaintive, lingering song of the fairy lovers' drifts in at every opportune moment, interceding and underscoring Qu's heroic passion and his longing for ultimate return. Ehuang's and Nüying's songs are love songs. They sing of undying attachment, endless waiting and dried up tears. Their addressee, the "lover," is unspecified and uncertain, never more than a general "he." But Qu feels the call, though it is a summons the "weaker subjects"—his sister and the old boatman—cannot hear. For Qu the siren song holds a twofold attraction: in the song he sees himself as the long lost lover, an acknowledgement of his suffering and unrequited devotion; also, in identifying with the hero-king as the fairies' love object, he feels a reaffirmation of the terror of darkness, and therefore the sublimity of his own place and aspiration. Qu's sympathetic identification with the Xiang fairies' singing transforms their elusive tears from a shadowy backdrop to the center of the play: the singing figures as the structure and intimation of Qu's "pathological association" and the complexity of Guo's aesthetic pursuit.

One can understand the ambivalence and contrary implications of the relationship between Qu's sublime sentiments and the beautiful, feminine allure of the fairies as the Hegelian symbolic. This is often posited by mainstream Guo criticism, which traces the poet's fascination with symbols and its necessary suggestive ambiguity of meanings and emotions to the influence of Goethe (see J. Wang; Long; and M. Huang). Or, alternately, one can see the contrary threads of Guo's aesthetic tendencies as his Romantic partiality to the quest of the unrepresentable, the uncanny, and the limitless. While the latter reading may not be far amiss in characterizing Guo's general aesthetic schema, it fails to shed light on the immediate concern and particular implication of the figuration of Qu and the meaning and structure of his sentiments in relation to the river fairies' song. If Qu's dread is of compromise, which will undermine his ideal of epic heroism as well as the affect of his poetry, and if a death wish is the only defense against the prospect of compromise, then the temptation of yielding to the fairies' tearful and tender soul beckoning complicates the wish. Such a temptation compromises the refusal to compromise. If undying and unrequited love belongs to the realm of the sublime, feminine love itself is by no means unproblematic. The disruptive force of femininity is figured most prominently and of major concern throughout the genealogy of the modern Chinese sublime (see B. Wang). Behind the betrayal and persecution of Xiu Zheng, Qu's ex-patron admirer, a consort of the King of Chu who caused his banishment, Qu also finds undying and unrevealed love not only for himself but also for his poetry. In his vision, however, this treacherous love that leads to rage and betrayal is indistinguishable from the love of the Xiang fairies. Qu is altogether wary of the treachery of feminine love, which for him seems to lead to nothing less than whoring and threatens his very being in the world: "Qu Yuan: . . . It is true that I long to return! But, oh, but how can I stand the very transaction? Am I not the prodigal son of heaven? Am I not born ordained? . . . I, who am inspired and upright, how can I bear to apprentice myself to the whoring trade? My poetry, my poetry are my life! How can I offer my life, this ultimate and treasured life of mine, to be trampled by myself and other men?" (Guo, *Xianglei* 18-19).

In his attempt to figure Qu and his poetry as the very ideal of the sublime, Guo bestows upon them qualities that necessarily gesture toward the majestic, the limitless, and the beyond and stresses their qualitative difference, their incomparability. Compelled nonetheless to render such transcendent qualities translatable, which is requisite for any sympathetic identification, Guo simultaneously figures the classical poet's susceptibility to and his comparable need for understanding. He also prominently figures the solace of that tender, feminine embrace that beckons his hero's soul home. This is probably why Guo dramatizes Qu's fantasies and longings as pathological, and places the saneness of that pathology on the "higher" plane of less worldly ideals. The sublime affect of Qu's presence and his lines of passion thus seem both to depend on and are imperiled by the shadowy accompaniment of the feminine beautiful. It is at once the soul companion, the undying, unrelenting lover of the poet with his lofty ideals, and the beguiling peril of the compromising comfort of returning. And one should bear in mind that in the first half of *Lisao*, Qu had himself figured the Chu king as the ideal, the "fair one," and the licentious, maliciously insidious aristocracy as a flock of women. The attraction to the beautiful and fear of its treachery to the ideal of the sublime, seem to have passed down from the classical poet of original difference to his modern heir, whose ambition in refiguring the former as the epic culture-hero is aimed at a revolution that will result in a modern Chinese culture. If Guo's vision depends on the affect of a sublime play, in *Xianglei*, the poet's contrary impulses towards the sublime as well as the beautiful are not resolved. And this may have accounted for Guo's own complaint that the dramatic verse is "not all together satisfactory," even though his subsequent critics have lauded the complementary presence as an aesthetic "balance," a stylistic and affective achievement in itself.

Guo's play, for the moment, ends in tears. Immediately after Qu castigates his sister by steadfastly refusing any hint of poetic or personal compromise and reaffirming his ideal of aesthetic and historical sublimity, thereby reducing her to silent weeping, he again hears the soul-beckoning of the fairies:

> Singing from the water:
> The white clouds on the Jiuying Mountain gather and spread
> The rushing tides of the Dongting Lake ebb and flow.
> The sad mist in our hearts, oh!
> The teary waves in our eyes, oh!
> They will never dissolve!
> They will always flow!
>
> Qu Yuan: Ah, what mournful strains! It has even moved me to tears. Flow! Gush! The spring of my life! Once you stream forth, the fiery blaze engulfing my body and soul seems to be extinguished. I am feeling again the prime of my youth, as if afloat the Yangtze River in burning summer hazes. You the unbelievable invisible spring of soul, you my resurrector! Oh, my sister! Are you also crying? Have you also heard the plaintive song? (*Xianglei* 19-20)

What eventually extinguish the flame that burns the poet's soul, that makes him mad, terrible but sublime, and that constitutes the play's very gesture beyond are the fairies' feminine and beautiful tears. Their teary entreaty proves infectious and universally appealing: both Qu and his sister, and even the old boatman (even if he professes no comprehension) are moved to identical action—weeping. The act of being immersed in tears suddenly seems to Yuan Qu, the poet of sublime standing and epic ambition, no longer a threat of feminine weakness but recourse for rejuvenation. If the tears have washed away his fire of unyielding defiance, they have also cleansed him of his madness. Unlike the ending of "Nirvana of the Phoenix," where the male and female phoenixes redeem both themselves and the world with their lonely, heroic, and in the eyes of the mundane, futile defiance, the denouement of Guo's first refiguration of Qu as the poetic epic culture-hero comes as a reconciliation, although Qu and the "weaker subjects," his sister and the old boatman, have not come to a shared understanding of his sublime act, the ways of the world, and the meaning of "the plaintive song," they are nevertheless identically affected. What finally enables any semblance of sympathetic correspondence between the characters, and more importantly for Guo the poet-playwright, affective identification between Qu and the audience, is the shedding of tears: non-discriminating, all-embracing, all-cleansing tears. These tears may be Guo's dramatic ploy to let Qu, and therewith his sublime play, avoid the fate of the burning phoenixes scorned by the mundane multitude. Or perhaps it is the only possible ending since Guo both exalts his exemplary poetic predecessor's terrible but sublime state of being and figures it as something akin to a pathological state. Through Qu's final monologue, and in sharp contrast to the earlier Yangtze River soliloquy, Guo glorifies the affect of overflowing tears, both in the world of being and in the realm of poetry: "Qu Yuan: People who can shed tears are invariably good people. Poetry that causes tears is invariably good poetry. It is like this that poems affect deeply and dearly. Now, and only now I begin to understand the true value of a poetic vocation. You serene and exquisite melody, please sing and murmur on. I will dedicate to you my lotus crown" (*Xianglei* 20-21).

Qu's first exit from Guo's poetic career certainly reflects a change of strains as well as a change of heart. Or is this merely a poetic resolve of compromise? Actually, this is not the first or only time that Guo "frolic(ed) with the waves" ("Juan'er ji xu" 161) of beautiful feminine tears in his enlistment of classic origins as part of the project of modern cultural redemption. In her study of the folklore movement in the May Fourth cultural revolution, Haiyan Lee has noted that in Guo's free-verse rendition of the love songs in *Shijing* (The Book of Songs), his "version is entirely cast in the female voice" (Lee 57). He based his translation of the classic texts as archaeology of primordial folk feelings on the tears and lamentations of the often deserted heroines. And "much of the expansion—the 'translation' is almost three times the length of the original—is devoted to delineating feminine emotions and desires which point to a strong presence of female/romantic/modern subjectivity" (Lee 58). This, however, Lee also points out, is not so much indication of Guo's figuration of female agency, but rather for him "this is because millennia of cultural ossification have deeply buried the beautiful spirit of the ancient people or destroyed it beyond recognition. Only an archaeology as translation—transfiguring whatever is excavated—allowed him to retrieve that spirit in its true essence" (58). Feminine tears, then, embody the beautiful spirit of the primordial sources for Guo's project of a sublime cultural modernity that he has to invoke and enlist, even though they also unleash forces that he cannot always come to terms with. However, if tears are the only affective promise and resolution that Guo could summon for his first dramatization of the ideal classical poet as the original Chinese epic culture-hero, and all he could envision for the sublime vocation of poetry, he certainly does not stop at it. After two decades of settling for the composition of "serene" and "exquisite" "small wave" poems, his longing for the "volcanic" and the explosion of the heroic sublime descends upon him again, attacking him like a thunderstorm and hay fever (see Yan): "I have been expecting with all my heart that one day the seizure of real poetry will attack me again, that like a dormant volcano I will re-erupt. When that day comes I will eulogize the deeds of heroes in heroic tones" (Guo, "Wode zuoshi jingguo" 148). Not surprizingly, his renewed attempt to eulogize heroic deeds with heroic tones comes in the form of the five-act poetic-historical play *Qu Yuan* (January 1942).

The dramatic transformation of Guo's *Qu Yuan*

Both Guo and his critics account for this resurrected passion for the sublime ancient poet, and the resulting play's equally impassioned reception in the early 1940s as the culmination of the agitation and emotions of the times. The play was written, published and performed in the war-time capital of Chongqing during the "darkest" period of the War of Resistance against Japan, a period marked by a shared sense of impending national doom and often described in PRC accounts as one of political oppression and cultural censorship. Guo, in his preface to the Russian translation of his play, called this period a time of tragedy, just like the times of Qu: "I saw in front of me numberless tragedies of the times, big and small. . . . Progressive people all over China were suffering from the sense of rage. That is why I resurrected the anger of the times to the epoch of *Qu Yuan*. In other words, I have borrowed Qu Yuan's times to symbolize our own" (Guo, "Xu erwenyiben *Qu Yuan*" 158). As always, to don the robe of the ancients to express one's own longings and sentiments is to establish bonds—it both relocates the origin of a sublime tradition and places one in that original tradition. But this time however, it is also, ironically, a necessity—a consequence of censorship, part of the timely tragedy.

Xun Lu redefines tragedy of his times as "the display of the destruction of all that is invaluable in life" (Lu 192). Guo's second poetic-dramatic refiguration of Qu seems to concur with this, although, like his earlier eulogy to the nirvana of the Phoenix, it is a figuration of the terror of destruction as a sublime gesture. However, to cast Qu's story and times as tragic seems to strike a dissonant note in the paean to the progress of history championed by self-conscious Chinese modernists like Guo. It sets Qu's personal and national tragedy, his betrayal and the destruction of the kingdom of Chu, against the triumph of historical progress in the transition from the system of slavery to feudalism and the necessary unification of China. Guo discounts the tension by pointing out in his historical research (he is a known historian and archeologist) the contingency of history and insisting that *Qu Yuan*, like the earlier *Xianglei*, is lyrical rather than historical. His insistence on lyrical continuity reaffirms the centrality of the figuration of Qu in the establishment of a modern Chinese sublime. It also stresses that the concern of the modern figuration of Yuan Qu is not in the past, but rather in the present redress of the past. It is, literally, to don the robe of history to express one's own longings and sentiments, in particular the "anger of the times." Guo's fascination with Qu and his times is therefore not a representation of the ancient poet as an historical figure or a dramatization of historical events. His insistence on dramatic lyricism and an abstraction of Qu as the archetypal tragic figure makes it evident that his interest lies in the aesthetic value of history as tragic drama rather than history in and for itself. In his interest in history as drama, though, Guo does seek certain faithfulness, a faithfulness of "spirit" rather than detail (Yan 440). This faithfulness lies in the figuration of the spiritual and characteristic sublimity of Qu as an ideal hero, which are both historical and contemporary at the same time. For this reason, Guo concentrates on recovering the tragic qualities of Qu and foregrounds their possibility for ideal perfection against the background of the terrors of history, and on the aesthetic affect at the display of the ideal's destruction as a gesture beyond.

The new *Qu Yuan*, simultaneously lyrical and dramatic, is considered in modern Chinese literary history as the poetry-drama of sublimity par excellence. Apart from its claim and general reception as the resounding expression of the fury and terror of the times, the sublimity of the play is at least partly achieved by the playwright's new balancing act between his propensity for the sublime and the beautiful. The contrary tendencies in the earlier play have not so much disappeared as they have been restructured with the subsumption, or rather, translation of the beautiful into the sublime. The movement of the play, as it builds up toward the sublime moment, is a process of transfiguring the lyrical-beautiful into the dramatic-tragic, of rewriting a "noble" femininity while ridding it of its beguiling and erotic entrapment.

The play begins with Guo's translation of Qu's original poem "Ju Song (Ode to the Orange)," in which the fragrant and homely loveliness of the orange tree and its immobility are eulogized as an ideal for man.

> Oh glorious orange tree, with your splendid foliage.
> You grow in the south, steadfast and unflinching.
> With leaves green, flowers white, and thorns piercing.
> Oh, you lovely, full-bodied fruit!
> From verdant to golden, hues magnificent!
> But inside you are pure as snow, fragrant beyond comparison.
> Deep-rooted, you can withstand ice and thunder thick and fast.
> Resolute as nature endowed, you are an exemplar of a man of lofty ideals.
> (*Qu Yuan* 151-52)

In Qu's ode that begins Guo's play, the lofty ideal of man is embodied in the steadfast but domestic beauty of the southern orange. What stands out in the playwright's new figuration, however, is not only the fusion of the sublime aspiration of man, and local, homely, "full-bodied" beauty, but also the shift in the addressee of the poem. In the play, the master poet Qu first bestows his longing and hope for a deep-rooted, unflinching loftiness of man upon his young apprentice and fellow poet Yu Song by addressing the ode to him. Song however, finds the dedication flattering but daunting. By imposing his noble conviction upon his chosen disciple, Qu sets up the interpretation of the ode as an educational project, an important part in his cultural monument building. To comprehend the gravity of Qu's imposing aspiration,

Yu Song, the addressee, like the audience of the play, needs further elaboration. Qu explains to his pupil that his partiality to the orange as an outstanding metaphor for human nobility is because it is at once common and uniquely uncompromising. Its beauty is modest and unassuming: "However if you thus declare they are . . . there merely to please, without backbone of character or integrity, you are far mistaken . . . Look all around them; aren't they covered by prickly thorns? (Pointing to the tree on stage) They are inviolable and resilient" (*Qu Yuan* 154). The qualities Qu attributes to the orange are not unlike the qualities Guo attributes to him as the exiled poet in *Xianglei*, namely, a thorny and uncompromising immobility.

However as sung in the new ode this time and in its further elaboration, these qualities are manifested in marriage to a purified, modest, and homely beauty, a beauty pleasing but devoid of any beguiling potential, erotic or otherwise. Qu as well as Guo's message here is again a dread of and a warning against whoring, which is feared as the ultimate betrayal to their sublime mission, as Qu painstakingly explains to Yu Song: "When it comes to the moment of crisis, of ultimate test, you will not compromise or drift along. You have to learn from the ancient sage Boyi who starved himself on top of the Shouyang Mountain. One should rather starve than whore. I know you'll understand me?" (*Qu Yuan* 155). Besides eulogizing the pure and uncompromising beauty of the orange, Qu, like his modern day heir, also feels the need for the lineage of traceable epic culture-heroes and the exemplar of original champions for his sublime cause. Thus Act I of the play becomes an extended scene of historical, poetic and heroic education, in which Qu elaborates on the historical and cultural meaning of the martyrdom of Boyi, the ancient man of uncompromising nobility. And where he also elaborates on the nature of his new poetry as exemplified by "The Ode to the Orange," in which he attempts to create a pure, artless, and noble beauty and rid it of any trace of slavish conventional elegance. This, he claims, is accomplished by learning from the ballads and speeches of the "commoners" and "children."

What impedes and complicates Qu's first sublime and educational act is that his chosen disciple, Yu Song, although bright and compliant to his mentor's aspirations, turns out to be his ultimate betrayer. At the moment of crisis, by choosing to leave his master and join his powerful enemies (it also turns out that he had long looked forward to reaching beyond and replacing him), Song proves himself the antithesis of the ideal man, the very incarnation of guile and compromise. Qu's panegyric and its follow-up lesson for Song would look like nothing more than self-irony and would degenerate into the merely absurd if not for Chanjuan's timely entrance on the scene. Chanjuan, Qu's hitherto neglected young maidservant, suddenly takes on dimensions of gigantic proportion in the drama. Only then does the audience come to realize that all along she would be a better object for Qu's idealization and recipient of his pedagogical project, as she is visibly the personification of Qu's ideals: humble, pure, and beautiful but artless while at the same time unfalteringly uncompromising in her dedication. Qu's failure to recognize the true object upon which to bestow his vision certainly sows seeds of doubt about his judgment. Then again, Chanjuan is only his young maidservant, outside his world of poetry and not yet even a woman. While anxious to pass on the monument of his poetic ideal to his chosen cultural heir, the beautiful young man-poet, Qu's attraction to the feminine is not unlike what was depicted earlier in *Xianglei*. That is, he is incapable of resisting the lure of the erotic and the beguiling, masquerading as female worship and tenderness. In fact, this is what leads to his entrapment and undoing by Queen Nan (Xiu Zheng), the artful and immoral Queen of Chu, a finality that not only causes his personal downfall but also the destruction of the kingdom of Chu.

Chanjuan's ascendance to dramatic importance occurs when she throws herself onto center stage at the moment of crisis. She has to assert herself to become his sole defender, an act that transforms her common humility to what is akin to the sublime: "Chanjuan: . . . My master is the beam of the kingdom of Chu, between heaven and earth he is its indomitable pillar . . . I am a girl from the common stock, I am only my master's handmaiden. My calling in life is to serve my master, to sweep, dust, and tidy up the hall and the courtyard. I can neither compose poetry nor chant a lofty song. I cannot discourse on the rise and fall of the State. But I for one know that the life and death of my master is the life and death of Chu, for he is nothing less than its very soul. If you destroy him, you destroy our beloved kingdom" (*Qu Yuan* 216-17). The rest of the play seems a fulfillment of her prophecy, thereby making her an unwitting, naive seer of a higher truth. Chanjuan's transposition from inconsequential girlhood to the handmaiden of a sublime course represents the subsuming of guileless, uneroticized femininity to the mastery of the manly and the great. It is a process that involves self-sacrifice as agency. Chanjuan is able to offer herself, despite her inconsequentiality and humble origin, by thrusting herself at the altar of her master's ideal of uncompromising martyrdom; by making herself the embodiment of his aspirations and their sacrificial lamb in the flesh. As the handmaiden to her master's course, she has proven herself more than immovable. She refused to be tempted by either Song's guile or Prince Lan's threat when she was imprisoned for defending Qu. She convinces Song that she is even more obstinate in her single-minded devotion than her mentor-master, who, because of his very humanity and manliness, cannot rid himself of all the worldly trappings. Thus Chanjuan, in her uncontaminated, uneroticized, and therefore unthreatening femininity, in her relentlessly uncompromising but totally sympathetic dedication, replaces Song and completes the other complimentary theme of the beautiful in Qu's ideal and Guo's play. Her subsumption into the figuration of her master as the sublime poet is complete: she literally dies for him by drinking the poisoned wine intended for him: "But I . . . I am very happy . . . very happy! [Showing signs of exhilaration] That I can go instead of my master, to save your life. I am blithe beyond words! . . . Sir, I am the daughter of a commoner . . . I love our kingdom, so I cannot not love you . . . Today I dedicate my humble life to the preservation of your noble existence. Oh sir, I am fortunate indeed! . . . Indeed! . . . I am happy beyond words!" (*Qu Yuan* 263).

In the tribute to Guo's unflinching patriotism (as the play is generally regarded as a potent part in the anti-Japanese war effort), as symbolized by Chanjuan's unquestioning and unquestionable loyalty to her master and their shared undying loyalty to the kingdom of Chu, it is strange that neither the progressively minded nor the class-conscious critics minded the ambiguity of Guo's figuration of the master-handmaiden relationship, as this is what underscores the nature of her devotion and their immovable but rather questionable (if only according to the logic of historical progress) loyalty to the feudal kingdom of Chu. It is also rather hard not to notice that in Guo's play, Chanjuan's beautiful sacrifice not only supplements Qu's thundering sublime but also proves part of its founding structure. It is her single-handed and single-minded dedication that brings about the play's sublime ending, allowing Qu both the proximity to and a narrow escape from death and all that is dark and threatening, which is the requisite of any sublime play. It also redeems Qu's ideal from being a mere fit of madness. Finally, somewhat belatedly, Qu does realize his late maid's full worth and understands that she is the only soul with whom he can achieve true sympathetic identification. He therefore recasts their relationship as that of mentor-pupil, father-daughter, instead of master and servant: "She is someone who truly respects me, she looks up to me as her father, her teacher. In her eyes I am more important than her life. [Moment of silence] She is the one who comforts me most. And I also regard her as my own daughter, my most beloved pupil" (*Qu Yuan* 261). Consoled by her final dedication, her unquestioning sacrifice, which alone constitutes the confirmation of his sublime poetic and historical ideal, Qu rededicates his "Ode to the Orange" to her: "Chanjuan, you are the one who truly deserves this. Oh, if I had only known, my 'Ode to the Orange' is and has always been a eulogy to you" (265). Qu's rededication, as elegy to his handmaiden's sacrifice, redeems the ode for its uncompromising ideal and reestablishes the possibility of sympathetic identification in the cause of the sublime. It is accomplished by Guo's shift of the addressee of Qu's ode, a process in which the lyrical-beautiful is made tragic-noble, and rid of the beguiling and artful, thus translatable to the sublime.

Guo's poetic resolution in "Leidian Song (Thunderstorm Monologue)"

The most sublime passage in Guo's play is not the "Ode to the Orange" as embodiment of Qu's poetic and human ideal but the "Leidian Song (Thunderstorm Monologue)" of the last act. As the most dramatic and explosive eruption of Qu's righteous rage and Guo's "timely' sentiments, the monologue is structured and functions as the climax of the play. It brings about the dramatic denouement, and thus justifiably considered the dramatic and lyrical peak of the play. This is only true, however, if one accepts the suggestion that the movement of the play is the resurrection and development of the theme of the "anger of the times." In this sense, act 1 becomes the laying out of the stormy times against which we witness Qu's attempt to erect the monument of an uncompromising human ideal. Acts 2, 3, and 4 are the gradual display of the destruction of Qu as poet and righteous politician, who cherishes and aspires to and thus symbolizes "all that is invaluable in life." These three acts are a display of all that is dark, obscure and terrible—prerequisites for the attainment of the sublime. The tragedy that unfolds is one in which Qu is betrayed and sacrificed by the intrigue and treason of his fellow courtier and Queen Nan, a betrayal that shatters Qu's dream of a "beautiful polity" and leads to his own destruction and that of his beloved kingdom of Chu. It is also a betrayal that by its very caprice, guile and treachery actually casts Qu as the embodiment of his own noble, relentlessly uncompromising, and sublime ideal. In other words, through Guo's dramatic depiction of the destruction of all that is invaluable in life, that is, all that Qu aspires to and stands for, Qu becomes "the great sublime he draws."

The unfolding of Qu's tragedy is thus made analogous to the tragedy and terror of Guo's times. Qu's betrayal and the national crisis of the besieged Chu, his explosive expression of pain and wrath, are where the audience hears the poet's rage over his personal wrongs, but more emphatically, his protest against the evil that has befallen his country, and his declaration of an undying, unequivocal loyalty to his endangered kingdom: "Oh, Queen Nan! I'd never imagine that you would wrong me in such foul scheme! Heaven above, and earth below, ancient kings and old sages, all my ancestors and fathers, what you've wronged is not me, but you yourself, our king and kingdom of Chu, our dominion majestic and sacred!" (*Qu Yuan* 189). Qu's unequivocal identification with "our dominion majestic and sacred," as the heir apparent and aspiring future father of its "ancient kings" and "old sages," "ancestors and fathers," is received immediately by Guo's critics and the audience as an historical and transcendental patriotism whose continuity links his sentiments with their very own "anger of the times." The rage of the classical poet, in this sense, is not only identifiable with but also becomes a direct expression of the sentiments of the times as well as the nation. The "Thunderstorm Monologue," the acknowledged passage great and sublime is thus situated historically and set up dramatically as the culmination of the rage of the times.

The monologue, like Guo's "tidal wave" poems in *Nüschen*, is a turbulent and "volcanic eruption." It erupts at "the darkest moment of the darkest times," of the poet's overflowing sentiments and feelings with their attendant phantasmagoric imagination, their resounding tone, and cataclysmic expressions. As an ode to the savage turbulence of one of nature's mighty terrors: the flash and lightening of the thunderstorm, the blast of roaring winds, its imagery of the sound and fury of nature is infused with the wrath and vehemence of the poet:

> Qu Yuan: [To the wind and thunder] Wind! You roar! You blast! You keep on roaring with all your might! In times of Cimmerian darkness, when everything is sleeping, is dead, or sunken in nightmares, it is time you roar in rage, roar in thundering blast and rage! . . . Though your blare cannot awaken them from their slumbering dream, your fury resurrect the dead; you cannot blow away the darkness that is heavier than the iron cast before our eyes, but you can at least carry away some smothering dust, puff away the stray sand, stir the flowers, grass, and trees. You can make the Dongting Lake, the Yangtze River, and the rolling waters of the East Sea heave and surge, heave and surge like you in roaring waves! . . . Oh lightening, how I

revere and worship your brightness . . . I know that fire is your essence, you, the greatest in the universe, oh, fire! You are beyond the horizon, you are in front of my very eyes, and you are everywhere around me. I know you are the life of the world, you are the life of me, and you are I! My blazing, burning life, the wrath in me that is exploding, can it be true that it will no longer burst forth with light? (*Qu Yuan* 253-54; unless indicated otherwise, all translations are mine)

Qu's celebration of the mighty forces of nature and the expression of his longing to traverse with them to the sublime beyond dwells more on a sense of fusion with nature than on the desire for self-expansion, as compared to *Xianglei*. In his enumeration of the different faculties of power in nature, the blasting wind can only "blow away some smothering dust, puff away the stray sand;" the roaring thunder can temporarily carry the poet to the realm of transcendence; the flashing lightening is capable of no more than slashing open the darkness of the moment. However, together the disparate phenomena constitute nature's mighty power and generate "the boundless fire of wrath:" a fire that will blaze away all that is dark and evil, and a fire of righteous destruction. Thus the dominant imagery of the passage is not made up of any singular phenomenon of nature, though its individual power is enumerated and eulogized. It is made up of the sum total of its sense of might, of a boundlessness that only comes from the amalgamation of its tempestuous, erupting motions. Here the poet is no longer afraid of being identified with the small Dongting Lake, because its raging tide links it to the Yangtze River and flows all the way to the East Sea. Here nature in Qu's reevocation and Guo's reimagination, in its dark, obscure and all embracing disruptive power, is vast and boundless. The image of the bound and boundless might of nature which Qu celebrates and identifies with here may well be symbolic of the corresponding, sympathetically identifiable sentiments—the sense of terror and rage, of the "people" and the "times." What it evokes and venerates is the correspondence between and the infusion of the poet's passion and historical sentiments with the turbulent expression of a vast, binding and almighty nature. It is from such tempestuous, shifting, disruptive but nonetheless coalescent images and motions that the passage derives its affective power.

However, it is the destructive force and its terror that each of the natural phenomena unleashes that structures and accentuates the lyrical and the dramatic power of the passage. In Qu's cosmology, the greatest essence of universe is fire, an angry, all-consuming fire. And such raging fire of boundless destruction is not only the central image of the explosive monologue but also its link to the other devastating and sublime poems such as the "Nirvana of the Phoenix," though the "Thunderstorm Monologue" itself promises no sublime beyond in its passion and evocation of destruction:

Oh, the greatest poems in the universe! You, the wind, thunder, and lightening. You roar in darkness . . . You the greatest artists, express with all your might, and vent your endless rage, to explode, to blast away the dim, melancholy and insidious universe! . . . Oh, lightening! You the most incisive sword of the universe! . . . You strike, strike and strike! Split the darkness as hard as iron, strike, strike and strike! . . . Explode, my body and soul! Blow up, the whole world! Let the naked fire roll, like the wind, like the sea, roll, let all shapes, all form, all filth, scorch, burn, to ashes and dust! Let the flame blaze away all that is dark and evil! . . . Oh, blow, you wind! Roar, you thunder! Strike, you lightening! Blaze away all that is sleeping in darkness, destruction, destruction, and destruction! (*Qu Yuan* 254-57)

Like the incineration of the phoenixes in the "Nirvana," Qu's invocation of destruction here is all inclusive and all consuming. But unlike it, it does not promise resurrection or any sense of redemption. Even the celebration of the great universal essence—fire, which was habitually associated in *The Goddess* with brightness and regeneration, here no longer offers glimpses of transcendence. Guo's summons of the raging fire, like his elicitation of the roaring thunder and blasting wind, is for its destructive power, for its nondiscriminating savage incineration. The lasting imagery in the bombarding "Monologue" is darkness heavier than iron and everything sleeping in nightmarish stillness, and the mad, blazing raging of a thunderstorm and lightening, and a fire that clearly calls forth associations of an inferno and hell fire. It is truly dark, obscure, and terrible, but stops short of transforming into the sublime. The outburst is saved from a mere fit of madness only by the translation and rededication of the beautiful. It is made sublime at the end of the play only by subsuming the sacrifice of Chanjuan, which redeemed the "Ode to the Orange" as the truly noble human ideal, and which in turn reframes and supplements the "Monologue" in realizing its potential for the sublime.

By highlighting Guo's wrath as the expression of the "anger of the times," his critics could no longer categorize the lyrical eruption of the "Monologue" as an exposition of a "positive Romanticism." Although it seems a direct demonstration of the Kantian dynamic sublime, whose affective power dwells upon the motion of the might in nature, and contains all the elements of the Burkean prerequisites for the dark, obscure, and terrible, it suggests neither mastery nor transcendence. The might in nature and the poet's wrath stay at the limit of the terrible, which might have heightened the tension of the dramatic conflict but do not bring about its affective denouement—it cannot rescue the passage from appearing a mere outburst of madness. In other words, it does not redeem the ancient poet's passion from the "pathology" ascribed to it in the earlier *Xianglei*. Guo's sublime aspiration is realized only at the end of the play through the rededication of the "Ode to the Orange," which restored the wrath of the poet from pathological to ideal and epic dimensions. The rededication of the ode to Chanjuan after her sacrifice and Qu's narrow escape, and with him his historical and poetic ideal, is a process of purification and transformation. Guo himself has suggested that Chan for him symbolizes a certain exquisite nostalgia, but he is certainly understating the case ("Wozenyang xie *Qu Yuan*" 308-09; "*Qu Yuan* yu *Lierwang*" 317). Once Chan's life is understood as symbolic, both the reiteration of the "Ode" as dedication to her as well as the ending of the play take on added meaning. The ode's imagery poeticizes and consecrates her humble being to a pure embodiment of beauty. Chanjuan becomes the personification of the "Ode" and rescues the latter half of the play—the more direct expression of exaltation of the poet's lofty longing and aspiration—from fantasy. Only after her consecration as referent to the poem, is its 'human' dimension restored. Chan, in this sense, has become truly "the soul of the poem," the "symbol" of Qu's Ode.

The appearance of the "Thunderstorm Monologue" and the "Ode to the Orange" in the same act, as contrary expressions of Guo's pursuit of the aesthetic ideals of the sublime and the beautiful, may not have worked for Guo's original intention. He had declared in his 28 March 1942 letter to friend and fellow poet Chi Xu that "*Qu Yuan* is a lyrical play. But it is sublime, not beautiful" ("*Qu Yuan* yu *Lierwang*" 316) immediately upon its production. But this juxtaposition actually endows it with a needed sense of equanimity. The translation of the lyrical-beautiful into the noble-tragic, and its reframing and subsumption into the sublime, restores Qu's poetic wrath to its ideal quality and corroborates it with the passions of history and the "anger of the times." Thus it rescues such dramatic outburst from the threat of the mere bathos of personal pathology. When Qu holds Chanjuan's body and rededicates the "Ode to the Orange" to her as a sacrificial offering, "flames of wrath rekindle in his eyes," just like the raging fire that destroys the East Imperial Temple. And so is the poet's "thunder and storm" character infused through the corresponding fire with the spirit of the Orange. Chanjuan's body is incinerated together with the manuscript of the "Ode" in the same all-consuming fire, transcending and becoming the cleansed and redeeming essence of beauty in the flame. And so does Yuan Qu the epic poet's sublime poetical and historical spirit. However, the sublime rendered in this process of translation and transformation, and in the refiguration of Qu as the original epic culture hero, is neither the Kantian mastery nor the moment beyond. Though it is realized through the evocation of nature's might. Instead, the process is an amalgamation of the movement of unlimitation on the border of the limit, and of the identification, the transfusion between things and beings, subject and object after the moment of awful encounter. In other words, Guo's transformation of what is arguably a modern Chinese sublime (for a comprensive treatment of the subject, see K. Wong), comes about as a consequence of his aesthetic and cultural sojourn elsewhere: his translation of the Romantic sublime, and his unacknowledged journey back to his own past, such as the great originary poetic fathers from Qu to Bai Li. Guo's refiguration of Qu literally hinges upon the limit—he declared later that the significance of reevoking the classic poet is that the latter had been pushed by the forces of evil to the very limit of madness and had striven to maintain a certain dignified equilibrium. And such a precarious position of being perpetually on a cliff, for the poet himself, is not only a moment of a terrible historical situation but also a conscious, even ideal, state of being, if not as an historical figure at least as a dramatic persona. Just as Qu told his warden in the play, the ultimate state of being human is to be "both sacred and mad, or as mad as sacred." The poet refigured in such a state is on the one hand forever in the near pathological condition of extreme stimulation and agitation, thus feeling, thinking and behaving like one possessed by madness; on the other, he is in saintly control of his passion, all the time clinging to and fueling it with an almost exaggerated sense of reality, thus imbuing the overflow of pathos with a historically sanctified purpose, channeling it to a greater end. It is because Qu the driven poet is always on the verge of the limit that he is able to drift between, to transfuse himself with, the "thunder and storm;" to identify with other forces of nature's might, which in turn restores his project to sublimity by a totaling that swallows up the lesser things. Paradoxically, it is Guo's sojourns elsewhere—his espousal and translation of the movement of unlimitation, his uncontrollable passion for destruction for the sake of a revolutionary modernity—that has occasioned and enabled a return to, a reformation of an originary but unwanted past. This is probably the only way to resolve the dilemma between his aspirations for the erection of a savage, unrelenting, translated Chinese sublime and its corresponding need for sympathetic identification. Or is it again a resolve of poetic and historical compromise?

Guo's project of a sublime poetics thus indeed unleashes the original aspirations and burdens of the Romantic sublime, in that it fully displays the possibilities and limitations of the modern "aesthetic reprieve" of history. If Wordsworth ends with suspensions and beginnings that point to something ever more about to be, and imagines historical redirection by weaving his "spots of time" between nature and culture, texts and revolution, Guo tries to resolve his poetic and cultural dilemma by supplementing and transfiguring "pathos" and "the spirit of the times," beautiful tears and sublime terror, tradition and modernity. And at the center of their negotiation of a poetic modernity lies the Burkean establishment of correspondence as the principle of the modern sublime. The modern poet figured as such seems indeed an original translator. And like the figure of the Longinian sublime, he scatters and lifts up in an endless movement to begin again imaginatively both his poetry and with it our shared modern history.

Conclusion

The modern refiguration of the aesthetics of the sublime—which propagates in equal measures the cognition and feelings for greatness and ferocity—is indeed a "historical aestheticism" with manifest cultural ambitions. It was emphatically so in the transformation of the Romantic sublime as a cultural reaction to modern history from eighteenth- to nineteenth-century Europe to early twentieth-century China. While the European and the Chinese transformations are different in geo-cultural interests and traditions of precedents, they are motivated similarly by a shared modern history with its attendant sense of crisis. A critical study of aesthetic treaties and literary texts as diverse as Burke's *Inquiry into the Origins of Our Ideas of the Sublime and Beautiful*, Wordsworth's *Prelude*, and Guo's experimental poem "Fenghuang Niepan (Nirvana of the Phoenix)" and verse drama *Qu Yuan* in their historical and comparative contexts show that these modern aesthetic practices are a deliberate hyperbolization of literary agency. Such an agency is in turn constructed imaginatively and affectively as a means to redress different cultures' traumatic encounter with modernity. And this comparative commensurability is historically aesthetic in the sense that both the earlier European reformulation of the sublime and its later Chinese transformation are movements dependent on the historical situation at the moments of their figuration, as well as on the excessive and capacious nature of the sublime as an aesthetic property.

Nancy defines the sublime in philosophical terms as an aesthetics of movement and this movement of unlimitation is not concerned with a potential infinity or a progression without end, but an act that signals new formations (37). Although for Nancy this aesthetic gesture of offering something new alongside the border of limit is a motif with self-generating and self-vexing properties within modern European aesthetical philosophy, it is nonetheless a structural construction that promises historical developments. In this sense it continues in post-Kantian terms both Kant's and Burke's characterization of the sublime in their respective philosophical and historical projects. That is, the sublime is a cognitive as well as an affective effort in relation to the sense of limit. It is a historical-aesthetic gesture that stresses a striving movement and builds on the sentiment of the limit. For Kant, the sublime offering—mounting the abyss—is the act of freedom in thought. For Burke, it is the motion of

Conclusion

possibilities for refiguring both the distinction and correspondence between things, human beings and feelings, hence the possibilities of history. And for Wordsworth, it helps "history" to "rise once more" imaginatively and poetically at a moment of historical and literary impass.

While terror is at the centre of the construction of the sublime sentiment, its propencity for excess, that is, the "flash" that scatters and lifts up as Longinus elaborated long ago, promises the structural possibility of suspension and consequitivity. As we can see the rise of history is both the result and constituting part of Wordsworth's literary modernity. The relation between its possibility and the redemptive sublimity of poetic power is a process of translation from moments (of poetic resuolution) to consecutivity (history), and from beginnings to ends. Thus the modus operandi of the modern sublime is an aesthetic structure and an imaginative agency to enable fresh historical beginnings at moments of cultural crisis. This is how and why the sublime came to be the central aesthetic-philosophical, poetic and literary property in the building up of a cultural modernity from late eighteenth- into mid-nineteenth-century Europe. In a simultaneous celebration of and desire to guard the disruptive, it typifies the historical direction of the aesthetic turn which Romanticism is often associated with. For all their conceptual and methodological differences, the sublime's leading theorists and practitioners have nevertheless espoused the kind of cultural avant-guardism that Schiller spells out for historical redirection. The sublime, as the aesthetic construction that preoccupies them in their encounter with a distraught modernity, is indeed a movement of unlimitation that sets up its own legislative function in the act of crossing over and passing on.

One can conclude that the modern sublime in its eighteenth- and early nineteenth-century European formulation is built on its aesthetical-structural possibilities. They are seen as the cornerstones of a new cultural imagination. This Romantic construction of the sublime is in turn stressed as a capacious aesthetic property that can lend itself to redress the modern cultural and historical crisis. It is refigured as an aesthetics of disruption and at the same time a grounding movement by which historically ambitious philosophers, aesthets, and poets can come face-to-face with and rectify the terrors of modernity: from colonial to revolutionary violence and to the radical reordering of human society and perception. Because of these aethetical-historical promises, the sublime is also transformed and invoked as the timely spirit of a new Chinese poetics. This transformation is similarly predicated on the disruptive as well as exemplary potential of the sublime as an aesthetic structure. Its choice in early twentieth-century China highlights the nature of cultural translation as the act of making transcultural equivalences, foregrounding sympathy, judgement, and precondition. It calls emphatic attention to comparable historical anxieties and needs at related but differently configured modern moments. Guo, as an exemplary modern Chinese poet, was certainly inspired by many a poetic and cultural figure from Anglo-America to India and Japan, but what he was inspired with is not any discernable "parallel lines" but a translatable aesthetic and poetic spirit, underwritten and motivated by his and their historical cultural situations. This translatable spirit led him to rediscover his own poetic and historical tradition although his declared end is to recreate a modern Chinese poetry through an affectively as well as formally revolutionized poetics.

The Romantic sublime is transformed as the timely spirit of a terrible but necessary Chinese cultural modernity because it captures the affective and perceptual ferocity of modern history; and because it offers promises of beginnings in its propensity for excess. The preoccupation with the sublime in the modern Chinese poetic revolution owes as much to its aesthetic protocol, with attendant ethical and political implications, as to the terrible modernity (at least in the eyes of the aesthete-poets) as its historical grounding. With these preconditions, the sublime is refigured as a passage that allows both disruption and continuity with the fear of, as well as fascination with, terror and destruction at its center. The transformation and practice of a Romantic poetics of the sublime in early twentieth-century China begins with a "crash" that aims to "drag to earth" not only its own tradition but also the crisis-ridden modern world, figured by Guo and celebrated by his fellow New Culturalists in the poetic abandon of the "Nirvana of the Phoenix." It also consigns "the otherness of things" in the original of the cultural translation into "quiet being" (Wordsworth, *Nutting* 43-48) through processes of historically motivated eclectic appropriation and reinvention. Influences are thus but misnomers for sources and resources historically necessitated and limited but nonetheless at one's disposal at a cost.

Guo's transformation of a sublime poetics indeed unleashes the original aspirations and burdens of the Romantic sublime, in that it fully displays the possibilities and limitations of the modern "aesthetic reprieve" of history. If Wordsworth ends with halting beginnings that point to something ever more about to be, and imagines historical redirection by weaving poetic resolutions and passages between nature and culture, texts and revolution, Guo tries to resolve his poetic and cultural dilemma by supplementing and transfiguring "pathos" and "the spirit of the times," beautiful tears and sublime terror, tradition and modernity. For this he needs the liminal figure of the originally (the first ever named) great Chinese poet Yuan Qu, whose exemplary poetic power is nonetheless conversant with the spirit of Guo's times, as both the ground and denouement for his sublime modern poetics and historical vision. As Qu, his life, poetry and death (suicide), has always symbolized the aesthetic intervention of history writ large. Guo hyperbolized Qu's agency and imbued it with the roaring passions of his own times, highlighting the possibility of poetic greatness and ferocity. At the center of Guo's (just as Wordsworth's) negotiation of a poetic modernity, lies the Burkean establishment of correspondence as the principle of the sublime. The modern poet figured as such seems indeed an original translator. And like the figure of the Longinian sublime, he scatters and lifts up in an endless movement to begin again imaginatively both his poetry and with it our shared modern history. But Guo stops right before Qu's actual (recorded) suicide, which had made him an epic culture hero in both Chinese intellectual history and folklore in the first place, and ends instead with the latter's narrow escape from madness and death as the most sublime moment in his own modern play. One might argue that this is a successfully poetically orchestrated denouement, which resolves historical tragedies into aesthetically and affectively uplifting ends, stressing the sublimity of poetry composed in proximity to extremities in historical and personal situations. But by the same token, is Guo and his fellow New Culturalists' construction of a Chinese poetic and cultural modernity but a narrow escape from the traumas of their times? Their attempts to figure an ideal poetic and cultural sublimity in historical crisis a traumatic choice? If the Romantic sublime allows the English (pre-)Romanticists and Chinese modern poets to reconstruct history from primeval ground by imagination, thus allowing them a new ideal role for aesthetic and literary culture, this aesthetic historical ambition also persists in the melancholy and destruction of the sublime's excess.

Works Cited

Abrams, M.H. *The Mirror and the Lamp.* Oxford: Oxford UP, 1953.
Abrams, M.H. *Natural Supernaturalism: Tradition and Revolution in Romantic Literature.* New York: Norton, 1971.
Arac, Jonathan. *Critical Genealogies: Historical Situations for Postmodern Literary Studies.* New York: Columbia UP, 1989.
Aristotle, Horace, and Longinus. *Classical Literary Criticism.* Trans. T.S. Dorsch. New York: Penguin, 1965.
Averill, James H. *Wordsworth and the Poetry of Human Suffering.* Ithaca: Cornell UP, 1980.
Benjamin, Walter. "Thesis on the Philosophy of History." *Illuminations.* Trans. Harry Zohn. New York: Schocken Books, 1969. 253-64.
Bernstein, J.M. *The Fate of Art: Aesthetic Alienation from Kant to Derrida and Adorno.* University Park: The Pennsylvania State UP, 1992.
Bersani, Leo. *The Culture of Redemption.* Cambridge: Harvard UP, 1990.
Bian, Zhilin. "The Development of China's 'New Poetry' and the Influence from the West." *Chinese Literature: Essays, Articles, Reviews* 4.1 (1982): 152-57.
Blakemore, Steven, ed. *Burke and the French Revolution: Bicentennial Essays.* Athens: The U of Georgia P, 1992.
Bloom, Harold, ed. *Poets of Sensibility and the Sublime.* New York: Chelsea House, 1986.
Bourke, Richard. *Romantic Discourse and Political Modernity: Wordsworth, the Intellectual and Cultural Critique.* New York: St. Martin's, 1993.
Bové, Paul A. *Mastering Discourse: The Politics of Intellectual Culture*, Durham: Duke UP, 1992.
Brinkley, Robert, and Keith Hanley, eds. *Romantic Revisions.* Cambridge: Cambridge UP, 1992.
Bromwich, David. *A Choice of Inheritance: Self and Community from Edmund Burke to Robert Frost.* Cambridge: Harvard UP, 1989.
Bromwich, David. *Hazlitt, the Mind of a Critic.* New York: Oxford UP, 1983.
Burke, Edmund. "To the Earl of Charlemont, 9 August 1789." *The Correspondence of Edmund Burke.* Vol. 6. Ed. A. Cobban and R.A. Smith. Cambridge: Cambridge UP, 1967. 9-12.
Burke, Edmund. "To Lord Loughborough, 27 January 1793." The Correspondence of Edmund Burke. Vol. 7. Ed. A. Cobban and R.A. Smith. Cambridge: Cambridge UP, 1967. 344-45.

Burke, Edmund. *A Philosophical Enquiry into the Origin of Our Ideas of the Sublime and Beautiful*. Ed. James T. Boulton. Oxford: Basil Blackwell, 1987.

Burke, Edmund. *Reflections on the Revolution in France*. Indianapolis: Hackett, 1987.

Butler, Marilyn. *Romantics, Rebels and Reactionaries: English Literature and Its Background 1760-1830*. Oxford: Oxford UP, 1981.

Carlyle, Thomas. *On Heroes, Hero-Worship, and the Heroic in History*. Ed. Murray Baumgarten. Berkeley: U of California P, 1993.

Castle, Terry. *The Female Thermometer: Eighteenth-Century Culture and the Invention of the Uncanny*. Oxford: Oxford UP, 1995.

Chandler, James K. *England in 1819*. Chicago: U of Chicago P, 1998.

Chandler, James K. *Wordsworth's Second Nature*. Chicago: U of Chicago P, 1984.

Chen, Li. "Shengming shengdian de chengzuikuanghuan (Intoxication in the Carnival of Life)." *Guo Moruo zuopin duoyuanhua jiedu* (Pluralist Interpretations of Guo Moruo's Major Works). Ed. Li Chen Li and Xiaocun Chen. Chengdu: Sichuan daxue xhubanshe, 2006. 8-24.

Chen, Sihe. *Zhongguo Xinwenxue Zhengti Guan* (A Comprehensive Review of Chinese New Literature). Taipei: Yeqing chubanshe, 1990.

Chen, Xiaoming. *From the May Fourth Movement to Communist Revolution: Guo Moruo and the Chinese Path to Communism*. Albany: State U of New York P, 2007.

Chou, Ying-hsiung, ed. *The Chinese Text: Studies in Comparative Literature*. Hong Kong: The Chinese UP, 1986.

Chow, Tse-tsung. *The May Fourth Movement: Intellectual Revolution and Modern China*. Cambridge: Harvard UP, 1960.

Claridge, Laura. *Romantic Potency: The Paradox of Desire*. Ithaca: Cornell UP, 1992.

Coleridge, Samuel Taylor. *Biographia Literaria*. Ed. J. Shawcross. 2 vols. London, 1907.

Coleridge, Samuel Taylor. *Samuel Taylor Coleridge: Selections*. Ed. H.J. Jackson. Oxford: Oxford UP, 1985.

Copley, Stephen, and John Whale, eds. *Beyond Romanticism: New Approaches to Texts and Contexts 1780-1832*. London: Routledge, 1992.

De Bola, Peter. *The Discourse of the Sublime: Readings in History, Aesthetics, and Subject*. Oxford: Blackwell, 1989.

Deguy, Michel. "The Discourse of Exaltation: Contribution to a Reading of Pseudo-Longinus." *Of the Sublime Presence in Question*. Ed. Jeffrey S. Librett. Albany: State U of New York P, 1993. 5-24.

de Man, Paul. "Phenomemality and Materiality in Kant." *Aesthetic Ideology*. Ed. André Kaminski. Minneapolis: U of Minnesota P, 1996. 70-90.

de Man, Paul. *The Rhetoric of Romanticism*. New York: Columbia UP, 1984.

Denton, Kirk A., ed. *Modern Chinese Literary Thought: Writings on Literature, 1893-1945*. Stanford: Stanford UP, 1996.

Derrida, Jacques. *Acts of Literature*. Ed. J. Attridge, London: Routledge, 1992.

Derrida, Jacques. *Of Grammatology*. Trans. Gayatri Charkravorty Spivak. Baltimore: The Johns Hopkins UP, 1974.

Doar, Bruce. "Images of Women in the Dramas of Guo Moruo: The Case of *Empress Wu*." *Drama in the People's Republic of China*. Ed. C. Tung and C. Mackerras. Albany: State U of New York P, 1987. 254-92.

Eagleton, Terry. "Aesthetics and Politics in Edmund Burke." *History Workshop* 28 (1989): 53-62.

Eagleton, Terry. *The Ideology of the Aesthetic*. Cambridge: Blackwell, 1990.

Ellison, Julie K. *Delicate Subjects: Romanticism, Gender, and the Ethics of Understanding*. Ithaca: Cornell UP, 1990.

Fang, Achilles. "From Imagism to Whitmanism in Recent Chinese Poetry: A Search for Poetics that Failed." *Indiana University Conference on Oriental-Western Literary Relations*. Ed. Horst Frenz and G.A. Anderson. Chaple Hill: U of North Carolina P, 1955. 177-89.

Fay, Elizabeth A. *Becoming Wordsworth*. Amherst: U of Massachusetts P, 1995.

Ferguson, Frances. *Solitude and the Sublime: Romanticism and the Aesthetics of Individuation*. New York: Routledge, 1992.

Foucault, Michel. *The History of Sexuality*. Trans. Robert Hurley. 3 vols. New York: Pantheon Books, 1978.

Freeman, Barbara Claire. *The Feminine Sublime: Gender and Excess in Women's Fiction*. Berkeley: U of California P, 1995.

Furniss, Tom. *Edmund Burke's Aesthetic Ideology: Language, Gender and Political Economy in Revolution*. Cambridge: Cambridge UP, 1993.

Gálik, Marián. *The Genesis of Modern Chinese Literary Criticism, 1917-1930*. London: Curzon, 1980.

Gálik, Marián. "Kuo Mo-jo and his Development from Aesthetico-Impressionist to Proletarian Criticism." *The Genesis of Modern Chinese Literary Criticism, 1917-1930*. Ed. Marián Gálik. London: Curzon, 1980. 28-62.

Gao, Yang. "Lishijingshen yu Yishugouxiang—Lun Guo Moruo Lishiju de Xinnitezheng (The Historical Spirit and Aesthetic Structure—On the Psychological Characteristics of Guo Moruo's Historical Plays)." *Guo Moruo yanjiu* (Guo Moruo Studies) 4 (1998): 8-15.

Gibbons, Luke. *Edmund Burke and Ireland*. Cambridge: Cambridge UP, 2001.

Gill, Stephen Charles. *William Wordsworth: A Life*. Oxford: Clarendon, 1989.

Gilpin, William. *Observations on Several Parts of Great Britain, Particularly the High-Lands of Scotland, Relative Chiefly to Picturesque Beauty, Made in the Year 1776*. London: T. Cadell and W. Davies, 1808.

Guo, Moruo, "Fenghuang Niepan (The Nirvana of the Phoenix)." *Guo Moruo xuanji: Shige* (Selected Works of Guo Moruo: Poetry). Vol. 3. Chengdu: Sichuan renmin chubanshe, 1982. 22-34.

Guo, Moruo. "*Geming shiren Qu Yuan* (Qu Yuan the Revolutionary Poet)." *Moruo wenji* (Collected Works of Guo Moruo). Vol. 12. Beijing: renmin wenxue chubanshe,1959. 43-46.

Guo, Moruo. "Geming yu wenxue (Revolution and Literature)." *Moruo wenji* (Collected Works of Guo Moruo). Vol. 10. Beijing: renmin wenxue chubanshe, 1958. 312-23.

Guo, Moruo. "Guanyu shide wenti (On the Question of Poetry)." *Moruo wenji* (Collected Works of Guo Moruo). Vol. 11. Beijing: renmin wenxue chubanshe, 1958. 105-07.

Guo, Moruo. *Guo Moruo lun chuangzuo* (Guo Moruo on Creation). Shanghai: Shanghai wenxue chubanshe, 1983.

Guo, Moruo. *Guo Moruo quanji: Wenxuebian* (The Complete Works of Guo Moruo: Literature). 38 vols. Beijing: renmin wenxue chubanshe, 1984.

Guo, Moruo. Juan'er ji xu (Preface to Cocklebur Collection). 1923. *Guo Moruo yanjiu zhiliao* (Reference Materials for Guo Moruo Studies), Ed. Xunzao Wang, Zhengyan Lu, and Hua Shao, Beijing: Zhongguo shehui kexue chubanshe, 1981. 161-62.

Guo, Moruo. "Lunshi sanzha (Three Letters on Poetry)." *Moruo wenji* (Collected Works of Guo Moruo). Vol. 10. Beijing: renmin wenxue chubanshe, 1958. 199-213.

Guo, Moruo. *Qu Yuan, Guo Moruo xuanji: Lishiju* (Selected Works of Guo Moruo: Historical Drama). Vol. 4. Chengdu: Sichuan renmin chubanshe, 1982. 151-240.

Guo, Moruo. "*Qu Yuan* yanjiu (On Qu Yuan)." *Moruo wenji* (Collected Works of Guo Moruo). Vol. 12. Beijing: renmin wenxue chubanshe,1959. 331-430.

Guo, Moruo. "*Qu Yuan* yu *Lierwang* (*Qu Yuan* and *King Lear*)." *Moruo wenji* (Collected Works of Guo Moruo). Vol. 3. Beijing: renmin wenxue chubanshe, 1957. 313-22.

Guo, Moruo. "Renmin shiren Qu Yuan (Qu Yan the People's Poet)." *Moruo wenji* (Collected Works of Guo Moruo). Vol. 17. Beijing: renmin wenxue chubanshe, 1963. 138-48.

Guo, Moruo. "Shinian chuangzuo (Ten Years of Creation 1918-1923)." *Moruo wenji* (Collected Works of Guo Moruo). Vol. 7. Beijing: renmin wenxue chubanshe, 1957. 15-164.

Guo, Moruo. "Tan shige chuangzuo (On Poetic Creation)." 1920. *Guo Moruo yanjiu zhiliao* (Reference Materials for Guo Moruo Studies). Ed. Xunzao Wang, Zhengyan Lu, and Hua Shao, Beijing: zhongguo shehui kexue chubanshe, 1981. 137-38.

Guo, Moruo. "Wenxue de benzhi (The Nature of Literature)." *Moruo wenji* (Collected Works of Guo Moruo). Vol. 10. Beijing: renmin wenxue chubanshe, 1958. 214-24.

Guo, Moruo. "Wenyi de shengchan guocheng (The Production Process of Literature and Art)." *Moruo wenji* (Collected Works of Guo Moruo). Vol. 10. Beijing: renmin wenxue chubanshe, 1957. 97-99.

Guo, Moruo. "Wenyi zhi shehui shiming (The Social Task of Literature and Art)." *Moruo wenji* (Collected Works of Guo Moruo). Vol. 10. Beijing: renmin wenxue chubanshe, 1958. 83-88.

Guo, Moruo. "Wode zuoshi jingguo (My Poetic Career)." *Moruo wenji* (Collected Works of Guo Moruo). Vol. 11. Beijing: renmin wenxue chubanshe, 1958. 137-48.

Guo, Moruo. "Wozenyang xie *Qu Yuan* (How I Wrote *Qu Yuan*)." *Moruo wenji* (Collected Works of Guo Moruo). Vol. 3. Beijing: renmin wenxue chubanshe, 1957. 306-12.

Guo, Moruo. *Xianglei. Guo Moruo xuanji: Shige* (Selected Works of Guo Moruo: Poetry). Vol. 3. Chengdu: Sichuan renmin chubanshe, 1982. 12-21.

Guo, Moruo. "Xu erwenyiben *Qu Yuan* (Preface to the Russian Translation of *Qu Yuan*)." *Moruo wenji* (Collected Works of Guo Moruo). Vol. 17. Beijing: renmin wenxue chubanshe,1963. 157-59.

Guo, Moruo. "Xu (Preface)." *Chuangzao jican* (The Creation Quarterly) 1.1 (1921): 1-3.

Guo, Moruo. "Yinxiang yu biaoxian (Impression and Expression)." *Guo Moruo yanjiu zhiliao* (Reference Materials for Guo Moruo Studies). Ed. Xunzao Wang, Zhengyan Lu, and Hua Shao. Beijing: zhongguo shehui kexue chubanshe, 1981. 195-202.

Guo Moruo yanjiuhui (Guo Moruo Studies Association), ed. *Guo Moruo bainian danchang wenji* (Collections for the Centennial of Guo Moruo). Beijing: shehui kexueyuan wenxianchubanshe, 1994.

Harrison, Gary. *Wordsworth's Vagrant Muse: Poetry, Poverty, and Power*. Detroit: Wayne State UP, 1994.

Hartman, Geoffrey H. *Wordsworth's Poetry, 1787-1914*. Cambridge: Harvard UP, 1987.

Hazlitt, William. *The Spirit of the Age, 1825*. Menston: Scholar, 1971.

He, Qifang. "Shige xinshang" (Poetry and Its Appreciation)." *He Qifang wenji* (The Collected Works of He Qifang). Beijing: renmin wenxue chubanshe, 1983. 442-63.

Hegel, Georg Wilhelm Friedrich. *The Phenomenology of the Mind*. Trans. J.B. Baillie. New York: Harper and Row, 1967.

Hertz, Neil. *The End of the Line: Essays on Psychoanalysis and the Sublime*. New York: Columbia UP, 1985.

Hu, Shi. "Bishang liangshan huiyi wenxue geming (Driven to Rebellion—Recollections of the Literary Revolution)." 1934. *Hu shi xueshu wenji: xinwenxue yundong* (Collected Academic Works of Hu Shi: The New Literature Movement), Ed. Jiang Yihua. Beijing: Zhonghua shuju 1993: 193-215.

Hu, Shi. "Zixu (Forward)." *Changsiji* (Attempts). 1920. *Hu shi xueshu wenji: xinwenxue yundong* (Collected Academic Works of Hu Shi: The New Literature Movement). Ed. Jiang Yihua. Beijing: Zhonghua shuju 1993. 369-83.

Huang, Manjun. *Guo Moruo zuoping xinshang* (Appreciations of the Poetic Works of Guo Moruo). Guiling: Guangxi renmin chubanshe, 1986.

Huang, Ziping, Pingyuan Chen, and Liqun Qian. "Lun Ershi Shiji Zhongguo Wenxue (On Twentieth-Century Chinese Literature)." *Wenxue Pinglun* (Literary Criticism) 5 (1985): 3-13.

Jacobus, Mary. *Romanticism, Writing, and Sexual Difference: Essays on the Prelude*. Oxford: Clarendon P, 1989.

Jacobus, Mary. *Tradition and Experiment in Wordsworth's Lyrical Ballads (1798)*. Oxford: Clarendon P, 1976.

Jameson, Fredric. *The Political Unconscious: Narrative as a Socially Symbolic Act*. Ithaca: Cornell UP, 1981.

Jameson, Fredric. "Third-World Literature in the Era of Multinational Capitalism." *Social Text* 15 (1986): 65-88.

Kant, Immanuel. *Critique of Judgment*. Trans. J.H. Bernard. New York: Hafner, 1951.

Kant, Immanuel. *Observations on the Feeling of the Beautiful and Sublime*. Trans. John Goldthwait. Berkeley: U of California P, 1965.

Kelly, Theresa M. *Wordsworth's Revisionary Aesthetics*. Cambridge: Cambridge UP, 1988.

Kowallis, Jon. *The Subtle Revolution: Poets of the "Old-School" during Late Qing and Early Republican China*. Berkeley: Institute of East Asian Studies, 2006.

Lacoue-Labarthe, Philippe, and Jean-Luc Nancy. *The Literary Absolute: the Theory of Literature in German Romanticism*. Trans. Philip Barnard and Cheryl Lester. Albany: State U of New York P, 1988.

Larson, Wendy. *Literary Authority of the Modern Chinese Writers*. Durham: Duke UP, 1991.

Laughlin, Charles, ed. *Contested Modernities in Chinese Literature*. New York: Palgrave Macmillan, 2005.

Lee, Haiyan. "Tears that Crumbled the Great Wall: the Archaeology of Feeling in the May Fourth Folklore Movement." *The Journal of Asian Studies* 64.1 (2005): 35-65.

Lee, Ou-fan. "In Search of Modernity: Some Reflections on a New Mode of Consciousness in Twentieth-Century Chinese History and Literature." *Ideas across Cultures*. Ed. Paul A. Cohen and Merle Goldman. Cambridge: Harvard UP, 1990. 109-35.

Lee, Ou-fan. *The Romantic Generation of Modern Chinese Writers*. Cambridge: Harvard UP, 1973.

Levenson, Joseph R. *Confucian China and its Modern Fate: The Problem of Intellectual Continuity*. Berkeley: U of California P, 1958.

Levine, George, ed. *Aesthetics and Ideology*. New Brunswick: Rutgers UP, 1994.

Li, Zehou. *Mei de licheng* (Stages on the Way to Beauty). Beijing: Wenwu chubanshe, 1981.

Li, Zehou. *Meixue lunji* (Essays on Aesthetics). Shanghai: Shanghai wenxue chubanshe, 1980.

Li, Zehou. *Zhongguo xiandai sixianshi lun* (Essays on Modern Chinese Thought). Beijing: dongfang chubanshe, 1987.

Li, Zehou, and Liu Gangji. *Zhongguo Meixue Shi* (A History of Chinese Aesthetics). Beijing: Zhongguo shehuikexue chubanshe, 1987.

Lin, Julia C. *Modern Chinese Poetry: An Introduction*. Seattle: U of Washington P, 1973.

Liu, Alan. *Wordsworth: The Sense of History*. Stanford: Stanford UP, 1989.

Liu, Kang, and Xiaobing Tang, eds. *Politics, Ideology, and Literary Discourse in Modern China: Theoretical Interventions and Cultural Critique*. Durham: Duke UP, 1993.

Liu, Lydia H. *Translingual Practice: Literature, National Culture, and Translated Modernity—China, 1900-1937*. Stanford: Stanford UP, 1995.

Liu, Ruoqiang. "Whitman's Soul in China: Guo Moruo's Poetry in the New Culture Movement." *Whitman East and West: New Contexts for Reading Walt Whitman*. Ed. Ed Folson. Iowa City: U of Iowa P, 2002. 172-86.

Long, Quanming. *Zhongguo xinshi liubianlun* (On the Trends and Changes of the Chinese New Poetry). Beijing: Renmin wenxue chubanshe, 1999.

Longinus. *On the Sublime*. Trans. D.A. Russell. Oxford: Clarendon, 1964.

Lu, Xun. *Moluo shili shuo* (On the Power of Mara Poetry). Tianjin: Tianjin renmin chubanshe, 1982.

Lu, Xun. *Nahan* (Call to Arms). Beijing: Xin Chao She, 1923.

Malpas, Simon. *Jean-François Lyotard*. London: Routledge, 2003.

McFarland, Thomas. *Romantic Cruxies: The English Essayists and the Spirit of the Age*. Oxford: Clarendon, 1987.

McFarland, Thomas. *Romanticism and the Forms of Ruin: Wordsworth, Coleridge, and Modalities of Fragmentation*. Princeton: Princeton UP, 1981.

McGann, Jerome J. *The Romantic Ideology: A Critical Investigation*. Chicago: U of Chicago P, 1983.

Mellor, Anne K. *Romanticism and Gender*. New York: Routledge, 1993.

Mi, Jiayan. *Self-Fashioning and Reflexive Modernity in Modern Chinese Poetry*. Lewiston: Edwin Mellen, 2004.

Mishra, Vijay. *The Gothic Sublime*. Albany: State U of New York P, 1994.

Monk, Samuel Holt. *The Sublime: A Study of Critical Theories in Eighteenth-Century England*. Ann Arbor: U of Michigan Press, 1960.

Mu, Mutian. "Guo Moruo de shige (Guo Moruo's Poetry)." *Literature* 8.1 (1937): 8-16.

Nancy, Jean-Luc. "The Sublime Offering." Trans. Jeffrey S. Librett. *Of the Sublime Presence in Question*. Ed. Jean-Francois Courtine and Jeffrey S. Librett. Albany: State U of New York P, 1993. 25-44.

Ou, Hong. "Pantheistic Ideas in Guo Moruo's *The Goddesses* and Whitman's *Leaves of Grass*." *Whitman East and West: New Contexts for Reading Walt Whitman*. Ed. Ed Folson. Iowa City: U of Iowa P, 2002. 187-96.

Owen, Stephen. *Readings in Chinese Literary Thought*. Cambridge: Harvard UP, 1992.

Page, Judith W. *Wordsworth and the Cultivation of Women*. Berkeley: U of California P, 1994.

Paulson, Ronald. *Representations of Revolution, 1789-1820*. New Haven: Yale UP, 1983.

Pfau, Thomas. "'Elementary Feelings' and 'Distorted Languages': The Pragmatics of Culture in Wordsworth's Preface to *Lyrical Ballads*." *New Literary History* 24 (1993): 125-46.

Plaks, Andrew. *Archetype and Allegory in the* Dream of the Red Chamber. Princeton: Princeton UP, 1976.

Price, Martin. "The Picturesque Moment." *From Sensibility to Romanticism*. Ed. Frederick W. Hilles and Harold Bloom. New York: 1965. 259-92.

Prusek, Jaroslav. *The Lyrical and the Epic: Studies of Modern Chinese Literatur.* Ed. Leo Ou-fan Lee. Bloomington: Indiana UP, 1980.

Pu, Qinghua. *Guo Moruo yanjiu xinlun* (New Studies on Guo Moruo). Beijing: Shoudu shifangdaxue chubanshe, 1995.

Qin, Chuan. *Guo Moruo pingzhuan* (A Critical Biography of Guo Moruo). Chongqing: Chongqing chubanshe, 1993.

Rajan, Tilottama. *The Supplement of Reading: Figures of Understanding in Romantic Theory and Practice*. Ithaca: Cornell UP, 1990.

Roy, David T. *Kuo Mojo: The Early Years*. Cambridge: Harvard UP, 1971.

Ryan, Vanessa L. "The Psychological Sublime: Burke's Critique of Reason." *Journal of the History of Ideas* 62.2 (2001): 265-79.

Said, Edward W. *Beginnings: Intention and Method*. New York: Columbia UP, 1975.

Sakai, Naoki. *Translation and Subjectivity: On "Japan" and Cultural Nationalism*. Minneapolis: U of Minnesota P, 1997.

Saussy, Haun. *The Problem of a Chinese Aesthetic*. Stanford: Stanford UP, 1993.

Schiller, Friedrich. *Naïve and Sentimental Poetry and the Sublime*. Trans. Julius A. Elias Schiller. New York: Frederick Ungar, 1966.

Schiller, Friedrich. *On the Aesthetic Education of Man, in a Series of Letters*. Trans. Reginald Snell. New York: Frederick Ungar, 1965.

Schneider, Laurence. *A Madman of Ch'u: the Chinese Myth of Loyalty and Dissent*. Berkeley: U of California P, 1980.

Scodel, Joshua. *The English Poetic Epitaph: Commemoration and Conflict from Johnson to Wordsworth*. Ithaca: Cornell UP, 1991.

Shih, Shu-mei. *The Lure of the Modern Writing Modernism in Semicolonial China 1917-1937*. Berkeley: U of California P, 2001.

Sima, Qian. "The Biographies of Ch'u Yuan and Master Chia (*shi chi 84*)." *Records of the Grand Historian of China*. Trans. Watson Burton. New York: Columbia UP, 1971. 499-516.

Simpson, David, ed. *The Origins of Modern Critical Thought: German Aesthetic and Literary Criticism from Lessing to Hegel*. Cambridge: Cambridge UP, 1988.

Siskin, Clifford. *The Historicity of Romantic Discourse*. New York: Oxford UP, 1988.

Smith, Adam. *The Theory of Moral Sentiments*. Oxford: Clarendon P, 1976.

Spivak, Gayatri Chakravorty. *In Other Worlds: Essays in Cultural Politics*. New York: Routledge, 1987.

Sun, Fuyuan. "Du juben Qu Yuan (Reading the Play Qu Yuan)." *Zhongyang Ribao* (The Central Daily) Supplement. 7 February 1942: n.p.

Sun, Yixue. *Zhongwai langmanzhuyi wenxue daoyin* (A Synoptic Guide to Chinese and Foreign Romantic Literature). Shanghai: Tongjidaxue chubanshe, 2002.

Swann, Karen. "Suffering and Sensation in the Ruined Cottage." *PMLA: Publications of the Modern Language Association of America* 106.1 (1991): 83-95.

Tang, Xiaobing. *Chinese Modern: The Heroic and the Quotidian*. Durham: Duke UP, 2000.

Tian, Han, Baihua Zong, and Muoro Guo, eds. *Sanye Ji* (The Shamrock Collection). Shanghai: Shanghai shuju, 1982.

Tsu, Jing. "Perversions of Masculinity: The Masochistic Male Subject in Yu Dafu, Guo Moruo, and Freud." *Positions* 8.2 (2000): 269-316.

Wang, Ban. *The Sublime Figure of History: Aesthetics and Politics in Twentieth-Century China*. Stanford: Stanford UP, 1997.

Wang, David D.W. "Translating Modernity." *Translations and Creation: Readings of Western Literature in Early Modern China, 1840-1918*. Ed. David Pollard. Amsterdam: John Benjamins, 1998. 303-29.

Wang, Guowei. *Wang guantang xiansheng juanji* (Complete Works of Guantang Wang). Taibei: Wenhua chuban gongsi, 1968.

Wang, Hui. *Xiandai zhongguo sixiang de xingqi* (The Rise of Modern Chinese Thought). 4 vols. Beijing: Sanlian Shudian 2004-2009.

Wang, Jinghou. *Guo Moruo xueshu lunbian* (Controversy and Discussions of Guo Moruo). Chengdu: Sichuan wenxue chubanshe, 1989.

Wang, Yao. *Zhongguo xiandaiwenxue shilunji* (On the History of Modern Chinese Literature). Beijing: Beijing daxue chubanshe, 1998.

Weiskel, Thomas. *The Romantic Sublime: Studies in the Structure and Psychology of Transcendence*. Baltimore: Johns Hopkins UP, 1986.

Wen, Yiduo. "Nusen zhi shidai jingshen (The Timely Spirit of the Goddess)." *Chuangzao zhoubao* (The Creation Weekly). 3 June 1923: 3-7.

Wen, Yiduo. "Tade jingshen shishidaijingshen (His Spirit is the Spirit of the Times)." *On Guo Moruo*. Ed. Fang Xiangdong. Beijing: dacong wenyi chubanshe, 2001. 430-36.

Wen, Yiduo. *Wen Yiduo quanji* (Complete Works of Wen Yiduo). Hong Kong: Sanlian shudian, 1982.

Wong, Kin-yuen. "Negative-Positive Dialectic in the Chinese Sublime." *The Chinese Tex: Studies in Comparative Literature*. Ed. Chou Ying-hsing. Hong Kong: The Chinese UP, 1986.

Wordsworth, Jonathan. "Revision as Making." William Wordsworth, *The Prelude: 1799, 1805, 1850*. Ed. Jonathan Wordsworth, M.H. Abrams, and S. Gill. New York: Norton, 1979. 485-90.

Wordsworth, William. "Advertisement, Preface, and Appendix to Lyrical Ballads." The Prose Works of William Wordsworth. Vol. 1. Ed. W.J.B. Owen and Jane Worthington Smyser. Oxford: Clarendon, 1974. 130-219.

Wordsworth, William. "Essays upon Epitaphs." *The Prose Works of William Wordsworth*. Vol. 2. Ed. W.J.B. Owen and Jane Worthington Smyser. Oxford: Clarendon P, 1974. 49-80.

Wordsworth, William. *The Fourteen-Book Prelude*, Ithaca: Cornell UP, 1985.

Wordsworth, William. *A Guide through the District of the Lakes. The Prose Works of William Wordsworth*. Vol. 2. Ed. W.J.B. Owen and Jane Worthington Smyser. Oxford: Clarendon P, 1974. 151-240.

Wordsworth, William. "Letter to the Bishop of Llandaff." *The Prose Works of William Wordsworth*. Vol. 1. Ed. W.J.B. Owen and Jane Worthington Smyser. Oxford: Clarendon, 1974. 37-88.

Wordsworth, William. "Letter to Charles Fox with the 'Lyrical Ballads' and his Answer." *The Prose Works of William Wordsworth*. Vol. 2. Ed. Alexander B. Grosart. St. George's: Blackburn. 202-06. http://www.gutenberg.org/files/16550/16550-h/vol_ii.htm#g.

Wordsworth, William. "Letter to John Wilson." *Letters of William Wordsworth: A New Selection*. Ed. Alan G. Hill, Oxford: Oxford UP, 1985. 49-55.

Wordsworth, William. *Lyrical Ballads, and Other Poems, 1797-1800*. Ed. James Butler and Karen Green. Ithaca: Cornell UP, 1992.

Wordsworth, William. "MS. Drafts and Fragments 1798-1804." William Wordsworth, *The Prelude: 1799, 1805, 1850*. Ed. Jonathan Wordsworth, M.H. Abrams, and S. Gill. New York: Norton, 1979. 485-506.

Wordsworth, William. *The Poetical Works of William Wordsworth*. Ed. E. de Selincourt. Oxford: Clarendon, 1952.

Wordsworth, William. Preface to *Lyrical Ballads*. The Prose Works of William Wordsworth. Ed. W.J.B. Owen and Jane Worthington Smyser. Oxford: Clarendon, 1974

Wordsworth, William. *The Prelude, 1798-1799*. Ithaca: Cornell UP, 1977.

Wordsworth, William. *The Prelude: 1799, 1805, 1850*. Ed. Jonathan Wordsworth, M.H. Abrams, and S. Gill. New York: Norton, 1979.

Wordsworth, William. "The Sublime and the Beautiful." *The Prose Works of William Wordsworth*. Vol. 2. Ed. W.J.B. Owen and Jane Worthington Smyser. Oxford: Clarendon P, 1974. 349-60.

Wordsworth, William. *The Thirteen-Book Prelude*. Ithaca: Cornell UP, 1991.

Wordsworth, William, and Samuel Coleridge. *Lyrical Ballads: 1798, 1800*. Ed. R.L. Brett and A. R. Jones. London: Routledge, 1963.

Yan, Huang-dong. *Fenghuang, nushenjiqita: lun Guo Moruo* (Phoenix, Goddess and Others: On Guo Moruo). Beijing: renmin wenxue chubanshe, 1990.

Yeh, Michelle. "Chayi de youlu: yige huiying (The Anxiety of Difference: A Rejoinder)." *Jintian* (Today) 1 (1991): 94.

Yeh, Michelle. *Modern Chinese Poetry: Theory and Practice since 1917*. New Haven: Yale UP, 1991.

Yip, Terry, Siu-Han, and Kwok-Kan Tan. "European Influence on Modern Chinese Drama: Kuo Mo-jo's Early Historical-Problem Plays." *Journal of Oriental Studies* 24.1 (1986): 54-65.

Zhang, Longxi. *Mighty Opposites: From Dichotomies to Differences in the Comparative Study of China*. Stanford : Stanford UP, 1998.

Zhang, Yingjin. Ed. *China in a Polycentric World: Essays in Chinese Comparative Literature*, Stanford: Stanford UP, 1999.

Zheng, Yi. "The Figuration of a Sublime Origin: Guo Moruo's Qu Yuan." *Modern Chinese Literature and Culture* 16.1 (2004): 153-98.

Zhongguo xiandaiwenxue yanjiuzhongxin (Center for the Study of Modern Chinese Literature), ed. *Zhongguo xiandaiwenxue cuantong* (Modern Chinese Literary Tradition). Beijng: Renmin wenxue chubanshe, 2002.

Zhou, Yang. "Guo Moruo he tade nushen (Guo Moruo and His Goddess)." *Jiefang Ribao* (The Liberation Daily) 16 November 1941. *Guo Moruo yanjiu zhiliao* (Reference Materials for Guo Moruo Studies). Ed. Xunzao Wang, Zhengyan Lu, and Sao Hua, Beijing: Zhongguo shehui kexueyuan chubanshe, (1987). 208-15.

Zhu, Qikai, ed. *Zhongguo wenxueshi erbai sishi ti* (Two-Hundred and Forty Topics in Chinese Literary History). Jinan: Shangdong wenxue chubanshe, 1985.

Zhu, Xiang. "Guo Moruo jun deshi (The Poetry of Guo Moruo)." *Zhongshoji* (Collections of Zhongshu). Ed. Qian Zhongshu. Shanghai: Shenghuo shushe, 1934. 24-31.

Zhu, Zhiqing, ed. *Zhongguo xinwenxue daxi: shiji* (The Comprehensive Collection of New Chinese Literature: Poetry). Shanghai: Liangyou tushu gongsi, 1935.

Žižek, Slavoj. *The Sublime Object of Ideology*. London: Verso, 1989.

Zong, Baihua. "Letter to Guo Moruo 7 January 1920." *Guo Moruo yanjiu zhiliao* (Reference Materials for Guo Moruo Studies). Ed. Xunzao Wang, Zhengyan Lu and Sao Hua, Beijing: Zhongguo shehui kexueyuan chubanshe, (1987): 106-07.

Zong, Baihua. "Qingshi wenti (The Question of Love Poetry)." *Xinshi bao* (The New Current Post). *Xuedeng* (Learning Light) 8.22 (1920): n.p.

Index

Abrams, 49, 65, 66, 77
absences, 50, 51, 60
absolution, 49
adaptation, 3, 73
advent, 14, 75, 95
aesthetic barbarism, 16
aesthetic category, 4, 57
aesthetic choice, 73
aesthetic choices, 75
aesthetic culture, 2, 5, 8, 13, 22
aesthetic distance, 7
aesthetic doctrines, 13, 75
aesthetic experience, 14, 16, 25, 26, 29, 35
aesthetic figuration, 5, 8, 13, 14, 16, 68
aesthetic figure, 68
aesthetic formations, 2, 3
aesthetic ideal, 4, 5, 8, 11, 97
aesthetic ideals, 2, 4, 7, 8, 110, 122
aesthetic imperative, 10, 14, 15
aesthetic inqirury, 2
aesthetic judgment, 9, 19, 22, 24, 69, 85
aesthetic movement, 10, 11, 12, 14, 41, 78
aesthetic object, 17
aesthetic prelude, 47
aesthetic property, 2, 3, 68, 70, 124, 125
aesthetic protocol, 71
aesthetic redemption of history, 9
aesthetic reprieve, 14, 81, 123, 126
aesthetic resolution, 110
aesthetics, 2, 3, 4, 5, 6, 8, 9, 10, 11, 12, 14, 16, 17, 18, 27, 29, 30, 32, 34, 35, 37, 38, 39, 40, 41, 68, 69, 70, 74, 75, 79, 80, 82, 101, 124, 125
aesthetic schema, 111
aesthetics of greatness, 12
aesthetics of modernity, 35
aesthetics of the great, 6
aesthetics of the sublime, 2, 4, 8, 10, 11, 12, 16, 124
aesthetic sources, 1

aesthetic subject, 56
aesthetic tenet, 12
aesthetic turn, 70, 125
aesthetic value of history, 115
affect, 11, 13, 21, 22, 26, 28, 31, 33, 34, 35, 37, 39, 56, 81, 87, 91, 93, 97, 107, 109, 110, 111, 113, 115
affective, 5, 10, 16, 19, 20, 21, 22, 28, 58, 59, 60, 70, 71, 77, 80, 81, 84, 87, 88, 93, 94, 97, 102, 112, 113, 120, 121, 124, 126
affects, 20, 21, 31, 58, 65, 93, 94
agency, 4, 5, 11, 14, 15, 16, 26, 35, 40, 46, 48, 56, 72, 76, 82, 89, 90, 93, 94, 101, 113, 117, 124, 125, 126
ambivalence, 74, 110, 111
anachronism, 106
analogy, 32, 38
ancient customs, 44
anger, 80, 99, 114, 118, 119, 121, 122
anxieties of modernity, 10
anxiety, 11, 14, 15, 18, 22, 23, 32, 47, 49, 53, 54, 73, 80
apocalypse, 48
apology, 59
apparition, 54, 55, 58
appropriation, 32, 71, 73, 126
Arabian knight, 54
Arab phantom, 54, 55
Arac, 29, 30, 41, 49, 51, 63, 69
archetypal, 115
art, 5, 12, 16, 35, 36, 39, 42, 52, 68, 69, 77, 89, 90, 92, 93, 110
artificial system, 18, 22
artistic creation, 89, 90, 93
aspiration, 30, 39, 42, 77, 81, 106, 109, 110, 115, 121
asymmetry, 8
audience, 8, 13, 34, 36, 37, 39, 101, 107, 110, 113, 116, 119
avant-garde, 6, 40, 102

avant-guardism, 16, 30, 40, 70, 102, 125

baihua, 73, 75, 83, 87, 94, 95, 96, 105
Baihua Zong, 77, 85, 86, 87
ballad, 98, 99, 101, 106
Ban Wang, 77, 100, 109, 111
Baudelaire, 84, 88
beautiful, 9, 11, 20, 21, 27, 29, 35, 57, 69, 110, 111, 112, 113, 115, 117, 121, 122
beauty, 1, 12, 16, 28, 57, 60, 84, 115, 116, 122
beginning, 4, 6, 10, 18, 40, 41, 44, 46, 47, 48, 50, 55, 70, 71, 72, 74, 75, 78, 79, 89, 93, 96, 104, 105, 106, 108
beginnings, 1, 4, 7, 13, 14, 15, 40, 41, 42, 46, 47, 48, 57, 61, 62, 65, 67, 68, 69, 70, 71, 73, 82, 86, 123, 125, 126
Benjamin, 52, 61, 74
Bismarck, 87
body, 28, 29, 31, 32, 43, 44, 45, 65, 66, 67, 90, 91, 99, 112, 121, 122
body politic, 29, 32
boundaries, 15, 31, 56, 100
boundary crossing, 45
boundless, 18, 20, 98, 108, 110, 120
bourgeoisie, 13
bourgeois subject, 31
Bourke, 14, 56, 57, 75
Burke, 2, 3, 5, 6, 7, 9, 11, 12, 13, 14, 16, 17, 18, 21, 22, 24, 25, 26, 28, 29, 30, 31, 32, 33, 34, 35, 36, 37, 38, 40, 55, 57, 68, 70, 77, 80, 82, 124
Burkean sublime, 28, 30, 31, 32, 33, 34, 38, 42, 56, 57
Bushmin, 3
Byron, 76, 87, 102

capacious, 2, 4, 10, 11, 14, 26, 68, 70, 72, 124, 125
Carlyle, 80
catastrophe, 32, 36
catastrophes of history, 72
catastrophic events, 72, 73
celebration, 70, 82, 102, 106, 120, 121, 125
censorship, 22, 24, 114
Chandler, 78
Chanjuan, 116, 117
Chinese civilization, 99
Chinese cultural modernity, 73
Chinese Romanticism, 76
Chinese sublime, 2, 76, 81, 100, 109, 111, 114, 122
chivalry, 38

choice, 3, 9, 22, 26, 28, 29, 31, 32, 36, 38, 47, 48, 71, 73, 88, 90, 93, 99, 101, 125, 127
classical, 1, 16, 72, 79, 83, 92, 94, 95, 96, 97, 104, 105, 107, 111, 113, 119
classical Chinese poetry, 97
classical tradition, 104
classification, 17, 23, 24, 32
climax, 118
cognition, 27, 28
cognitive, 29, 56, 70, 77, 124
Coleridge, 24, 88
Coleridgean, 51, 63
colloquial, 99, 105
colonial terror, 82
commencement poetics, 10
common humanity, 34, 38
communication, 24, 33, 110
comparable cultural moments, 4
comparative context, 9
comparative taxonomy, 9
compromise, 11, 109, 110, 111, 112, 113, 116, 123
conjurer, 54, 60
consciousness, 21, 44, 58, 79, 89, 90, 94, 105
consecration, 122
consolidation, 56
contemporaneity, 5, 78, 84
continuity, 3, 14, 71, 82, 114, 119, 126
contrary impulses, 8, 102, 112
contrary tendencies, 11, 49, 115
corporal, 21, 29
corporeal, 21
correspondence, 7, 22, 24, 25, 27, 44, 45, 56, 60, 70, 74, 77, 90, 91, 92, 102, 110, 113, 120, 123, 125, 126
cosmology, 120
Creation Society, 76, 108
creative activities, 3
creative emulation, 83
creative formations, 74
crisis, 9, 12, 13, 14, 15, 17, 22, 32, 40, 71, 78, 100, 104, 108, 116, 117, 119, 124, 125, 126
critical freedom, 21, 22
cultural, 3, 5, 9, 10, 11, 49, 55, 59, 71, 78, 79, 92, 102, 126
cultural aspirations, 75
cultural assertion, 10
cultural distinction, 29
cultural heir, 117
cultural imagination, 5, 40, 42, 70, 125
cultural memories, 82

Index

cultural modernity, 2, 6, 9, 11, 41, 71, 72, 73, 85, 125, 127
cultural monuments, 104
cultural negotiation, 25
cultural precedence, 4
cultural preoccupation, 5
cultural rejuvenation, 9, 74
cultural revolution, 1, 6, 76, 77, 78, 113
cultural source, 103
cultural texts, 7, 9
cultural translation, 82
cultural vision, 88
culture building, 7
cultured youth, 76

Dai, 84
danger, 26, 30, 31, 33, 35, 49, 52, 60, 63
Dante, 87, 88
datong, 79
Datong shije, 102
death, 5, 27, 34, 39, 44, 45, 77, 81, 85, 97, 98, 101, 102, 105, 108, 109, 111, 117, 118, 126
deathlike, 44, 45
deceased, 43, 44, 45
dedication, 75, 115, 116, 117, 118, 121
deferral, 51
defiance, 11, 68, 77, 79, 99, 101, 102, 108, 112
degeneration, 37, 93
Deguy, 40, 41
dejection, 32
delicacy, 97
delight, 27, 30, 31, 33, 34, 35, 55
delightful, 27, 30, 31, 32, 59
de Man, 19, 21, 68
denouement, 112, 118, 121, 126
Derrida, 50
despair, 32, 99, 100, 101, 108
desperation, 80, 97, 107
destiny, 45, 58, 64, 68, 69
destruction, 6, 9, 11, 20, 31, 36, 55, 71, 76, 77, 80, 82, 97, 98, 101, 102, 105, 108, 114, 117, 118, 120, 121, 123, 126, 127
dialectic, 15, 20, 51, 81, 89
difference, 5, 7, 15, 22, 25, 31, 55, 61, 73, 74, 78, 88, 90, 92, 110, 111
disciple, 16, 115, 116
discourse, 6, 7, 29, 37, 41, 68, 73, 75, 77, 78, 109, 117
displacement, 14, 15, 29, 65, 66
disruptive, 29, 30, 70, 81, 82, 85, 97, 105, 125

distance, 15, 27, 30, 35, 40, 54, 101
distinction, 17, 24, 25, 27, 28, 29, 33, 34, 70, 78, 125
distraught modernity, 70, 125
dramatic importance, 117
dramatic lyricism, 115
dramatic poems, 96
dramatic resolution, 11
dramatization, 35, 37, 39, 113, 114
draperies, 38, 42
dream, 54, 119
dream-play, 54
dynamic sublime, 19, 121

Eagleton, 17, 57
earlier masters, 75
education, 15, 16, 43, 45, 54, 55, 77, 116
effect, 12, 17, 20, 24, 28, 30, 33, 35, 110
Ehuang, 110
elegy, 98, 118
elsewhere, 13, 16, 20, 35, 44, 49, 51, 52, 53, 54, 58, 65, 66, 74, 122
embodiment, 43, 76, 78, 86, 88, 96, 106, 117, 118, 122
emotion, 22, 33, 76
empirical, 18, 21, 22, 24, 25, 27, 33
empiricism, 17, 21, 22, 27, 33, 34
epic, 5, 30, 46, 49, 81, 89, 93, 98, 101, 104, 108, 111, 112, 116, 121, 122, 126
epic culture hero, 5, 11, 81, 101, 104, 106, 108, 112, 113, 122
epilogue, 102
epistemological, 15, 17, 31, 54, 68, 72
epitaph, 40, 44, 45
epitaphic poet, 44, 45, 58
equivalence, 72, 104, 106
equivocation, 33, 35, 38, 74
erotic, 109, 115, 116, 117
event, 13, 34, 51, 59, 95
exaltation, 58, 76, 99, 122
exalted discourse, 41
excess, 13, 26, 50, 51, 54, 71, 109, 125, 126, 127
excesses of revolution, 36
excessive, 2, 10, 11, 41, 42, 53, 61, 62, 66, 81, 97, 124
exemplary, 6, 17, 30, 34, 71, 78, 85, 113, 125, 126
exemplary actions, 17
exemplary aesthetics, 71
experiments, 83, 95, 97
expert reader, 44
external, 69, 89, 90

familiar modes, 75
fantasy, 98, 108, 122
fashion, 25, 68, 88
fear, 19, 20, 28, 32, 38, 41, 52, 53, 57, 73, 82, 112, 126
feelings, 9, 12, 15, 20, 21, 24, 25, 26, 35, 37, 39, 41, 45, 49, 59, 62, 63, 70, 76, 77, 80, 81, 84, 86, 90, 91, 92, 94, 96, 100, 107, 110, 113, 119, 124, 125
feminine, 57, 109, 110, 111, 117
feminine love, 111
femininity, 28, 109, 111, 115, 117
Ferguson, 14, 17, 18, 24, 25, 30, 33, 42
ferocity, 13, 71, 79, 80, 97, 124, 126
Fichte, 80
fiction, 31, 32, 36, 41, 53, 75
figuration, 2, 4, 7, 8, 9, 11, 17, 27, 32, 47, 58, 59, 68, 69, 74, 75, 79, 81, 97, 105, 107, 109, 111, 113, 114, 115, 117, 118, 124
figurative, 33, 35
figurative language, 39
figurative process, 33
figurative terms, 26
fire, 80, 102, 109, 112, 120, 121, 122
forefathers, 105
form, 3, 17, 21, 35, 36, 45, 65, 66, 67, 69, 75, 83, 85, 86, 91, 92, 94, 95, 96, 97, 99, 104, 105, 109, 114, 121
formal, 21, 71, 79, 95
Formalists, 84
formalist studies, 75
freedom, 15, 16, 19, 20, 21, 47, 69, 70, 76, 80, 95, 96, 97, 124
free verse, 75, 79, 96
French Revolution, 6, 7, 10, 13, 14, 32, 35, 37, 38, 64, 66, 87
Freud, 88
frustrations, 79
Furniss, 25, 26, 29, 30, 33, 80
future, 78

Gálik, 1, 3, 75, 84
gender, 109
genealogy, 22, 39, 40, 69, 106, 111
genius, 30, 81, 90
genres, 13, 74, 75, 102
German Romanticism, 13
Gibbons, 16, 32
Gilpin, 15
Goethe, 1, 76, 84, 87, 88, 102, 107, 111
grandeur, 2, 36, 60, 97
great, 11, 26, 30, 42, 59, 61, 75, 81, 83, 85, 86, 87, 94, 97, 107, 108, 117, 119, 121, 122

greatness, 2, 12, 28, 33, 36, 37, 64, 77, 86, 105, 106, 107, 109, 124, 126
Guangqian Zhu, 81
Guo, Moruo, 1, 2, 3, 4, 5, 6, 7, 11, 74, 76, 77, 79, 81, 83, 84, 85, 86, 87, 88, 89, 90, 91, 92, 93, 95, 96, 97, 98, 99, 100, 101, 104, 105, 106, 107, 108, 109, 110, 111, 112, 113, 114, 115, 116, 117, 118, 119, 120, 121, 122, 123, 124, 125, 126
Guofeng, 1, 104
Guowei Wang, 76, 100

habitual, 34
Haiyan Lee, 113
handmaiden, 117, 118
harmony, 15, 48, 55, 94, 97, 102
Hartman, 41, 47, 48, 49, 51, 61
He, 21, 26, 34, 35, 36, 38, 43, 44, 46, 47, 51, 53, 55, 64, 68, 77, 79, 80, 85, 86, 108
Heine, 76, 87
heritage, 75, 83
heroic, 33, 40, 76, 77, 81, 95, 102, 106, 110, 112, 113, 116
heroism, 76, 97, 101, 102, 106, 109, 111
historical aestheticism, 2, 4, 6, 12, 13, 14, 15, 16, 22, 39, 58, 70, 77, 100, 124
historical anxieties, 6, 10, 71, 125
historical aspiration, 5, 41
historical burden, 26
historical condition, 3, 39
historical crisis, 2, 5, 7, 9, 16, 32, 70, 107, 125, 127
historical destiny, 68
historical difference, 7, 8
historical drama, 37
historical events, 6, 7, 72, 114
historical ground, 69
historical imagination, 17
historical inheritance, 14, 75, 76
historical judgment, 37
historical linkage, 3, 8, 73
historical monument, 44, 95
historical practice, 44
historical problem, 17, 39
historical progress, 80, 114, 118
historical redress, 4, 76, 104
historical sentiments, 120
historical vision, 22, 103, 126
historicity, 19, 29, 35, 41, 75, 105, 106
history, 3, 4, 5, 6, 7, 10, 11, 14, 15, 16, 17, 22, 29, 32, 35, 36, 37, 38, 40, 41, 42, 43, 44, 45, 49, 50, 51, 53, 54, 56,

Index

58, 61, 65, 66, 67, 68, 70, 72, 73, 75, 76, 79, 80, 81, 82, 83, 85, 86, 88, 89, 95, 96, 97, 99, 100, 101, 105, 106, 107, 109, 114, 115, 122, 123, 124, 125, 126
history as theater, 36
Hu, 94, 95
Huang-dong Yan, 80
human bond, 43
humanity, 10, 15, 38, 43, 44, 82, 117
human nature, 58, 89
human ties, 44
human volition, 38
Huxley, 72
hyperbole, 97
hyperbolic, 4, 5, 11, 49, 94, 101, 102
hyperbolization, 5, 14, 15, 40, 76, 89, 124
hyperbolization of literary agency, 15

iconic, 64
iconoclasm, 104, 106, 107
iconoclastic, 1, 11, 74
idealism, 90, 98
idealist, 89, 93
ideology, 38
idioms, 92
imagery, 35, 84, 98, 99, 100, 102, 119, 120, 121, 122
images, 34, 53, 60, 76, 97, 98, 120
imagination, 15, 18, 20, 21, 26, 28, 38, 41, 49, 63, 64, 76, 80, 86, 91, 97, 98, 99, 102, 108, 119, 120, 127
imaginative, 2, 5, 8, 29, 125
imitation, 29, 89, 90
immortality, 44
impasse, 10, 53, 66
indeterminacy, 48, 51
individuation, 22, 24, 25, 29
inertia, 32
infinite, 69
infinity, 24, 45, 70, 124
influence, 2, 8, 20, 54, 72, 75, 81, 82, 84, 87, 89, 95, 96, 102, 106, 111
inheritance, 5, 32, 38, 39, 42
inscription, 42, 44, 45
inspiration, 1, 76, 89, 91, 92, 96, 107
intellectual, 1, 4, 6, 12, 21, 32, 73, 80, 85, 126
intelligentsia, 80
intention, 35, 46, 93
interplay, 19, 31, 60
interruption, 51

Jacobus, 34, 35, 36, 37, 42, 54

journey, 11, 47, 49, 50, 51, 62, 63, 110, 122
judgment, 18, 20, 21, 22, 24, 25, 29, 32, 43, 45, 56, 77, 116
Kant, 9, 16, 17, 18, 19, 20, 21, 22, 25, 31, 69, 70, 88, 91, 100, 124
Kantian critique, 13
Kantian sublime, 31, 39, 57
Keats, 76
kindred, 44, 106
knight errant, 54
Kong, 86

Lacoue-Labarthe, 13, 14, 75
lamentation, 37, 38, 99, 100, 108
late Qing, 83
Laughlin, 6
Lee, Ou-fan, 73, 76
Lee, 113
legacy, 21, 41, 44, 75, 91, 92
legends, 88, 98, 110
legislative function, 26, 30, 40, 70, 125
legitimation, 5
levelers, 38
Li, Jinfa, 84
libidinal energy, 57
liminal, 58, 126
limit, 9, 10, 15, 34, 47, 69, 70, 97, 101, 104, 121, 122, 124
limitation, 9, 69
limitless, 85, 94, 111
Lin, Julia, 72, 73, 75, 83, 84, 86
literary absolute, 14
literary culture, 2, 5, 10, 88, 92, 127
literary formulations, 72
literary model, 2
literary modernity, 1, 42, 68, 70
literati, 80
literature of decadence, 88
Liu, Alan 4, 7, 49, 50, 51, 73, 87
Liu, Lydia, 71, 73, 87
lofty, 20, 81, 115
Longfellow, 1
Longinian sublime, 41, 67, 123, 126
Longinus, 29, 40, 41, 42, 69, 109, 125
love, 28, 43, 44, 47, 49, 54, 58, 79, 102, 108, 110, 111, 113, 117
Lu, 87, 106, 107, 114
Lyotard, 12
lyrical, 81, 115, 118, 120, 121, 122
Lyricists, 84

madness, 108, 112, 118, 121, 122, 126
magnitude, 28
majestic, 81, 86, 105, 109, 111, 119
Malpas, 12, 14
Mao, 95
martyrdom, 116, 117
masculine, 110
mastery, 18, 21, 30, 31, 77, 84, 117, 121, 122
materialism, 90
maternal, 90
mathematical sublime, 18, 19
May Fourth, 1, 6, 8, 73, 77, 78, 79, 80, 83, 92, 96, 98, 102, 103, 105, 106, 107, 113
May Fourth spirit, 79
McGann, 15
meaning, 5, 7, 8, 28, 51, 53, 54, 57, 66, 88, 92, 100, 101, 111, 113, 116, 122
mediation, 18, 20, 27
megalomania, 108
melancholia, 80
melancholy, 9, 20, 32, 37, 60, 98, 121, 127
memory, 44, 46, 47, 52, 53, 54, 65
metaphor, 38, 90, 116
metaphorical participation, 33, 35
metaphysical, 21, 38, 49, 50, 51, 69
metaphysics, 26, 39
metonymy, 30, 42, 45, 81, 85, 90, 93, 96, 106
might, 3, 8, 9, 19, 20, 21, 22, 35, 38, 41, 51, 53, 65, 74, 76, 85, 97, 104, 119, 120, 121, 122, 126
Mill, 78
mind, 18, 20, 21, 28, 29, 31, 33, 45, 63, 64
modem figuration of the sublime, 4
modern aesthetic ideal, 11, 76
modern aesthetics, 14, 68
modern Chinese literary movement, 89
modern Chinese literature, 1, 2, 5, 72, 75, 76, 78, 81, 87, 96
modern Chinese poet, 1, 74, 75, 84, 85, 104, 125
modern Chinese poetry, 8, 72, 73, 74, 82, 83, 88, 95, 126
modern history, 3, 5, 8, 9, 13, 14, 15, 46, 47, 51, 71, 80, 87, 99, 123, 124, 126
modernism, 8, 84, 88
modernity, 1, 2, 3, 5, 6, 7, 8, 9, 10, 11, 12, 13, 14, 16, 17, 18, 19, 22, 32, 35, 37, 38, 39, 40, 41, 42, 43, 45, 47, 50, 51, 54, 59, 60, 67, 68, 69, 70, 71, 72, 73, 74, 75, 77, 78, 81, 82, 84, 85, 86, 88, 94, 95, 96, 104, 106, 113, 123, 124, 125, 126
modern sublime, 9, 10, 22, 68, 69, 70, 72, 80, 81, 82, 102, 123, 125
modern world, 43, 101
modus operandi, 4, 7, 9, 14, 44, 69, 70, 74, 125
momentum of the times, 95
Monk, 12
monologue, 107, 113, 118, 119, 120
monument, 44, 45, 107, 115, 117, 118
monuments, 5, 42, 45, 82, 104, 105
moods, 20, 76, 80, 84, 86, 95, 108
morality, 20, 22
moral judgment, 29
Moruo, 1, 2, 77, 83, 86
mourning, 99
movement of passage, 78
murder, 32, 33, 38

Nancy, 10, 13, 14, 39, 68, 69, 70, 75, 124
narrative, 63, 65, 79, 80, 98, 99
national doom, 114
natural, 10, 29, 32, 37, 65, 120
natural lore, 54, 55
nature, 2, 5, 7, 10, 12, 18, 20, 22, 23, 26, 27, 28, 32, 33, 35, 36, 38, 39, 40, 44, 46, 47, 48, 49, 52, 55, 58, 61, 64, 65, 66, 68, 71, 72, 79, 84, 89, 90, 91, 92, 97, 99, 115, 116, 118, 119, 120, 121, 122, 123, 124, 125, 126
necessity, 8, 19, 22, 24, 26, 27, 28, 29, 38, 53, 56, 68, 73, 110, 114
neo-Kantian tradition, 19
neo-Newtonism, 32
new Chinese cultural movement, 76
New Chinese poetry, 76
New Culturalists, 7, 11, 73, 75, 77, 78, 79, 80, 82, 85, 87, 89, 91, 92, 93, 103, 126, 127
New Culture Movement, 1, 3, 6, 8, 74, 76, 81, 83, 85, 92, 95, 96
new literature, 73, 87, 92
New Poetry Movement, 11, 74, 76, 82, 96, 106
new poets, 72
new prosody, 75
new province of literature, 86
new spirit, 76
new subject matter, 76
new verse, 75, 84, 86
new world, 80, 89, 90, 97
Nietzsche, 88
nirvana, 114

Index

nostalgia, 41, 121
Nüxu, 110
Nüying, 110

obscurity, 11, 15, 17, 18, 22, 24, 28, 29, 33, 39, 56, 100
off-stage, 37, 44
ontological, 9, 24, 25, 32, 94
origin, 1, 4, 10, 27, 32, 47, 59, 61, 63, 71, 74, 88, 90, 101, 103, 104, 105, 106, 107, 114, 117
origins, 1, 4, 7, 9, 26, 29, 40, 42, 45, 66, 67, 102, 104, 106, 113
orthodoxy, 83, 92

pain, 11, 12, 24, 26, 27, 28, 30, 31, 53, 80, 86, 97, 99, 100, 101, 119
Paine, 37
pantheism, 86
paradox, 18, 95, 101
parallel cases, 9
parricide, 38
passion, 9, 26, 27, 28, 30, 33, 60, 61, 73, 80, 88, 92, 99, 102, 108, 110, 111, 114, 120, 121, 123
passions, 25, 26, 27, 31, 37, 49, 56, 59, 76, 80, 81, 84, 95, 96, 97, 98, 100, 122, 126
past, 16, 38, 41, 52, 61, 73, 75, 78, 99, 114
pathological association, 108, 110
pathos, 79, 81, 87, 94, 105, 123, 126
Paulson, 35
perception, 7, 9, 12, 14, 27, 33, 71, 74, 81, 101, 125
performance, 35, 89
personification, 116, 122
Pfau, 58, 59
philosophical motif, 69
philosophical response, 17
philosophy, 9, 12, 13, 14, 17, 39, 68, 69, 70, 93, 124
philosophy of art, 12
physiological, 21, 29
picturesque, 16
pleasure, 12, 24, 25, 27, 28, 31, 32, 33, 34, 35, 92
poetic, 10, 42, 48, 49, 52, 53, 58, 59, 65, 77, 83, 91, 96, 98, 107, 113, 126
poetic act, 11, 42
poetic audacity, 97
poetic awakening, 1
poetic creation, 9, 91
poetic expulsion, 43
poetic form, 75, 76, 83, 92, 105
poetic ground, 6
poetic ideal, 83, 107, 117, 121
poetic impact, 1
poetic imperative, 10, 62
poetic passage, 10, 49
poetic reform, 83
poetic rejuvenation, 3
poetic revolt, 75
poetic revolution, 8, 12, 71, 75, 83, 88, 92, 94, 97, 105, 106, 126
poetics, 1, 2, 3, 4, 5, 7, 8, 10, 11, 40, 41, 42, 49, 50, 51, 55, 56, 59, 60, 67, 71, 74, 77, 81, 83, 86, 123, 125, 126
poetic subject, 76, 95, 96, 97
poetic substance, 54
poetic substition, 11
poetic supplementation, 53
poetic trafficking, 49
political discourse, 17
postmodern, 12
potential director, 37, 39, 44
power, 10, 13, 18, 19, 21, 26, 28, 29, 34, 36, 38, 45, 55, 60, 61, 63, 64, 65, 66, 67, 94, 97, 109, 120, 121, 125, 126
precedence, 58, 61
precedents, 44, 75, 124
presences, 60
present, 8, 9, 16, 31, 35, 42, 48, 51, 52, 67, 78, 84, 99, 114
Price, 14, 16, 37
primeval, 10, 30, 32, 43, 45, 60, 127
primeval ground, 10, 32, 43
primordial, 5, 46, 55, 113
principle, 12, 21, 22, 26, 28, 44, 45, 51, 57, 59, 99, 123, 126
privileged locus of expression, 13, 14, 16
prodigal, 47, 96, 111
proliferation, 22, 24, 34
prophecy, 117
prosody, 75, 94, 95
protocol, 68, 71, 126
prototype, 83, 85, 95, 97
Prusek, 81
psychological, 21, 30, 32
public execution, 34
public executions, 17, 34

Qian, 86
Qu, 1, 5, 11, 84, 85, 97, 99, 102, 104, 105, 106, 107, 108, 109, 110, 111, 112, 113, 114, 115, 116, 117, 118, 119, 120, 121, 122, 124
quotidian, 81

Qu Yuan, 1, 5, 11, 84, 85, 104, 105, 106, 107, 108, 111, 112, 114, 115, 119, 122, 124, 126

radicalism, 79
radical modernity, 13
rage, 11, 99, 102, 109, 111, 114, 118, 119, 120
rationality, 15
ravishment, 41, 42, 43
reason, 18, 20, 21, 22, 25, 28, 37, 39, 43, 44, 45, 57, 69, 115
rebellion, 75, 79, 95, 97
reciprocal play, 39
reciprocity, 31, 48, 61, 92, 94, 110
reconcile, 51, 63
reconciliation, 21, 113
redemption, 9, 13, 16, 49, 51, 77, 81, 100, 101, 102, 109, 113, 121
redemptive, 51, 66, 67, 125
redress, 2, 5, 6, 9, 10, 15, 30, 42, 70, 80, 96, 101, 114, 124, 125
refiguration, 4, 11, 26, 27, 74, 82, 89, 93, 104, 105, 109, 113, 114, 122, 124
refigures, 45
refinement, 75, 97
reflection, 13, 37, 89, 90, 91, 99
reformation, 73, 123
regeneration, 75, 79, 97, 98, 102, 104, 108, 121
regicide, 38
regulated forms, 76
reincarnation, 102
reinvention, 5, 7, 9, 71, 126
rejuvenation, 112
relaxation, 32
remembrance, 44
replacement, 29, 50, 67, 92, 101, 105
representation, 18, 21, 33, 35, 36, 38, 74, 84, 89, 90, 114
representation of reality, 36
representation of revolution, 36
residual, 33
resources, 9, 126
restlessness, 10, 48
restoration, 41, 51, 65
revisionist, 79
revolution, 10, 35, 36, 37, 39, 49, 50, 56, 58, 64, 66, 71, 73, 76, 82, 83, 92, 94, 95, 96, 102, 105, 106, 112, 123, 126
revolutionary violence, 37, 71, 125
ritual, 98, 101
Rolland, 88
Romantic, 2, 4, 5, 7, 8, 9, 10, 11, 12, 13, 14, 15, 16, 18, 22, 24, 26, 40, 47, 48, 49, 50, 51, 54, 55, 56, 62, 63, 68, 70, 71, 72, 74, 75, 76, 77, 78, 79, 83, 84, 86, 87, 88, 89, 90, 91, 93, 97, 101, 105, 106, 107, 111, 122, 123, 124, 125, 126
Romantic criticism, 49
Romantic Formalist, 83
Romantic historicism, 78
Romanticism, 2, 4, 13, 14, 15, 35, 36, 37, 48, 54, 68, 74, 76, 80, 84, 89, 97, 98, 105, 108, 121, 125
Romanticists, 76, 77, 88, 93, 101
romantic lyricism, 84
Romantic sublime, 86, 97, 127
Rong Nie, 97
Rousseau, 50, 87, 88
ruggedness, 97
ruination, 32
ruins, 10, 15, 16, 29, 32, 44, 82, 97, 98, 104
ruins of traditions, 104
rupture, 58, 72
ruse, 33, 34, 35, 42, 57, 59, 79, 100, 101, 107

Said, 4, 15
Saigyo, 88
savagery, 80, 81, 97
Schiller, 5, 9, 14, 15, 16, 70, 82, 125
Schopenhauer, 77, 93, 100
seizure, 43, 114
self-hatching poet, 54
seminal, 1, 10, 46, 47, 48
sensation, 12, 21, 28, 45
sensationalist, 29
sensations, 21, 24, 27, 28, 29
sense of urgency, 78
sensibilities, 73, 84, 91, 94, 97
sensibility, 2, 3, 22, 76, 85, 95, 97, 105
sensuousness, 15
sentiment, 11, 25, 70, 76, 77, 83, 86, 96, 100, 124, 125
sentimental, 37
sentiments, 16, 37, 76, 84, 87, 92, 95, 97, 111, 114, 118, 119, 120
series, 6, 9, 18, 26, 28, 29, 31, 35, 59, 72
Shelley, 76, 87, 102
Shih, 3, 8, 88, 103
Shijing, 1, 105, 113
Shonin, 88
Shu Lin, 72
Sima, 106
simplicity, 27, 97

social agreement, 22, 24, 25
social and moral order, 38
social diseases, 32
social function, 5, 13, 14, 75, 81, 89, 93
social leveling, 38
social transaction, 42, 45
sojourner, 47, 54
Song, 1, 98, 99, 102, 115, 116, 117
sonnet, 75
sorrow, 99, 100, 106, 110
sources, 4, 5, 7, 27, 32, 41, 45, 52, 53, 55, 65, 84, 88, 90, 91, 94, 104, 105, 107, 113, 126
spatial, 8, 11, 30, 51, 74, 82
spectacle, 13, 34, 36, 37, 52, 53, 55, 66, 101
spectators, 33, 34, 36, 101
spectator sport, 34
spectral sublime, 51, 53, 56
speculative, 69
Spivak, 64, 66
stripping, 38, 41, 42
structures of intentions, 15
Su, 72
subject, 9, 13, 18, 31
subjectivity, 89, 113
sublime, 2, 3, 4, 5, 7, 9, 10, 11, 12, 13, 16, 17, 18, 19, 20, 21, 22, 24, 26, 27, 28, 29, 30, 31, 32, 33, 35, 36, 39, 40, 41, 42, 53, 55, 56, 57, 60, 64, 66, 68, 69, 70, 71, 76, 78, 80, 81, 82, 83, 85, 86, 87, 88, 97, 98, 100, 101, 105, 106, 107, 109, 110, 111, 113, 114, 115, 117, 118, 119, 120, 121, 122, 124, 125, 126
sublime aesthetics, 2, 3, 4, 5, 7, 10, 11, 32, 34, 35, 68, 69
sublime construction, 45, 70
sublime discourse, 5
sublime gesture, 70, 102, 114
sublime movement, 68
sublime poet, 117
sublime poetics, 10, 11
sublime ruse, 33, 34
supplementarity, 26, 50, 60, 65
supranationalism, 3, 88
surplus, 25, 50, 60
suspension, 41, 42, 50, 56, 58, 63, 64, 66, 67, 70, 125
swan song, 99, 108
symbiosis, 35, 79
Symbolists, 84
symmetry, 97
sympathetic identification, 110, 111, 118, 123

sympathy, 34, 59, 65, 110, 125
synonym, 106
synonymous, 78, 96

Tagore, 1, 84, 88, 102
Tang, 81
taste, 22, 24, 25, 26, 30, 38, 42
tastes, 17, 22, 24, 25, 45
tears, 77, 85, 99, 100, 109, 110, 112, 113, 123, 126
temporal, 2, 4, 5, 7, 8, 11, 30, 47, 51, 57, 74, 82
temporality, 31
temptation, 111
tendencies, 13, 16, 29, 40, 45, 67, 92, 104, 106, 111
terrible, 16, 27, 28, 29, 30, 31, 35, 52, 56, 71, 80, 81, 85, 100, 112, 118, 121, 122, 126
terror, 5, 9, 11, 12, 16, 20, 26, 27, 28, 30, 31, 32, 33, 37, 39, 52, 53, 55, 57, 58, 71, 72, 77, 81, 82, 99, 100, 101, 107, 108, 110, 114, 115, 119, 120, 123, 125, 126
textuality, 65
theory of art, 35
theory of history, 35, 36
threat, 9, 18, 22, 27, 30, 34, 38, 57, 59, 71, 72, 109, 112, 117, 122
Tian, 87
timely spirit, 6, 10, 71, 74, 75, 78, 79, 80, 125, 126
tour, 49, 50
tradition, 1, 3, 5, 6, 9, 11, 19, 25, 29, 32, 42, 71, 73, 74, 75, 78, 79, 80, 82, 83, 85, 89, 91, 94, 95, 97, 104, 105, 106, 107, 114, 123, 126
traditional bondage, 75
tragedy, 34, 35, 36, 37, 81, 105, 107, 114, 119
tragic hero, 105, 107
tragic time, 105
transcendence, 33, 48, 49, 99, 100, 102, 120, 121
transcendental, 17, 19, 21, 22, 29, 48, 69, 81, 94, 119
transcultural equivalences, 71, 125
transference, 7, 14, 35, 39, 42, 53, 55
transformation, 2, 3, 4, 5, 6, 7, 11, 20, 29, 71, 72, 73, 74, 82, 97, 104, 114, 121, 122, 124, 125, 126
translation, 3, 5, 7, 10, 11, 14, 16, 26, 27, 28, 53, 59, 60, 62, 66, 67, 71, 72, 73, 74, 82, 84, 87, 104, 105, 110, 113, 115, 121, 122, 125, 126

translator, 8, 10, 42, 53, 58, 60, 67, 87, 91, 94, 123, 126
transposition, 7, 19, 31, 78, 105, 117
trauma, 2, 5, 7, 9, 22, 46, 77, 80, 86, 96, 101
traumatic modernity, 75
traveling, 8
Treitschke, 87
tribute, 45, 117
truth, 49, 61, 69, 117
turbulence, 97, 119

uncanny, 52, 53, 82, 111
universal bliss, 102
unlimitation, 10, 11, 69, 70, 122, 124, 125
usurpation, 48, 64

vanguard, 16, 81, 96
vernacular, 73, 75, 84, 104, 105
verse drama, 5, 11, 96, 105, 107, 108, 110, 124
violence, 20, 31, 38, 41, 42, 48, 72, 77
Voltaire, 87

Wang, David, 72, 73
wardrobe of inheritance, 42
weaker subject, 101
Wen, 79, 83, 85, 96
wenyan, 73, 75, 94
Western forms, 75
Whitman, 1, 4, 76, 81, 87
woman, 38, 109, 117
Wordsworth, 3, 5, 6, 7, 10, 30, 37, 40, 41, 42, 43, 44, 45, 46, 47, 48, 49, 50, 51, 53, 54, 55, 57, 58, 59, 61, 63, 64, 66, 67, 68, 70, 71, 76, 82, 87, 104, 107, 123, 124, 125, 126
Wordsworthian sublime, 56, 57
world, 6, 15, 17, 25, 27, 39, 41, 44, 57, 85, 89, 90, 91, 99, 101, 102, 104, 109, 111, 112, 120

Xiang Zhu, 86
Xie Liu, 107
Xiu Zheng, 111, 117
Xu, 76, 83
Xun Lu, 87

Yan, 72, 80, 88, 89, 93, 95, 96, 114, 115
Yeh, 3, 73, 82
Yingjin Zhang, 9

Zehou Li, 81
Zheng Nie, 97

Zhou, 79, 80, 85
Žižek, 18
Zong, 77, 81, 87, 88, 91, 107